EDUCAT
POLITICS

Also by Jack Demaine

BEYOND COMMUNITARIANISM: Citizenship, Politics and Education (*with Harold Entwistle*)

CONTEMPORARY THEORIES IN THE SOCIOLOGY OF EDUCATION

SOCIOLOGY OF EDUCATION TODAY

Education Policy and Contemporary Politics

Edited by

Jack Demaine
Department of Social Sciences
Loughborough University

palgrave

First published in 1999
Reprinted in paperback with corrections 2002

Published by PALGRAVE
Houndmills, Basingstoke, Hampshire RG21 6XS and
175 Fifth Avenue, New York, N.Y. 10010
Companies and representatives throughout the world

PALGRAVE is the new global academic imprint of
St. Martin's Press LLC Scholarly and Reference Division and
Palgrave Publishers Ltd (formerly Macmillan Press Ltd).

ISBN 0–333–68250–5 hardback
ISBN 0–333–68251–3 paperback

This book is printed on paper suitable for recycling and
made from fully managed and sustained forest sources.

A catalogue record for this book is available
from the British Library.

10   9   8   7   6   5   4   3   2   1
11   10   09   08   07   06   05   04   03   02

Typeset by Integra Software Services Pvt. Ltd., Pondicherry, India
www.integra-india.com

Printed and bound in Great Britain by
Antony Rowe Ltd, Chippenham, Wiltshire

Contents

List of Contributors

Miriam David is Professor of Policy Studies in Education and Director of the Graduate School of Social Sciences at Keele University. Her publications include *Parents, Gender and Education Reform* (1993), *Mother's Intuition? Choosing Secondary Schools* (with Anne West and Jane Ribbens) (1994) and *Educational Reforms and Gender Equality in Schools* (with Madeleine Arnot and Gaby Weiner) (1996). She is co-editor of the *Journal of Social Policy* and an executive editor of the *British Journal of Sociology of Education*.

Jack Demaine is Senior Lecturer in the Department of Social Sciences at Loughborough University. His publications include *Contemporary Theories in the Sociology of Education* (1981) and *Beyond Communitarianism: Citizenship, Politics and Education* (with Harold Entwistle) (1996). He is a member of the editorial board of *International Studies in Sociology of Education*.

Tony Edwards is Emeritus Professor of Education at the University of Newcastle. His publications include *The State and Private Education: An Evaluation of the Assisted Places Scheme* (with John Fitz and Geoff Whitty) (1989) and *Specialisation and Choice in Urban Education: The City Technology College Experiment* (with Sharon Gewirtz and Geoff Whitty) (1993).

David Gillborn is Professor of Education and Head of Policy Studies at the Institute of Education, University of London. His publications include *Racism and Antiracism in Real Schools* (1995) and the Ofsted Report on *Recent Research on the Achievements of Ethnic Minority Pupils* (with Caroline Gipps) (1996). He is founding editor of the journal *Race Ethnicity and Education*.

Denis Gleeson is Professor of Education in the Institute of Education at the University of Warwick. His publications include *The Paradox of Training* (1989), *Training and its Alternatives* (1990), *Truancy and the Politics of Compulsory Schooling* (with Pat Carlen and Julia Wardhaugh) (1992), *Knowledge and Nationhood: Education, Politics and Work* (with

James Avis, Martin Bloomer, Geoff Esland and Phil Hodkinson) (1996). He is a member of the editorial board of *The Sociological Review* and the *British Journal of Education and Work*.

Peter King is Director of the Teacher Education Unit at Loughborough University. His publications include *The Challenge of English in the National Curriculum* (with Robert Protherough) (1995).

Bob Moon is Professor of Education at the Open University. His publications include *The National Curriculum: Straightjacket or Safety Net* (with Peter Mortimore) (1989), *School Inspection* (with Tim Brighouse) (1995), *Education in France* (with Anne Corbett) (1996), and *A Guide to the National Curriculum* (1996). He is Honorary Editor of the British Curriculum Foundation.

Roger Murphy is Professor of Education and Director of Research in the School of Education at the University of Nottingham. His publications include *Evaluating Education: Issues and Methods* (1987), *The Changing Face of Educational Assessment* (1988), *Changing Educational Assessment: International Perspectives and Trends* (1990), and *Effective Assessment and the Improvement of Education* (1995).

Sally Power is Professor of Education at the Institute of Education, University of London. She is co-author of *Grant Maintained Schools: Education in the Market Place* (with John Fitz and David Halpin) (1993) and *Devolution and Choice in Education: The School, the State and the Market* (with David Halpin and Geoff Whitty) (1998). She is a member of the editorial board of *International Studies in Sociology of Education*.

David Reynolds is Professor of Education at the University of Exeter. His publications include *School Effectiveness: Research, Policy and Practice* (with Peter Cuttance) (1992), *Advances in School Effectiveness Research and Practice* (1994), *Making Good Schools* (1996), *Worlds Apart* (with Shaun Farrell) (1996), and the *International Handbook of School Effectiveness Research* (1998) (with Charles Teddlie). He is an editor of the journal *School Effectiveness and School Improvement* and a member of the editorial board of the *British Journal of Sociology of Education*.

Stuart Sexton was adviser to Secretaries of State Mark Carlisle and Keith Joseph (1979–86) and adviser to the Conservative Party in Opposition (1975–79). He is Director of the Education Unit of the Independent

Primary and Secondary Education Trust. His publications include *Our Schools: A Radical Policy* (1987), *Our Schools: Future Policy* (1992) and *Reform of University Funding* (1997).

Geoff Whitty is Director of the Institute of Education, University of London. His publications include *The State and Private Education: An Evaluation of the Assisted Places Scheme* (with John Fitz and Tony Edwards) (1989), *Specialisation and Choice in Urban Education: The City Technology College Experiment* (with Sharon Gewirtz and Tony Edwards) (1993) and *Devolution and Choice in Education: The School, the State and the Market* (with David Halpin and Sally Power) (1998). He is a member of the editorial board of *International Studies in Sociology of Education* and the *British Journal of Sociology of Education*.

Phil Wild was formerly Head of the Department of Education at Loughborough University. He has written widely in the field of IT and education. His publications include *GCSE Technology* (1990). He was a founding member of the IT in Education Management Working Group of the International Federation for Information Processing.

John Wilmut is a special lecturer at the University of Nottingham and a visiting research fellow at the University of Bristol. His publications include *Agreement Trialling* (1994) and he has contributed to a number of reports on assessment issues for the DfEE, SCAA, NVCQ and QCA. He is a member of the British Educational Research Association and of the International Association for Educational Assessment.

Acknowledgements

I would like to thank Linda Auld and her associates for their outstanding work on the proofs of this book, and Lorraine Culley and Sue
Bryman for reading parts of the text. Thanks to Tony Hodgson for technical assistance with computer files, and to all of the contributors for
their prompt and helpful responses to my queries. Thanks also to those
students and colleagues at Loughborough, and at other universities, who
have made invaluable contributions through numerous critical discussions
of the issues raised in this book.

Introduction
Jack Demaine

Education is said to be at the core of the new Labour project. In the 1997 election campaign Tony Blair used the phrase 'education, education, education' as clarion call and as a promise of a new future, insisting that 'education will be the passion of my government'. But, of course, education had been something of a passion for the Conservatives too during their eighteen years in government and, on returning to power in 1997, Labour inherited an education system very different from the one in place when they lost power in 1979. During the intervening years there has been increasing centralization of power coupled with the devolution of aspects of administrative and financial responsibility to individual educational institutions, and a consequent decline both in the power and responsibility of local education authorities. Labour has inherited a quasi-market system of educational provision which the 'new right' regards as a 'half-way house' on the road to a 'free market' system of educational provision. In Chapter 1, Jack Demaine examines the process of change in education and prospects for the future.

In Chapter 2, Tony Edwards, Geoff Whitty and Sally Power pose a range of questions concerning Labour's new directions, with particular reference to the issue of 'selection' and the provision of educational opportunity. Their chapter, 'Moving Back from Comprehensive Secondary Education?' argues that new Labour does not appear intent on reviving the 'old' Labour ideal of 'truly' comprehensive non-selective schooling. They point out that Labour's first education White Paper celebrates *variety* and displays an enthusiasm for *modernizing* comprehensive secondary education rather than addressing the question of selection.

In Chapter 3, 'Educational Reforms, Gender and Families', Miriam David examines discourses about *mothering* in relation to children's achievements in the context of educational reform. She argues that mothers are key to their children's education: they have contributed positively to the improvements in girls' educational achievements and to the closing of the 'gender gap' in educational performance. Mothers' aspirations for both their sons and their daughters are now given official legitimation through a variety of new Labour policies, but Labour does not give explicit recognition to mothers' voices, which remain occluded.

1

In Chapter 4, 'School Effectiveness, School Improvement and Contemporary Educational Policies', David Reynolds is also concerned with improvements in educational achievement. He argues that research into school effectiveness and school improvement has become a central influence on the educational policies being pursued in England and Wales. Labour's White Paper shows the influence of the 'effectiveness and improvement paradigm on virtually every page' but Reynolds outlines a range of doubts over existing educational policies, arguing that they might not be sufficient to achieve Labour's stated aims.

In Chapter 5, 'Race, Nation and Education: New Labour and the New Racism', David Gillborn recalls how, in September 1996, an Ofsted report written by him and Caroline Gipps had briefly 'punctured the deafening silence that had grown in policy-making circles around issues such as racism and equal opportunities'. The Ofsted report argued that the education system is still scarred by racism, that significant inequalities of opportunity persist, and that in some areas the situation is getting worse, not better. Despite such injustices, many young people from ethnic minority backgrounds *do* succeed in the education system, but a failure to consider ethnic diversity has been one of the most striking and consistent features of recent education reforms. Gillborn argues that a convergence in Labour and Conservative policy discourse may foreshadow a new phase of 'ethnic assimilationism'.

In Chapter 6, 'Beyond the Bell Curve: New Politics for the National Curriculum', Bob Moon argues that outmoded conceptions of the human mind and intelligence underpin too much of recent educational policy making. Moon suggests that the problem is particularly acute in relation to primary and secondary schooling but that many of the assumptions spill over into attitudes towards higher and adult education, influencing policy making across the political spectrum. A very different approach to the curriculum from that adopted in recent years is required if schools are to contribute significantly to the development of articulate and confident young people.

Educational assessment, testing and examinations have come to be a major focus of debate about education over the last twenty years. In Chapter 7, 'Educational Assessment in an Era of Reform', Roger Murphy and John Wilmut argue that powerful interests are invested in arguments for carrying out assessments in particular ways. But the assessment genie is out of the bottle now, and the interests of a few can no longer be secured by pretending that assessment is some kind of obscure science based on a secret knowledge held by a small band of assessment experts. The challenge now is to build learning and assessment opportunities which *promote* rather than inhibit widespread improvements in lifelong learning.

Lifelong learning is also the concern of Denis Gleeson who, in Chapter 8, 'Challenging Tripartism: Class and Inequality in Post-Compulsory Education Policy', maps out the dramatic changes in patterns of post-sixteen participation over the past decade. He challenges the tripartism that has remained a central feature of post-compulsory education policy and provision and argues for a different vision of post-compulsory education; one that will sustain personal development, encompassing a broad vision of citizenship and learning of all. The present tripartite system, he argues, does not provide the best structure for the learning society of the 21st century.

In Chapter 9, 'Education and IT Policy: Virtual Reality?' Phil Wild and Peter King question the capacity of British IT policy to deliver education in the learning society of the 21st century. Elsewhere, in Singapore for example, decisive action is already being taken to resource the IT infrastructure and to train teachers to use it effectively. Wild and King argue that Britain's present *ad hoc* developments will leave it far behind other countries and that government needs to take a much firmer lead in implementing a national strategy for IT in partnership with educationists.

In Chapter 10, Stuart Sexton also looks towards the prospects for the 21st century, but through rather different eyes. Once described as the *éminence grise* of Tory education policy, Sexton was the architect of the Assisted Places Scheme and later played an important role in advancing argument for the privatization of education, for the introduction of a free market and for education credit vouchers. Sexton is undaunted by recent political events and sees the election of the new Labour government as no necessary obstacle to the eventual privatization of education. Indeed, he concludes his chapter, 'The Next Ten Years', by suggesting that the prospects for what he calls his *utopia* might be better served by Labour's 1997 victory than if the Conservatives had won.

In a book of this kind there are bound to be political differences, but I have also found myself at odds on issues of *style* as much as politics. In some cases my advice to contributors has been heeded and in others declined. So, whilst I take full responsibility for Chapter 1, the responsibility for other chapters lies entirely with their particular authors. The ten chapters encompass a wide range of issues although, of course, a fully comprehensive review of education policy is beyond the scope of a single book. However, this collection raises many of the most important questions of education policy that new Labour will face in the coming years.

1 Education Policy and Contemporary Politics

Jack Demaine

On 2nd May 1997 Tony Blair, surrounded by enthusiastic supporters, walked triumphantly along Downing Street as Labour Prime Minister with the largest parliamentary majority in modern times – the beneficiary and main architect of a 'landslide' election victory. Eighteen years earlier, during election day in 1979, the previous Labour Prime Minister James Callaghan, alone with his close aide Joe Haines, is said to have swept aside a comforting observation as to the Party's prospects. Callaghan perceived what he referred to as a 'sea-change' in politics, and, indeed, the following day Mrs Margaret Thatcher stood at the front door of 10 Downing Street as Conservative Prime Minister.

In those eighteen years between sea-change and landslide the political terrain, and with it education policy, changed dramatically. At the presentational level Blair ('call me Tony') transformed the Labour Party into a nationally electable force for the first time since Harold Wilson won the 1974 General Election. At a more fundamental political level, by building on the work already done by Neil Kinnock, Blair played a leading role in transforming Party structures, organization and ideology, so that many observers have come to regard 'new' Labour as a party of the centre seeking a 'Third Way' in politics. Whichever way it is to go, education is said to be at the core of the new Labour project. In his political rhetoric in the run-up to the 1997 General Election, Tony Blair used the phrase 'Education, education, education' as a clarion call and as a promise of a new future: 'Education will be the passion of my government'. Of course, education was something of a passion for the Conservatives, too, during their eighteen years in government. They were passionately concerned to reform education because, like Blair, they also regarded it 'as fundamental to Britain's prospects'.

This chapter discusses important aspects of education policy from Jim Callaghan's defeat to Tony Blair's victory; from sea-change to landslide and beyond. In certain important respects, new Labour appears intent on following a similar policy-line on education to that of the Conservatives when they were in office: albeit a line modified and adapted

to the politics of the 'real world' in which Labour wants to appear new
and different, but at the same time pragmatic and 'down to earth'. For
example, with respect to the management of schools and the 'policing'
of teachers' work, new Labour is hardly distinguishable from the Tories.
But there are also aspects of policy where Labour is rather different. For
example, embarking on a £1.2 billion programme of school repairs and
building work really is new and different, and Labour's proposed changes
to modes of support for students in higher education are something
from which even the Tory Right shied away.

The chapter begins with a brief account of aspects of the politics of
education at the end of the Callaghan era, and traces important political
developments during the eighteen years of Conservative administration
up to the new Labour politics of education and the idea of a 'Third Way'.
The chapter does not subscribe to the widely-held view that Callaghan's
intervention was the 'cause' of all that was to follow in educational politics; neither does it suggest that there is a particular 'way' that Labour
must look to follow into the new millennium. Rather, what came about
during the 1980s and 1990s was the consequence of a complex combination of political conditions and ideology and not 'determined' by
some single force, principle or idea. Of forces, ideas and principles there
are many, and some of them may be regarded as more significant than
others, but their interplay produces outcomes which cannot simply be
'read off' from any one of them.

EDUCATION AND THE SEA-CHANGE IN POLITICS

Jim Callaghan is said to have been appalled by the events played out at
the William Tyndale Junior and Infants' School in Islington, North London between 1973 and 1975. The details of those events are set out in
the Auld Report (1976) and in the writings of those who disputed the
official report; they need not detain us here. The important political
issues raised by the William Tyndale affair were those of 'standards',
'accountability' and 'control of education' (see Demaine 1981). Soon
after he became Prime Minister, Callaghan made thinly disguised reference to the problems presented at the William Tyndale school in his
1976 Ruskin College Speech, but was careful to distance himself from
critics on the political right, saying explicitly that:

> My remarks are not a clarion call to *Black Paper* prejudices. We all
> know those who claim to defend standards but who in reality are

simply seeking to defend old privileges and inequalities (quoted in Ahier, Cosin and Hales 1996).

Nevertheless, some commentators at the time expressed surprise that a Labour Prime Minister should take up the issue of 'standards', which many had seen as a Tory slogan. But more significant is Callaghan's argument that:

It will be an advantage to the teaching profession to have a wider public understanding and support for what they are doing. And there is room for greater understanding among those not directly concerned (ibid.)

In the 1970s, some teacher trade unionists had regarded the notion of 'teacher accountability' as a threat to 'professional autonomy'. With the advantage of hindsight we can see that the issue of accountability was much more than a fashion, and more than a slogan, in a Britain where consumerism was fast gaining a strong foothold. Callaghan's thinking was well ahead of those teacher trade unionists who rejected the recommendations of the Taylor Report (1977) and, indeed, of some academic observers of education at that time (see Demaine 1980). The political issue that brought together the question of standards in education and the issue of accountability was, of course, the issue of 'control'. The William Tyndale affair appeared to demonstrate, night after night via the television screens in people's homes, that central government was not in control of education. Of course, central government had 'residual' powers that could be invoked, but the Education Act (1944) had placed much of the education system in the hands of the local education authorities (LEAs). Conservative governments' efforts during the 1980s were to be focused on shifting power away from the LEAs.

By present-day standards William Tyndale was a shocking affair. That it seems so now demonstrates how far education reform has moved on since Labour was last in office. The Auld Report had found a school out of political control and the Taylor Report sought to devise mechanisms through which schools might be made accountable to their local community. Callaghan's Ruskin College speech and his government's acceptance of the findings of the Auld Report (and subsequently the Taylor Report) set the context for aspects of reform that were to be enacted by the Conservatives when they came into office. As Batteson (1997) rightly argues, it is quite wrong to regard Callaghan's 1976 speech as somehow the 'cause' of those developments. Nevertheless, new Labour can now be seen to be continuing to develop policy-themes which were set out by old Labour and carried through by the Conservatives.

The Taylor Report had recommended a formal structure for the election of parents, teachers and community representatives to the governing bodies of schools. The new bodies would take on greater responsibility for overseeing the management of schools, although the 'day-to-day' management would remain in the hands of head teachers and their senior assistants. During the 1980s the Conservatives implemented many of Taylor's recommendations, although not in precisely the way delineated in the report. But of course, the Conservatives in office wanted much more. A major difference between Taylor's recommendations and the Tory plans for market-oriented school 'self-management' was the issue of school finance. Taylor had not recommended devolution of financial control to the individual school, although it did recommend that the local authorities 'involve' governors more in the drawing-up of expenditure plans along the lines of the 1945 'model articles' for school management (see Taylor Report, Chapter 7).

In contrast to Taylor's rather modest recommendations, radical proposals for financial self-management came from the so-called 'new right'. In modifying the radical right's policy proposals, the Conservatives found a way in which to appear to 'empower' the individual school whilst shifting more control to central government. The Tories used the radical right's rhetoric on 'liberalization' to wrench power from the hands of the LEAs. New Labour is now the beneficiary of 'central control of education'; a possibility that Stuart Sexton (1987) had always warned against. He and others on the neo-liberal right had wanted to see the development of a system of 'self-managed' schools 'free from State controls' (see Demaine 1990). What was actually to be developed during the 1980s and 1990s was the consequence of a complex combination of political conditions and ideology.

EDUCATION AND LABOUR IN OPPOSITION

In the period following Labour's defeat in the 1979 General Election the Party turned left and, in Denis Healey's view, thus condemned itself to further defeats in the next two general elections (Healey 1989). Callaghan resigned as Party Leader in 1980 and was replaced by Michael Foot, who led the Party to a disastrous defeat in the 1983 General Election. Gerald Kaufman described Labour's election manifesto as 'the longest suicide note in history' (rightly, according to Healey). Neil Kinnock became party leader just after the 1983 election and, although he took a leading role in making very important changes to the Party, he went on to lead Labour to further defeats in 1987 and 1992 before handing over to John Smith.

During the long years in Opposition, Labour had many critics both inside and outside the party. Although education had been regarded as one of its strengths, critics argued that even here Labour had lost its touch. In a paper titled *The Labour Party's Education Policy on Primary and Secondary Education 1979–89*, Bill Inglis (1991) maps out how he thinks Labour 'lost the initiative' to the Conservatives. He argues that for almost a decade between 1979 and 1987, and particularly during Giles Radice's tenure as Opposition spokesperson, the Party's approach to education policy was 'complacent' and there was a failure to prepare for the 'Conservative challenge' in the late 1980s. Radice's Fabian pamphlet, *Equality and Quality: A Socialist Plan for Education* (1986), and the discussion of education policy in his book *Labour's Path to Power* (1989), are said to be 'disappointing'. Later, according to Inglis, complacency was 'replaced by a mixture of acceptance and defensiveness' (Inglis 1991, p. 5). Inglis is most vitriolic in his attack on Neil Kinnock, who was Shadow Education Secretary in the early 1980s. Curiously, Kinnock's own book *Making Our Way* (1986) is ignored and instead Inglis refers to a much earlier piece on education policy published in Gerald Kaufman's *Renewal, Labour's Britain in the 1980s*. Kinnock's chapter in that book is said to involve 'a facile attack on the elitist academic tradition of British schools' and is 'suffused with a proselytizing optimism' (Inglis 1991, p. 13).

A different reading, of *Making Our Way*, would see Kinnock taking on the Conservatives in a way that could hardly be called complacent or defensive, as Inglis asserts. Indeed, readers will find a Labour Party leader coming to terms with the need for change and recognizing both the significance and the danger of consumeristic thinking. Whilst attacking the Conservatives and insisting that, as far as Labour is concerned, education should not go to market, Kinnock argued perceptively that:

> The objectives of *choice, standards*, and *relevance* must be central themes of education. They have been debased by the present government in order to mobilize prejudice, feed propaganda and provide excuses for narrowing and reducing provision – and therefore choice, standards and relevance – for the great majority of school children.

The expansion of choice, the raising of performance standards, the increase of relevance, together with other objectives of education like social and cultural enlightenment, good behaviour, responsibility, self confidence, the encouragement of the appetite for knowledge, the fulfilment of potential, the development of the individual regardless of sex, or race, or economic circumstances, are desirable. But they are only significant if they are supported and reinforced by adequate resources and implemented in a partnership with the professionals that can foster success. Choice is mocked as the pressures of shortages push another generation into old, narrow avenues, and when confrontation rather than co-operation informs relationships among government, teachers and education administrators. (ibid., p. 139, emphasis in the original).

Kinnock does not simply reject the consumerism that the Conservatives were keen to extend to education. He accepts that choice is important but turns the argument against his opponents. Conservative policy gives choices to the few as shortage of resources reduces choice and educational opportunity for the majority. Solutions lie in better co-operative relationships together with adequate resources, and Kinnock makes several points that are not dissimilar to those made by A. H. Halsey in a paper titled *Democracy for Education?* (Halsey 1981).

Halsey is significant here because he had long been regarded as one of the most important academic influences on Labour's education reform programme during the 1960s. His commitment to comprehensivization was beyond question but in 1981 he began to argue that modern education systems were becoming 'formidably bureaucratic'. He expressed concern about the 'negative effects of administrative and professional organization' and argued for more 'parent power plus direct grants for all'. Halsey suggested that self-managed schools financed by central and local taxation could make

every school a direct grant school. School government could be simultaneously reformed along the lines recommended in the *Taylor Report*, with more power to parents (Halsey 1981, p. 347).

Halsey's proposals presented something of a challenge to those on the left who were locked into thinking that provision of education via the local education authorities could be the only acceptable means through which to organize schooling. But, like Kinnock, Halsey differs from the Conservatives on the question of the market, and he suggests that a direct grant system of schools could be adapted to provide extra funding for schools with children from less well-off families.

A. H. Halsey and Neil Kinnock's writing shows that Labour did not ignore the Conservative challenge, nor did they display lack of interest, complacency, defensiveness or lack of initiative on education policy as Inglis asserts (see Demaine 1992). Their real problem was that they were unable to win general elections. Under Kinnock's leadership the Labour Party took its electoral predicament very seriously indeed, and in the wake of defeat in the 1987 General Election began a thorough review of its policy. In the Final Report of Labour's Policy Review for the 1990s, *Meet the Challenge: Make the Change* (1989), and in the pamphlet *Parents in Partnership* (1988), Labour committed itself more firmly than ever to the idea of partnership between parents, schools and LEAs and to the recommendations of the Taylor Report. Indeed, *Parents in Partnership* goes so far as to suggest that parents are the 'cornerstone of a school's success and a pupil's progress' and that 'Labour wants to build a firm bridge between home and school'. The Labour Party has a well-established record of seeking to develop the themes of involvement and partnership, in contrast to the right's relatively recent rhetoric on 'parent power', and 'parental choice'. We now turn to the right.

THE CONSERVATIVES AND THE NEW RIGHT

Consumerism, and in particular the notions of 'parental choice' and 'the market', became important themes in Conservative education thinking during the 1980s. The government appeared to be attracted to a line of argument set out by the 'new right', although they did not follow it slavishly, as we shall see in a moment. The term 'new right' (see Bosanquet 1983) refers not to any specific group but to a movement represented by a collection of lobby groups concerned, amongst other things, to bring about the 'liberation' of public services from 'excessive state control' through their 'privatization'. The political philosophy of the new right is that of 'liberalism', defined in F. A. Hayek's (1960) sense of limiting the powers of government in the interests of the liberty of the individual and a 'free society' (see Hindess 1987). As far as education is concerned, the new right seeks the transformation of school systems, so that individual schools would become individual self-managing 'private' institutions. As one leading proponent of new right thinking explains, 'the plan is to create, as near as practicable, a "free market" in education. To use a popular term, it is in some sense to "privatize" the State education system' (Sexton 1987, p. 10).

The new right argues that education must be regarded as a commodity: teachers are to be regarded as producers and parents (rather than children) as the consumers. Education provides an inadequate service when it suffers from the effects of 'producer capture'. According to the right wing Adam Smith Institute's *Omega Report: Education Policy* (1984), producer capture is evident when education serves the interests of teachers and administrators rather than the interests of consumers. The hallmarks of producer capture of education are said to include 'employment laxity, giantism and resistance to change' (p. 3). The new right sees producer capture as a central characteristic of 'Welfare State Socialism', and the post-war British comprehensive school system as a clear example. The remedy is said to be an 'education voucher' and a system of self-managed schools in which parental interests are strongly represented, and governing bodies are 'free to hire and fire' teachers. The new right argues that the provision of such arrangements would 'liberate' schools, and place them into market relationships leading to an improved education 'service'. Some on the right see the liberation of education as *a possible task still to be achieved*.

The idea of education vouchers is not new, and there are differences between the various proposals that have been put forward. Schematically, the suggestion is that every parent or legal guardian of a child of school age would be issued annually with a voucher on its behalf. The value of the voucher, sometimes referred to as a 'credit' or 'entitlement', would be that of the average *per caput* cost of schooling within a specific locality, taking into consideration differences in costs for children of different ages. Schemes recommended by the new right suggest that parents should be allowed to 'top up' the value of the voucher with cash and spend both in a 'free market' for education (Sexton 1987). According to the new right, one of the obstacles to the development of a free market is the way in which teachers' pay and working conditions are determined. In a future that is imagined by the new right, privatized self-managed schools would need to be able to appoint teachers on fixed-term contracts if they so wish, and hire and fire very much more easily than has been the case so far. In a free market, teachers' salaries would 'no longer be determined on a national basis, but by each school. Schools might wish to institute different grades of salary for different qualities of teacher' (Adam Smith Institute 1984, p. 7). But whilst teachers' pay and conditions are thought to present a serious obstacle, the main obstacle is the 'state provision of education', as such, because it has established a context which has the effect of frustrating consumer choice.

The right concedes that in Britain the development of a system of private self-managed schools where the producers are exposed to the rigours of the market, and where the paying customers exercise their consumer rights, cannot be achieved overnight and could not be achieved without the political force of central government. Some observers regard this as something of a paradox; the 'liberation' of schools from 'political control' and the creation of independent self-managed schools could only be brought about by the political power of central government. For the libertarian right this presents an obvious danger. As Stuart Sexton argues, centralization of control of education is 'unsatisfactory and objectionable, especially in England where the whole concept is alien to our ideas of personal liberty and freedom' (Sexton 1987, p. 7). Nevertheless, centralization might be thought tolerable in the short term, if it held out the prospect of eventual liberty for the consumers in a market for education. But once central government had taken control it might not let go. As we shall see, Stuart Sexton's worst fear was that Conservative central government might seize power in the name of liberty, only to lose it to an incoming 'socialist' government.

Now, although it is important not to overestimate the extent and capacity of centralization to bring about effective reform, it did provide the Conservatives with mechanisms through which to curtail the activities of LEAs and to steal political control from Labour councils during the 1980s and 1990s. Understandably, centralization was the focus of much criticism from both the left and the right. As far as the education voucher is concerned, the Conservatives began to distance themselves from the idea in the early 1980s following damaging publicity surrounding a feasibility study carried out by the then Conservative-controlled Kent County Council. Sir Keith Joseph, Secretary of State for Education and Science, told the 1983 Conservative Party Conference that 'the voucher, at least in the foreseeable future, is dead.' (quoted in Seldon 1986).

Following Sir Keith Joseph's speech, the new right in Britain had to concede that the introduction of vouchers and privatization would not be achieved quickly because 'politically and financially it would not be possible or desirable to make a sudden change' (Sexton 1987, p. 30). Stuart Sexton set about devising a plan for what I have referred to elsewhere as 'privatization by stealth' (Demaine 1989). In his influential pamphlet, *Our Schools: A Radical Policy* (1987), Sexton explains that there should be a 'phased introduction of educational credits, with every step a gentle step' (p. 46). He presents detailed plans for a process of gradual reform, delineating three distinct stages. What he refers to as 'gradualism' is required because by making slow progress towards privatization there will be less likelihood of 'offending the educationists and the bureaucrats' who are said to have 'enormous vested interest' in the *status quo* (p. 4). Since 'the public' needs to be introduced gently to the idea of paying for education in a 'free market', a step towards this long-term objective is the implementation of a scheme of direct grants from central government to the newly opted out self-managed schools. Once the cost of education is more fully understood and accepted by the public (something that has not really happened in Britain) the next stage would be to allow those direct grants to be transformed into education credit vouchers that parents would receive directly from government. Eventually there would be legislation to allow credit vouchers to be topped up with cash and used at any school competing for custom in the marketplace. The distinction between public and private, between 'state' and independent school, would eventually be dissolved, says Sexton.

During the 1987 election campaign Mrs Thatcher, clearly influenced by Sexton's pamphlet, thus played down the idea of education vouchers. She told an interviewer who asked about them that 'something much more simple is required', and suggested that instead 'a headmaster (sic) would get so much money per pupil and he would be free to spend a proportion of that how he liked' (see English 1987). Thatcher was alluding to the idea of the direct grant-maintained schools and to local financial management of schools which were to be legislated for in the *Education Reform Act* (1988). Later, Kenneth Clarke, who was Secretary of State for Education and Science in the run-up to the 1992 election, also played down the idea of vouchers and instead vigorously promoted the direct grant-maintained schools.

So as the Conservatives pressed on with their programme of reform, the voucher was not to be found at the cutting edge of policy. However, as Hywel Thomas (1990) observed, what emerged was a 'voucher economy' without the need actually to print the vouchers; the children themselves became a kind of 'walking voucher'. For political reasons, vouchers and privatization had been kept off the official agenda whilst 'market forces' were gradually brought to bear on education. This cautious approach, a sort of 'ultra-gradualism', frustrated sections of the right; Arthur Seldon, for example, argued that the Conservatives had 'implemented half-measures, in education, opting out by schools rather than parents, that will delay the best solution by a decade' (Seldon 1988). His 'best solution', to *force* schools to privatize, was ignored, and soon after the 1992 election new legislation was introduced which only went as far as making opting out easier. Whilst in power the Conservatives remained committed to the idea of self-managing schools in the context of a system of central government funding and supervision. From the new right view-point there was far more centralization than liberalization and (most cruelly of all, as they see it) a Labour government was able to inherit newly acquired 'central power' over education.

THE 'THIRD WAY' IN EDUCATION?

John Smith died in May 1994 and Tony Blair was elected Leader of the Labour Party. His intention to focus on education, and particularly on 'standards in schools' (Blair 1994), was evident from the very start of his tenure as Leader. By the time he became Prime Minister, in May 1997, schools were more deeply involved in their own management than had ever been the case when Labour was last in power. However, the self-management exercised by the governors, managers and heads of educational institutions has to be seen in the context of very much tighter Treasury controls over education expenditure and the activity of various agencies and quangos deployed by the Department for Education and Employment (Df EE) to oversee the curriculum and inspect standards in schools, colleges and universities. New Labour had no plans to turn the clock back to the 1970s.

Now, neither the principle of centralized control nor that of co-operative self-management is anathema to traditional Labour thinking: there is no *necessary* conflict between them. As we already seen, Halsey argued long ago for school self-management within the context of a national system for education. Of course, the 'new way' suggested by Halsey in 1981 has certainly not been achieved because of his advocacy of it. Rather, the Conservatives found their *own way* as they tried to combine the ideas of neo-liberalism with those of the traditional 'preservationist' Tories (see Knight 1990). The Education Reform Act (1988) combines the idea of a *National* Curriculum and *national* policy with plans for the *devolution* of the management of educational institutions and market reform of education, and although there is a certain amount of 'tension' between the different principles involved in the Act, this does not *in itself* make the Act unworkable. Of course, there are other issues raised by the question of the process of implementation of policy which are discussed by Ball and his associates (see, for example, Ball 1990; Bowe, Ball and Gold 1992). But a broader question arises as to whether the 'new way' Halsey recommended in 1981, and that followed by the Conservatives between 1987 and 1997, amounts to a 'Third Way' that new Labour will also follow now that it is in power.

Julian Le Grand (1998) argues that the government 'is too swamped by the day-to-day preoccupations of office to engage in the necessary reflection' that would afford it the capacity to confirm or deny that it had found or was following a new 'Third Way'. He suggests that we can only try to draw conclusions from what Labour has actually done in respect of the welfare state and local government. 'And here there does indeed seem to be something of a pattern. Moreover, it is one that is not neo-liberal or social democratic, but something different: a true Third Way'. Le Grand argues that new Labour is not the new right in new clothes – nor is it 'socialism', of course – but 'in many of the government's actions there is clearly a belief in the value of *community*, especially local community' (p. 26). Labour's consultation paper, *Modernising Local Government* (1998) is concerned with making local government more accountable; hence the need for more parental representation on LEAs as well as on school governing bodies. For Le Grand, the themes of community, opportunity, responsibility and accountability spell 'Cora: a worthy rival to Mrs Thatcher's Tina – There Is No Alternative'. Tony Blair's Third Way is said to provide a 'real alternative' and, although it would not necessarily be Le Grand's way, he suggests that it represents a set of values that Labour hopes will go down well with readers of 'the *Sun, Mirror* and *Daily Mail*, for that is where the next election will be won' (Le Grand 1998).

According to several observers, Labour is still searching for a Third Way (see Lloyd and Bilefsky 1998; Walker 1998). In some areas of social welfare 'new ways' are only just being unveiled to public gaze, but as far as education policy is concerned it might be argued that giant strides along a Third Way appear to have been taken already. However, there is no monopoly on policy analysis, and Steven Teles argues that what really lies at the core of new Labour's philosophy is an American import: *new paternalism*. He suggests that like all paternalistic approaches it 'uses the state to enforce, rather than merely encouraging individuals to conform to values that are generally non-controversial' (Teles 1998). This is clearly so for much of Labour's education policy; few 'sensible middle-class parents' would disagree with much of *Excellence in Schools* and nor would readers of the *Sun, Mirror* and *Daily Mail*.

Not withstanding these new perspectives, Labour's education policies involve an overriding *pragmatism* which takes advantage of the prevailing political conditions. If Blair's way is neither old left nor new right, and proves acceptable to such a wide range of voters, this is at least in part due to the effects of the policies of previous governments. Teachers and teacher unions have been stripped of much of their power and influence, so that what Blair's government can do now is very different from what was possible for Callaghan's government. Whilst the policies for the policing of teachers and present modes of management of schools do appear to fit comfortably into the idea of a Third Way, in an important sense there are no 'ways' but only *possibilities* contingent on a range of circumstances themselves partly the products of earlier conditions. Labour is able to make progress on education not because it has invented some new third way but because its pragmatism is built on a recognition of the way that educationists have been treated over the last two decades and on the way education system has already been reformed.

The management of schools in the new era

Whilst the new right was politically active and forceful in arguing for education reform, others, who made no claim to right-wing credentials, were writing enthusiastically about school self-management. For example, Caldwell and Spinks in their book *The Self-Managing School* (1988) and Hill, Oakley Smith and Spinks in *Local Management of Schools* (1990), amongst others, argue that the proper management of schools is best achieved through partnership and the co-operative participation of parents, teachers, local politicians and community representatives, within the context of national policy. In their book *The Self-Managing School*, Caldwell and Spinks (1988) define a self-managing school as

> one for which there has been significant and consistent decentralization to the school level of authority to make decisions related to the allocation of resources. This decentralization is administrative rather than political, with decisions at the school level being made within a framework of local, state or national policies and guidelines. The school remains accountable to a central authority for the manner in which resources are allocated (p. 5).

Caldwell and Spinks see no necessary contradiction between school self-management and accountability to a central authority. Enthusiasm for such an arrangement can be found in the early British literature which saw local management of schools (LMS) as presenting 'new opportunities' and a 'challenging environment' in which to deliver the education service (see Coopers & Lybrand 1988). By the mid-1990s these arguments had been largely accepted and, although it is recognized that LMS imposes new demands on head teachers and school governors, budget devolution has been welcomed by many institutional leaders (Cauldwell and Reid 1996). There can be no doubt that carefully planned and well-resourced individual school self-management can appear very attractive, particularly to the heads and governors of schools that are the winners in the education market. A national policy and framework for self-managed community-oriented schools is regarded as having the *potential* to make available the energy and enthusiasm which both the right and the left argue is locked out of the schools by the effects of bureaucracy and by unacceptable 'professional' practice. Such a framework affords an opportunity to develop the principles of 'social justice' and 'stakeholding' through renewed co-operative endeavour on the part of both local and national agencies. Of course, it remains to be seen to what extent co-operative endeavour and the pursuit of social justice will be allowed to take precedence over exigencies of the market.

If the new Labour government is to address the question of social justice in education, it must take seriously the evidence of the effects of poverty and inequality on educational opportunity (see for example, Smith, Noble and Smith 1995). Limited moves in the direction towards social justice for children at their schools will not provide them with 'really equal' educational opportunity because the latter involves much more than schooling. Thirty years ago, in a seminal paper commissioned by the Joint Education Committee of the New Jersey Legislature, James S. Coleman (1969) demonstrated convincingly that the notion of equality of educational opportunity is 'a mistaken and misleading concept'. Coleman is no right-wing elitist. Indeed, he wants to strengthen, and make more meaningful, the 'spirit' or ethos which the phrase 'equality of educational opportunity' represents. Coleman suggested that this can best be attained by using an alternative phrase, 'reduction in inequality' – he does not add the words 'of educational opportunity' to the end of this phrase because he regards inequality as involving a wide range of social conditions and institutions, and not just schools. In Britain, too, it is recognized that educational opportunity is conditioned by a range of factors, many of which are outside the influence of teachers and schools. Although schools which serve children from the poorest families cannot be expected to 'compensate' entirely for the 'deprivations' they endure, a government which calls itself Labour is expected to make serious efforts in the field of education and in educational expenditure policy, and to combine these with other appropriate welfare policies.

Labour's White Paper, *Excellence in Schools* (Cmnd. 3681) signalled what might be regarded as a small step in the direction of social justice by proposing the targeting of schools 'in need' through a policy for Education Action Zones (see Bilefsky 1998; Wilby 1998). But, of course, much will depend of the precise detail of the conditions involved in establishing such zones (EAZs), and there is a rather different prospect at hand for the so called 'failing schools'. Labour has indicated the *possibility* that the running of such schools or groups of schools might be handed over to private companies, as has happened in some states in America (Wilby 1998). In Britain, the National Union of Teachers has pledged 'to block any scheme under the government's EAZ initiative to allow private companies to run schools' (Bilefsky 1998). New initiatives which recognize and utilize opportunities to target appropriate funding and expertise to schools and children in need, rather than the profits of private companies, would be the way forward for a government that attached a high priority to the notion of social justice.

Changes in the structure of financing of schools need to be accompanied by serious consideration of the quality of school life. The now well-established National Curriculum necessarily provides the starting point for future reform. Although there is broad consensus between the main political parties over the notion of a National Curriculum, there remains scope for argument over the detailed content (see for example, Levine 1996) and particularly over the forms of assessment involved (see Murphy and Wilmut in Chapter 7 of this book). There are technical and pedagogic matters on which much further consultation is needed with teachers, their representatives and other knowledgeable parties. Labour needs to create new structures for its review of the school curriculum beyond 2000 and these are likely to involve the new General Teaching Council. As well as the technical and pedagogic issues raised by assessment, there is the issue of the publication of test and examination results and the drawing-up of league tables which have been regarded as one of the main tools in the attempt to establish and operate a market in education.

In Opposition David Blunkett had argued that the Labour Party was 'not shy of the benefits of information about schools' but added that 'it is important that league tables are used to help to lever up standards in schools that are underperforming – and not damage them' (Blunkett 1994). The potential for damage in league tables lies in what he referred to as their employment 'as the public hand of a market system in education'. Now in government, Labour has an opportunity to address some of the differences between schools which have been accentuated by the development of a quasi-market. Labour has an opportunity to address aspects of social inequality in pursuit of social justice and to concern itself with *structures* as well as schools – a point to which we will return shortly. To say as much is not to suggest that principles of social justice will always take precedence either in the minds of those parents who have the opportunity to assert their preferences in the education market, or indeed in the minds of leading politicians. Labour is not likely to develop its education policy by making a simple choice between social justice and the market but by trying to combine them in new ways.

In fact, Tony Blair has demonstrated that he is personally committed to the effective expression of parental preference but also to aspects of the argument on social justice. The Blair family choice of a grant maintained school for their children's secondary education understandably offended those Labour Party activists who had campaigned long and hard against opting out and achieved considerable success in mustering anti-opting-out votes at individual schools. But, of course, one of the political effects of Blair's decision was to send a signal to others whose votes he and his Party needed to win the general election that old Labour thinking had been supplanted by new Labour. Blair reinforced the message when he supported a close Cabinet colleague on a similar personal decision. But, one of the problems for *ordinary* parents who are successful in placing their children in the 'right school' is that in so doing they secure no guarantee over the qualities and capacities of the individual persons who will actually teach their offspring. The question of the qualities and capacities of the teaching workforce is addressed by recent discussion of the recruitment, appraisal and 'training' of teachers (Hartley 1998) and more broadly in the discussion over the question of the introduction of a General Teaching Council.

A General Teaching Council and the policing teachers

The idea of a General Teaching Council involves setting up a new body with the aim of enhancing the 'professional' status of teaching. The idea has support across a wide spectrum of opinion beyond the political mainstream. The radical right supports it although, as we shall see, what they have in mind is rather different from what is proposed by the teaching unions and professional associations. During the 1980s the idea of a GTC was discussed under the umbrella of the Universities Council for the Education of Teachers (UCET) but its working party was, at that time, unable to find sufficient consensus on the issue, mainly due to the opposition of the National Association of Schoolmasters and Union of Women Teachers (NASUWT) which refused to accept, 'either in principle or in detail', the working party proposals set out in a consultative document on the roles and functions of a GTC (see Sayer 1989). Those proposals envisage a GTC that would be concerned with teachers' qualifications, registration, supply, initial training, induction, in-service education, professional discipline, research and with 'external relations' but recommend that 'salaries, pensions and conditions of service should remain firmly matters for employers and unions'.

Now, this is a rather different notion of a GTC from that envisaged by the likes of Dame Mary Warnock, a Conservative Party adviser on education policy, who argues for a GTC on the grounds that 'teachers would gradually cease to be predominantly unionized' and that instead they would become 'professionals comparable to doctors or lawyers'. Indeed, the title of the proposed body mimics that of the GMC – the General Medical Council – although attempts to equate teachers' work with that of doctors, or lawyers, have never been particularly helpful (see Demaine 1995). Stuart Sexton elaborates the new right view on a GTC as part of a more general political argument on the privatization of the education system. As we have already seen, the new right regards the break-up of teachers' capacity for trade union activity as an important prerequisite of privatization. The new right elaborates a notion of 'professionalism' which refers to teachers' status as 'producers of services in a market'. Sexton argues that a GTC should be established by Royal Charter and that teachers could win their membership and retain their 'professional status' only by keeping to a 'no strike' contract. Teachers taking 'unprofessional action' and breaking such a contract would 'by their own self-selection, be weeded out'. The *true professionals*, on the other hand, would be allowed to have 'letters after their name, perhaps Fellow of the College of Teachers' (Sexton 1987).

The perceived threat to traditional trade union rights formed a significant part of the NASUWT objection to the idea of a GTC, but they eventually dropped their opposition to discussions and UCET was later able to announce that all of the 'major professional associations were in broad agreement on the roles and functions for a GTC'. The teacher unions are willing to engage in detailed discussion about a GTC, although not, of course, on the terms presented by the right. Not surprisingly, the teacher unions want a GTC 'alongside' rather than as an alternative to teacher trade unionism.

In their 1997 election manifestos all the main parliamentary parties gave qualified support for the consideration of the idea of a GTC. Much earlier, in its policy review for the 1990s, the Labour Party had said that it would 'consider carefully the establishment of a GTC' – indicating that it would seek to secure and enhance the status of the teaching profession. In July 1997, the new Labour government published *Teaching: Higher Status, Higher Standards: General Teaching Council: A Consultation Document* (DfEE 1997) in which the promise was made that

> by 2000 there will be a General Teaching Council which will: act as a single voice for the teaching profession; be independent of government; assist in the raising of standards in the classroom; advise on the quality of those entering the profession; give guidance on the framework for assessing a new entrant's induction year; have a role in barring individuals from the profession; advise on the standards of medical fitness to teach; establish agreed standards of conduct; and promote teaching as a career (DfEE 1997, p. 4).

The consultation document was generally well received, and *Excellence in Schools* confirmed the government's intention to legislate to establish a GTC. The White Paper also made what now appears to be an obligatory reference to the General Medical Council and the Law Society, followed by a statement that 'Teachers' professional standing should be underlined by the establishment of a General Teaching Council'. However, in early 1998 those institutions involved in recruiting people to courses leading to qualified teacher status (QTS) were reporting 'shortages' of candidates and there was much talk of 'a crisis in recruitment'. There was no such crisis in recruitment to the supposedly comparable professions of law and medicine. Serious questions remain over teachers' rates of pay and working conditions – especially the perception of an occupation overburdened by bureaucracy and continuously under supervision – and it is clear that government needs to do much more than assert the professional status of teaching. A GTC is unlikely to be sufficient in itself to raise the status of teaching and, of course, there are those who will caution Labour to be wary of completing another element of the right-wing agenda for the policing of teachers. The effect on teacher recruitment and teaching quality might not be of the kind the government wishes to achieve, especially if a GTC is allowed to develop even more aggressive mechanisms for the policing of teachers which might be regarded as a further *denial* of professionalism. To say as much is not to argue for 'teacher autonomy'. But there is a real danger that the assertion of the professional status of the occupation of teaching will fail to match potential recruits' perceptions, and that the references to law and medicine will merely have the effect of highlighting the *status difference* of teaching. What really matters to teachers, and potential recruits, is the support they might expect to receive, their working conditions, their rights as well as their responsibilities as workers and their prospects for decent rates of pay during their careers, and not pretentious and spurious comparisons with other occupations or having a few extra letters after their names.

Labour's promises for education in 2002

New Labour made a list of promises to the electorate during the 1997 election campaign, as part of what Tony Blair referred to as 'my contract with the British people'. In fact, there were differences in the promises made to the electorates in different parts of the Kingdom, but in England the 'five early pledges' included policy on 'fast track' punishment for persistent young offenders; cuts in NHS waiting lists; getting under-25-year-olds off benefit and into work; setting 'tough rules' on government spending and borrowing to try to ensure low inflation and strengthen the economy; and for schools, there was a specific promise of cuts in class size to thirty or under for five, six and seven-year-olds by the year 2002. *Excellence in Schools* set out a very much longer and more detailed list of promises, insisting that by the year 2002 'there will be greater awareness across society of the importance of education and increased expectations of what can be achieved' and that 'standards of performance will be higher'. Labour's 'overall approach to policy will be underpinned by six principles: education will be at the heart of government; policies will be designed to benefit the many, not just the few; the *focus will be on standards, not structures*; intervention will be in inverse proportion to success; there will be zero tolerance of underperformance; and government will work in partnership with all those committed to raising standards' (Cmnd. 3681, p. 5, emphasis added).

Labour's promises involve a way of thinking about education that Tony Blair sums up by the phrase 'schools not structure' in his book *New Britain: My Vision of a Young Country* (Blair 1996). The phrase is reproduced in Labour's 1997 election manifesto and reappears in a slightly modified form in *Excellence in Schools*. The phrase tells us much more about new Labour ideology than the mantra 'education, education, education'. Blair's argument is that the focus should be on schools rather than on the social context in which they are to be found, or on the question of the social range of difference between schools that has been encouraged to develop in recent years. Unlike Mrs Thatcher, Tony Blair knows all too well that there is such a thing as 'society', social difference and a wide social range of schooling opportunities. Why else would he have risked his personal political credibility within the Labour Party by exercising 'parental choice'? But rather than the mantra 'education, education, education', his slogan should read 'schools, schools, schools' and indeed Labour appears even keener on the question of standards in those schools than was Thatcher or Major, and very much more able to address the matter than was Callaghan's government. The focus on school standards and on the policing of teachers' work lies at the heart of Labour strategy for better education.

Whilst Labour hopes to be able to breath new life and a new 'spirit' into schools, Blair signalled his Party's intentions on 'standards' with an announcement well before the 1997 General Election: Mr Chris Woodhead, the Conservative-appointed Chief Inspector of Schools, would be retained in his post as the head of the Office for Standards in Education (Ofsted). The misgivings that Mr Blunkett had about league tables whilst in Opposition do not seem quite so urgent in Government, although, as promised, he does appear keen to make progress on the assessment of the 'value added' to the quality of a child's academic ability by attending school. And of course, physical structures can no longer be neglected; Labour has embarked on a £1.2 billion programme of school repairs and building work needed after eighteen years in which the Conservatives administered education. Money will also be released to pay for the promise of class-size reduction, in part, by gradually phasing out the Assisted Places Scheme.

During the 1997 election it was the promise of reducing the size of some primary school classes that was given prominence. In fact, Labour's promise on class size was breathtakingly modest, implying as it did that some children in the 5–7 age-range might still find themselves in classes of more than 30 in the year 2000–2001 and that children not in the 5–7 age-range might find themselves in classes of more than thirty even after 2002. Kirsty Milne (1998) points out that 'demography is in Labour's favour' because there is a small drop in the forecast number of primary-aged children between 1998 and 2000. Nevertheless, with a quarter of 5–7-year-olds (477,000) and a third of all primary school children being taught in classes of more than thirty in 1997–98, Labour's promise might be hard to achieve. Milne provides a detailed analysis which demonstrates the extent of the obstacles to this most modest of new Labour promises.

Writing before Labour's comprehensive spending review, which was announced by Chancellor Gordon Brown in the summer of 1998, Milne pointed to difficulties arising from Labour's electoral commitment to keep within old Tory spending limits during their first two years in government. She demonstrated that Labour's class-size policy could not be adequately funded by diverting public money released from the phasing-out of the Assisted Places Scheme (APS) as had been proposed. In the school year 1997–98 the APS had cost taxpayers around £146 million. But the money released by phasing-out was only to become available gradually because those eleven-year-olds starting on the APS in September 1997, for example, would continue to receive public finance until leaving the sixth form. The first tranche of money diverted from the APS, ring-fenced for reducing class sizes and amounting to only about £22 million, was announced in early 1998; subsequently, local authority schools would have had to be 'content with a drip-drip effect' (Milne 1998). A study in 1997 by the Chartered Institute of Public Finance and Accountancy had also showed that the APS saving would not be sufficient to cover the cost of the extra teachers required by Labour's class-size policy. Even in the longer term, phasing-out the APS would only have freed up a cumulative total of about £100 million by the year 2000, so it was necessary for the Chancellor of the Exchequer to make additional provision to fund Labour's class-size policy.

Labour hopes that, with the additional funding, their promise on class size will be secured by 2001–2, but another difficulty lies in what Milne refers to as 'the parable of the 31st child'. Even with sufficient money to pay for extra teachers to keep classes down to thirty, Labour might only be able to keep its promise by denying 'parental choice'. The parents of children who would have been the 31st child (and others) will have to find places in schools which are not their first choice. Milne points out that this is 'the untold story behind Labour's class-size pledge: it flies in the face of the Tories' much-vaunted policy on parental choice'. But, of course, thousands of parents had no real choice but to place their children in classes of over thirty during the years in which the Conservatives trumpeted the benefits of the market and parental choice. With additional funding, and through a range of policies for improving schools, Labour hopes to do much better and to regain its reputation as a party which regards education as a priority.

Many of Labour's promises about improving schools have little to do with questions of choice and the market and might appear more like old Labour interventionism. New Labour wants, quite properly, to intervene on the question of standards of numeracy and literacy and to establish centres of excellence to spread good practice rather than rely on market competition. Labour wants to improve the quality of education for children with special needs and to encourage more integration into mainstream schooling. Labour wants to encourage schools to promote racial harmony and raise the educational achievement of ethnic minority pupils. Labour wants a home–school contract in all schools, better partnership with parents and greater representation of parents on school governing bodies and LEAs. Labour wants 'Pandas' – performance and assessment reports – that will include benchmark targets related to pupils' family backgrounds, and Labour wants national guidelines on homework 'so that schools, parents and pupils realize its importance in raising standards' – and much more.

Labour's ambitious list of promises indicates that much needs to be done in education, and the year 2002 is set as a target date. But some of Labour's policy changes were already coming into effect in 1998, and in addressing the issue of funding for students in higher education, for example, the new Labour government has already dared to go much further than the right-wing Sir Keith Joseph and the left-of-centre John Smith. The Conservatives had floated the idea of radical reform during Sir Keith's period of office as Secretary of State for Education in the 1980s but shied away from it in fear of the electoral consequences, as did John Smith a decade later. In September 1997 the new Labour Government announced that from the academic year 1999–2000 'there will be no entitlement to maintenance grant' (DfEE 1997, p. 9) and laid plans for a system of 'up front' means-tested tuition fees and student maintenance loans to replace grants. Labour avoided the use of the phrase 'graduate tax', although the government is said to be 'looking at whether repayments might be collected through the Inland Revenue' (ibid. p. 8).

The notion of a 'graduate tax' had been on Labour's agenda in the early 1990s when Jeff Rooker was a Shadow Minister. His proposals (see Rooker 1993) were rejected by John Smith, who insisted that the idea could not be allowed to appear in Ann Taylor's consultative green paper on education, *Opening Doors to a Learning Society* (Labour Party 1993). Under Smith's leadership the issue was effectively suppressed and Rooker lost his role as Shadow Spokesperson on Higher Education. However, the Labor Government in Australia had introduced a graduate tax in the late 1980s, and when Blair took over the leadership of his Party the idea came back on to the agenda. Tony Blair and David Blunkett adopted a somewhat modified version of Sir Ron (now Lord) Dearing's proposals on student funding; but only *after* Labour had won the 1997 election.

Learning to Succeed, the Report of the National Commission on Education (1993), had argued that although the idea of a graduate tax had some 'immediate attractions' these had to be weighed against a range of complex technical problems involved in tax collection. Moreover, the Commission had concluded that 'the graduate tax is not a fair mechanism' (p. 264) and instead suggested that a 'pay as you go' repayment scheme 'is likely to be more attractive over the long run' (p. 265). Whether a repayment scheme is called a 'tax' or something else matters less than the detail, except, of course, to politicians wary of what they regard as a tax-sensitive electorate. Sir John Cassels, Director of the National Commission on Education, argued that the vast majority of taxpayers had not benefited from higher education and could not be expected to go on funding its expansion. He suggested that students would have to start contributing to the cost of their courses – but 'they must be able to defer payment until their earnings enable them to do so without hardship, through the tax system'. Cassels argued that Britain has 'one of the most expensive higher education systems in the world in terms of public expenditure per full-time student, and at the same time many of those students are at or near the poverty line'. He also pointed to 'another paradox' which is that 'well-off families in Britain actually receive more in education subsidies than poor families, because they use it much more and are so heavily subsidized to do so'. At the same time, he observed that 'many universities and colleges have clapped-out buildings' and 'much property that is shabby from undermaintenance and overuse'.

Cassels' observation about the social inequality involved in access to higher education is important, but other aspects of the argument are not entirely convincing. His suggestion that the vast majority of taxpayers have not benefited from higher education is true only in an immediate, individual sense. Most graduates do indeed benefit themselves to a certain extent, but many of them are also a benefit to the economic and social institutions which go on to employ them. Whilst the new Labour government recognizes the economic and social benefits of higher education and is keen to expand opportunities, it wants individuals and their families to pay more of the cost. The plan for students' families to pay up-front means-tested contributions to tuition fees excludes the poorest families who will pay no fees at all, whilst well-off families will pay £1000 per year from Autumn 1998. Ron Dearing was reported to be unhappy with Labour's modifications; his committee had not wanted any *up-front* means testing. But Labour and Dearing are agreed on the principle of replacing maintenance grants with student loans, and on the principle (but not the detail) of loan repayment on the basis of 'ability to pay'.

Well-off families who already sponsor their offspring's university education will be minimally affected by the changes, but no doubt there are some parents who will be pleased to find that students will have greater responsiblity for their own maintenance costs. The new arrangements do not fall easily into 'left' or 'right' categories and Labour appears to have calculated that whilst in politics it may not always be possible to please all of the people all of the time, the electoral consequences might not be quite as damaging as was once thought. Like the previous Conservative government, Labour claims to want to see more students taking up the opportunity of higher education, and it is widely acknowledged that this will mean persuading more students from less well-off families and more 'mature' students to consider applying to university. However, Labour's 'new way' in higher education and the prospect of substantial long-standing debt at the end of a three-year degree course may not prove attractive to such students.

CONCLUSION

On returning to power in May 1997 Labour inherited an education system very different from the one in place when the Callaghan Government was defeated in 1979. An important change during the intervening years had been the centralization of powers. At the same time, there was a transfer of aspects of the administrative and financial responsibility to educational institutions themselves, and a consequent decline of the power and responsibility of the local education authorities. Colleges of further education had been removed from local authority ownership and control, as had the polytechnics before gaining their new status as universities. Over a thousand schools had opted out of local education authority control to become direct grant-maintained schools and almost all of the rest had very substantial responsibility for the administration of their own financial affairs and other aspects of their management, albeit within the context of a system of central government policing. There can be little doubt that the new forms of management of schools and the policing of teachers' work goes down well with the voters of 'middle England' whose electoral support new Labour must secure in order to win general elections. However, we cannot be sure precisely what particular issues were in the minds of those who voted Labour in May 1997, and it is doubtful that education is quite the electoral issue it is sometimes made out to be (see McKenzie 1993). Labour's tremendous electoral achievement is acknowledged by even the most hostile of its opponents but, nevertheless, Labour's huge parliamentary majority, 65.2 per cent of the seats, was secured with only 44.4 per cent of the vote. Certainly no overall majority for Labour's education policy, as such, can be read off from the results of the poll.

At the end of the twentieth century the British education system stands at what the new right sees as a 'halfway house'. Over the last ten years much of the ground has been prepared for the kind of market system in education that the new right seeks to achieve. There is a quasi-market in which the users of education services have become what some observers regard as 'walking vouchers', so that funding is closely tied to participation rates. This does not appear to be unacceptable to new Labour, but it is a small step to a fully-fledged voucher system of the kind that the new right wants to see established and, given the opportunity, there is little that would prevent the new right from picking up where it left off. This is indeed the conclusion reached by Stuart Sexton in the final chapter of this collection. However, much will depend on future elections and on political circumstances. Labour itself might move much further towards the neo-liberal view on educational provision. And there is no knowing what might happen to the Conservative Party, or whether the new right will have influence through it in the future. Whilst it is not difficult to imagine Labour securing a second term of office, it is impossible to gauge the political terrain during the early 2000s.

There is, of course, much more to the politics of contemporary education policy than I have been able to refer to in this chapter. I have merely sketched out an argument about the changes of education policy over the last twenty years and provided some illustrations. I have left much of the detail on specific policy issues to the specialist contributors to the book – and in some respects a proper conclusion must be left till 2001–2, when we will be able assess the results of new Labour's promises and the electorate's verdict on the new Labour project as a whole.

ACKNOWLEDGMENT

I am grateful to Lorraine Culley for discussion of many of the important points in this chapter and for her reading of earlier drafts.

2 Moving Back from Comprehensive Secondary Education?

Tony Edwards, Geoff Whitty
and Sally Power

At times during several decades of spasmodic movement towards and away from comprehensive secondary education, a change of government has brought an abrupt shift in policy. Circular 10/65, issued by the Labour Government elected in 1964, seemed an important turning point, even though a majority of Local Education Authorities (LEAs) were already planning or considering the comprehensive reorganization which all of them were now 'requested' to make. In 1970, a Bill to make that request into a requirement was nullified by the Conservative election victory. The response of Ted Short, Labour's Secretary of State, to accusations of being dictatorial had been that a consistent national policy must take precedence over LEA autonomy: 'if it is wrong to select and segregate children', he argued, then 'it must be wrong everywhere' (quoted in Kerckhoff et al. 1996, p. 34). Yet his Conservative successor, Margaret Thatcher, promptly issued Circular 10/70 reaffirming LEAs' freedom to decide whether, when and how to end academic selection, although even her own high regard for grammar schools could not slow down what she later recalled as the 'roller coaster' of comprehensive reform. The 1974–79 Labour administration reaffirmed central government's commitment to a comprehensive system of state education by forcing the 'direct-grant' grammar schools to choose between remaining academically selective or continuing to receive public grants. Then, in 1979, the incoming Thatcher Government moved quickly to discard comprehensive education as national policy. It also introduced a publicly-funded scholarship ladder to assist 'clever children from poor homes' to escape neighbourhood (especially inner-city) comprehensive schools deemed incapable of providing the academic opportunities such children merited. In retrospect, the 1980 Education Act, which included this Assisted Places Scheme, has seemed to mark the beginning of that 'staged' return to academic selection which some have seen as implicit in parts of the 1988 and 1993 Education Acts and which was conspicuous in the Major Government's last (1996) Education Bill. So will Labour's election victory in 1997 reverse that 'reverse trend' which had doubled by 1996 the proportion of secondary schools which were private, or openly selective, or otherwise 'non-comprehensive' (Benn and Chitty 1996, p. 88)?

Certainly the intention of making a visible difference quickly was apparent in the first policy pronouncements of the Blair government. In particular, the prompt introduction of a Bill to end the Assisted Places Scheme was presented by David Blunkett, the new Secretary of State, both as an immediate return of resources to the public sector and as exemplifying the new Government's choice of 'high quality education for the many' over 'excellence for the few'. This might be taken as signalling a vigorous return to comprehensive secondary schooling. Yet a campaigning list of 'ten ways in which Labour will make a difference' to education had made no reference at all to academic selection (Labour Party 1997), nor is the issue prominent in Blunkett's first Education White Paper (DfEE 1997). Exchanging claims to pragmatism during the Commons debate about ending assisted places, the then 'Shadow' Secretary of State, Gillian Shephard, described the Government's action as 'driven by class-envy dogma' while the Education Minister (Stephen Byers) dismissed the Scheme itself as having been 'born out of dogma' (*The Times Educational Supplement* 6 June 1997). But, although Shephard extended her attack to what she described as Labour's persistent failure to 'recognize the contribution that choice, variety of school and variety of route make to raising standards', the Government's own White Paper also celebrates variety. It has retained the current distinction between LEA-maintained, voluntary aided and grant-maintained status in the renamed forms of 'community', 'aided' and 'foundation' schools. And, while it suggests that there will be no going back to the eleven-plus, no partial selection by general academic ability, and no misuse of special aptitudes as a substitute for it, the future of the remaining grammar schools is to be decided by local parents. The Old Labour view, that if selection is wrong then it is wrong everywhere, seems to have been quietly forgotten. Throughout, the White Paper displays an enthusiasm for 'modernizing' comprehensive secondary education, a trend seen to be in line with international moves to replace common schooling with a pluralist approach in which variety of school ethos, organization and curriculum is taken as the appropriate response to the multiple cultural identities of modern society (Hartley 1997; Whitty et al. 1998).

In its rejection of uniformity, the White Paper avoids the complex issue of how far traditional assimilationist objectives of comprehensive schooling should be replaced by a willing acceptance of cultural diversity. Even in the narrower context of curriculum specialization, it is uninformative about how special aptitudes are to be identified among eleven-year-olds, especially where the popularity of a school makes this a matter of competition for oversubscribed places rather than of simply expressing a preference. In a policy document published so soon after taking office and intended to define a new vision without being specific about policy details, some difficult problems are bound to be avoided or their possible solutions postponed. Nevertheless, we argue in this chapter that specialization is less easily distinguished from selection than the White Paper appears to assume. Choice is very much harder to argue against than selection. It may also seem obviously to require that secondary schools are different in kind, not merely better and worse versions of the same model. Choice should neither be denied not restricted, David Hargreaves (1996) has argued, unless the costs clearly outweigh the benefits *and* there are good grounds for believing that government intervention to avoid or reduce the costs would be effective. There is evidence however that, as various forms of open and covert selection have increased, so a steepening hierarchy of schools has added to the disadvantages of already disadvantaged groups. It is evidence which a Government committed to replacing a previously excessive faith in market forces with a firm (if modernized) view of education as a public service surely cannot ignore.

SPECIALISATION, NOT SELECTION

Even without that careful avoidance of ideological commitments which marked Labour's 1997 election campaign, the issue of selection has become complicated by those structural changes that enabled the last Conservative Secretary of State to argue that the old either-or terms of debate had become obsolete. Greater diversity in status, funding and accountability meant more schools controlling their own admissions policies and practices. Within the state sector, only forty per cent of English secondary schools are now both LEA-maintained and 'fully' comprehensive (Fitz et al. 1997). And, although successive Conservative efforts since 1980 to sponsor a 'staged return' to selection had still produced only a one per cent increase in the 'officially selective' school population (Benn and Chitty 1996, pp. 463–4), the 1996 Education Bill was intended to accelerate the trend and to move some way towards John Major's vision of 'a grammar school in every town'. Schools wishing to achieve or return to 'full grammar school status' were to be enabled to do so. Any secondary school could create a 'grammar stream' within an otherwise comprehensive intake, or could shape part of its entry by identifying applicants with an aptitude for its curriculum speciality. Even in 'ordinary' LEA-maintained comprehensives, the proportion so chosen could be as high as twenty per cent – a figure resembling the conventional eleven-plus pass rate too closely to be coincidental. In technology colleges and other specialist schools, it could be as high as thirty per cent; grant-maintained schools, the Conservatives' intended vanguard of innovation, were to be free to select up to half their entry by aptitude or general ability. What the 1996 White Paper termed 'an element of selection' was justified as a vital component in a system increasingly based on 'choice and diversity'.

Although a lively nostalgia for grammar schools and promises to revive them were a distinctively Conservative electioneering tactic in 1997, a considerable retreat from even the concept of the common secondary school was apparent in policy statements from all three main parties. It reflected the extent to which specialization has become accepted as a desirable (and legitimate) alternative to selection. In the Conservatives' 1992 White Paper, specialization is compared favourably with selection ('choice by schools') because it is 'parent-driven' and because encouraging schools to 'play to their strengths' would 'gear' schooling to 'local circumstances and individual needs' without creating 'tiers' unequal in esteem (DfE 1992, para.1.49). This is also how comprehensive secondary education is presented in Labour's 1997 White Paper, a sharp contrast in this respect being explicitly drawn with Old Labour policy. It is argued that while 'all-in secondary schooling rightly became the normal pattern' during the first wave of comprehensive reform, that approach to equal opportunity carried 'a tendency to uniformity' which has been unhelpful to raising standards and is not to be revived. The 'modernizing principle' is seen as indicating 'not a single model of schooling' but the active encouragement of schools to develop 'their own distinctive identity and expertise'. Nevertheless, certain conditions are to be imposed on this diversity. The spirit of co-operation which is now to replace an excessive faith in market forces requires specialist schools to make any distinctive expertise available 'as a resource for local people and neighbouring schools' and not merely use it for their own competitive advantage. Indeed, specialist schools are portrayed as 'magnets of excellence' with a special role in revitalising education and raising standards in those mainly inner-city areas to be designated as Education Action Zones. And while 'giving priority ... to relevant aptitude' is not to be misused as a substitute for selection by general academic ability, a further necessary departure from Old Labour's habit of associating 'excellence with elitism' requires that comprehensive schools should normally set by ability and provide 'fast-track' and 'accelerated' learning for pupils capable of benefiting from such provision. The dangers of reconstituting a tripartite system within schools are ignored.

Despite the appearance of decisively reversing recent Conservative policy towards selection by general academic ability, the new Government seems therefore to have inherited that comparison with specialization made in the 1992 White Paper (where selection by schools was contrasted very unfavourably with choice by parents), and the assumption made in the 1996 White Paper that parents should have 'greater choice in deciding the type of school that will best meet their children's interests and needs'. Yet there is little evidence yet that organizational diversity is bringing consumer-responsive innovations in curriculum, pedagogy, or ethos. Nor does research into children's and parents' reasons for choosing a secondary school show much evidence of choice being shaped by a preference for any educational 'style' significantly different from traditional models (Edwards and Whitty 1997: Glatter et al. 1997; Echols and Willms 1995). Market advocates sometimes explain this as a consequence of consumer demand having been suppressed for so long by the LEA 'monopoly' that the true causal relationships between choice and diversity have not yet had time to become evident. But at least in the short run, the conditions that several commentators have identified for 'specialization without selection' have not yet been created – namely, the distribution of school choices around a wide range of alternatives so that demand is not concentrated on popular schools to an extent which enables them to remain (or become) able to pick the more desirable applicants, and which leaves applicants very unequally placed in their chances of being chosen. From a market perspective, that is taken to be a necessary condition for not returning power to the producers by enabling popular schools to pick and choose (Tooley 1996). From a perspective concerned with equity, it is taken to be necessary to avoid competition for the more desirable school places being heavily skewed in favour of already advantaged applicants (Hargreaves 1996: Hirsch 1997). However, such competition is unavoidable where a local hierarchy of secondary schools is so largely determined by their positions on annual league tables of school performance.

In the quasi-market which the secondary sector has become in many areas, traditional academic values have tended to be emphasized to fill places and particularly to attract able middle-class children. The private sector continues to benefit hugely from marketing 'excellence' in that form, as do the surviving grammar schools and those comprehensives which try to resemble them (Edwards and Whitty 1997: Glatter et al. 1997). The creation of city technology colleges was interpreted in the 1992 White Paper as a significant step towards diversifying the range, because they were intended to offer (and stimulate demand for) a distinctively modern, high-technology version of secondary education in an environment embodying the best features of the enterprise culture. In practice, however, parents were more inclined to see them as having higher status than neighbouring comprehensive schools, as being at least partly selective despite an official requirement to recruit intakes representative of their catchment area, and as combining new technology with traditional values (Whitty et al. 1993, pp. 82–89). Grant-maintained schools were intended to use their freedom from Local Authority control to be innovative on a much larger scale, but what they have displayed more conspicuously in practice has been a 'reinvigorated traditionalism' (Halpin et al. 1997; Fitz et al. 1997). Certainly the first 'wave' of secondary schools seeking this new self-governing status was weighted towards the selective end of an increasingly complex continuum, having in comparison with the LEA sector a higher proportion of grammar schools and ex-grammar schools and tending more often to employ at least partial selection (Bush et al. 1993). Sampling what had then become a much larger category, Benn and Chitty (1996, pp. 142–3) found that while most grant-maintained schools 'positively wished to identify themselves as comprehensive schools', they were also significantly more likely than LEA-maintained schools to have sixth forms, relatively high proportions of middle-class pupils, and relatively low proportions of working-class, poor and ethnic minority pupils. The previous Government's frequent efforts to present this favoured category as academically superior to other secondary schools were intellectually dishonest in the absence of comparative data on 'value-added' performance, but have almost certainly influenced public perceptions. The proposals in the 1997 White Paper to identify the new category of 'foundation' schools even more closely with grant-maintained schools than was envisaged by Labour in Opposition (Labour Party 1995) makes it likely that the existing status hierarchy will be maintained. Indeed, the unfortunate choice of the terms 'community' and 'foundation' school may assist the latter to trade upon their traditionalist image even if their current advantages in terms of funding and control over admissions are removed.

Of course, schools can emphasize or develop a particular curriculum strength or distinctive ethos without making it a bid for competitive advantage or using it to select the more desirable of their applicants. Most of the 231 Technology, Languages, Arts and Sports Colleges currently receiving additional funding for their expertise remain more or less 'fully' comprehensive, as no doubt will the 21 recently added to that list. But the conclusion that 'specialization is unlikely to be achieved without selection in a fiercely competitive market' (Kerckhoff et al. 1996: 44) rests on substantial evidence that demand continues to be focused on the traditional academic model rather than becoming widely and variously dispersed. Where schools compete for custom, being 'like a grammar school' is an advantage not only in visible aspects of organization and ethos such as uniform but also in the curriculum being offered. So while the previous Government first actively encouraged schools to specialize in modern subjects such as technology, there is evidence of such specialisms being regarded as incompatible with notions of selectiveness and excellence which are more readily associated with a 'traditional liberal' curriculum (Fitz et al. 1997).

It might then appear logical to conclude that, if fierce competition for access to that curriculum is creating a disproportionate number of working-class 'losers', then the model itself should be expanded in a suitably updated version of Harold Wilson's 'grammar schools for all'. That is not a route which an energetically modernizing Labour Government could embrace wholeheartedly, because a 'grammar school education' is too closely associated with an elitist view of 'real' educational achievement as being 'naturally' restricted to the small minority academically capable of profiting from it. It is therefore contradicted by powerful political and economic arguments for a broadly-based Learning Society and against old divisions between the educated and the rest. In its commitment to 'excellence for all', the Labour Government will no doubt keep in mind that the Skills Audit carried out to support the 1996 *Competitiveness* White Paper once again identified levels of achievement in the middle and lower levels of academic ability as the main cause for national concern. Speaking at that time, Tony Blair dismissed the then Government's enthusiasm for grammar schools as a 'response to the needs of a vanished society', which required only a small educated class and a large supporting army of basically skilled and suitably deferential workers (Labour Party 1996). Yet, in some respects, the new Government has adopted a fairly conventional view of education and avoided some awkward questions about the selective nature and social functions of educational knowledge (Whitty 1985). Certainly an unexamined notion of 'standards' has been prominent in its rhetoric.

STANDARDS, STRUCTURES AND UNEQUAL OPPORTUNITIES

In his first major speech as Secretary of State for Education and Employment, David Blunkett declared himself 'interested in standards, not structures', in 'what works' and not in dogma. That pragmatic priority is restated in the White Paper. It is presumably intended to reassure apprehensive parents and teachers that the new Government will not engage in extensive restructuring of an education system which has suffered over the past ten years from a surfeit of dogmatic reform. But the separation of standards from structures is not tenable. Indeed it is denied, with direct reference to academic selection, in the White Paper itself when the endemic problem of the British education system is 'easily stated' as an undue concentration on 'excellence at the top' accompanied by a considerable neglect of the achievements of the many (DfEE 1997, p. 10).

It is true that comprehensive secondary education has not been universally accepted even in principle, so that necessary debates about what forms it should take have regularly been obscured by continuing objections to the 'cult of equality' (and 'tendency to uniformity') which the reform was seen by opponents to embody at a high cost to educational standards (Benn and Chitty 1996; Kerckhoff et al. 1996; Pring and Walford 1997). Confident counter-assertions that it is academic selection, not its absence, which 'raises standards for all' (Gillian Shephard, on the *Today* programme 21 April 1997) conveniently ignore the difficulties of supporting or refuting that claim when most comprehensive schools have had to co-exist with schools catering for much less than a comprehensive range of attainment. Public funds and school endowments assist attendance at private schools; some grammar schools have survived; some voluntary-aided schools have used their freedom to maintain a distinctively Christian character to shape their intakes academically; and some popular comprehensives have tried to attract a disproportionate share of the ablest children, to secure their market niche or to keep up with competitors. That these attenuating circumstances have been much less evident in Scotland largely explains the relative success of Scottish comprehensive schools in raising *average* levels of achievement and reducing social class inequalities (MacPherson and Willms 1987). In England, over half the schools surveyed by Benn and Chitty (1996) had fewer than fifteen per cent of their pupils in the top fifth of the ability range, a proportion widely taken as the threshold for a truly comprehensive school; over a third had no more than ten per cent, and only one in four could be considered to have fully comprehensive

intakes. Continuing disputes about the effects of comprehensive re-organisation on educational standards have therefore remained bedevilled by
the problems of finding 'fully' selective and 'fully' comprehensive systems
to compare.

They also reflect fundamental value differences in what conclusions
are drawn from evidence. One conclusion drawn from comparing the
secondary school attainments of the 1958 birth cohort followed up in
the National Child Development Study (NCDS) was that, when differences in the social composition of intakes were taken into account,
there was little difference overall in the academic outcomes of selective and non-selective systems. But the range of achievements was less
in non-selective systems because the less academically able did rather
better while the more able did rather worse (Kerckhoff et al. 1996:
245–6). That second conclusion might be cited as factual justification
for complaints about levelling down, and for reviving that association of
academic selection with special and perhaps indispensable meritocra-
tic opportunities for able children from disadvantaged backgrounds
which persisted within the Labour Movement long after a political
commitment to comprehensive secondary education appeared to have
been made. But subsumed within the objective of 'raising standards
for all', which had been the main driving force behind comprehensive
reorganization, was the belief that the persistently strong links
between social class and educational attainment would thereby be
weakened.

The egalitarian failure of a reform from which so much had been
hoped for is given a largely structural explanation by Alan Kerckhoff
and his colleagues (1997). They point to the greater tendency of Conservative-controlled and more middle-class local authorities to delay
reorganization, preserve grammar schools alongside comprehensive
schools, and to adopt patterns of secondary schooling that 'retained a
major class-related structural feature of the selective system'. In the
NCDS cohort, middle-class children were relatively more numerous in
those comprehensives which had been grammar schools, which recruited
at thirteen, and which retained sixth forms and the 'academic' orientation
associated with them. Even when differences in social composition and
in attainment at sixteen were taken into account, comprehensive schools
with sixth forms had produced far more graduates by the age of 23 than
those without. Their conclusion was that 'lower status and lower ability
students were placed in disadvantaged educational settings, with consequent reductions in their academic achievements' (Kerckhoff et al.
1996: 224). Now it is arguable that the continuing trend towards socially

segregated neighbourhoods would have polarized intakes to comprehensive schools even without the previous Government's discourage-
ment of catchment areas. Nevertheless, that further reinforcement of
'class-related structural features' of selection or partial selection which
seems to have marked recent education policy invalidates the separation
of structures from standards which characterizes the White Paper. In
particular, one effect of 'open' enrolment in some areas has been to
increase between-school differences in the composition of intakes with
middle-class parents gaining even more disproportionate access to the
'better' schools.

The marketing of academic excellence in the traditional forms which
we referred to earlier has been supported by annual performance tables
which embody a limited view of achievement and make no allowance
for the effects of more and less socially and academically selective
intakes. The consequent tendency to polarize 'good' and 'bad' schools
has had predictable effects on the social composition of their intakes, so
that if more of the top fifth of the ability range are in comprehensive
schools than was the case thirty years ago (which is one of the more
optimistic findings reported by Benn and Chitty 1996), they are increasingly concentrated in the more high-achieving, oversubscribed schools.
There is also some evidence of downward pressure on primary schools,
with unofficial forms of selection being used by those enjoying special
transfer arrangements with popular comprehensives (Menter et al.
1997).

It is arguable that committed, well-informed parents who are willing
and able to be 'active choosers' of their children's school deserve the
better opportunities which are likely to result (Tooley 1996). And there
are counter-arguments against giving 'well-resourced choosers ...
free rein to guarantee and reproduce their advantages' (Gewirtz et al.
1995: 23). Where choice falls heavily on some favoured schools, as it
often does in large urban areas, many children will be crowded out in
the competition for places and many parents will not even express a
first choice for a school they expect would reject their application. The
Audit Commission (1996) placed around twenty per cent of parents in
its survey in one or other of these two categories. In London, one in
three parents failed to get their first choice. That parents of higher
socio-economic status are more likely to apply for the 'better' comprehensive schools is another example of differentiation by candidature
which has long been part of the explanation for processes of social
selection – that is, knowledge of the likelihood of not 'succeeding'
in more 'ambitious' choices creates more 'realistic' ambitions and so

contributes to reproducing social class differences in participation and achievement.

Covert forms of selection are likely to produce even greater inequalities, because even greater demands are made on 'cultural resources' to decipher 'real' admissions criteria. Detecting them and constructing appropriate responses are more likely among better educated and otherwise socially advantaged parents. This strengthens the case for procedures that are straightforward and transparent (Jowett 1995: West et al. 1997). Although there is nothing covert about CTCs' consideration of applicants' suitability, because they are required to enquire into parents' commitment to extended full-time education, longer school hours and an 'enterprising' school environment, this evaluation of family suitability privileges attitudes which have traditionally served as a social filter. This may well have prepared the way for the sort of home–school contracts which, under the previous Government's proposals, could have been used by oversubscribed schools to exclude undeserving applicants. Concern about the wider implications of selection by interest and aptitude led Gewirtz et al. (1995) to suggest that 'unusual talent' in (for example) music and dance was being used by some schools to enhance the entry of academically able children from middle-class families. Such partial selection may of course make some inner-city comprehensives more academically comprehensive than they would have been otherwise, on the 'magnet' principle of attracting applicants across usual social and ethnic boundaries through the power of a specialized curriculum. But it also allows oversubscribed schools to decide which pupils to take after interviewing them with their parents, thereby enabling them to have 'an intake balanced by ability which has, however, weeded out any child/family that the school considers might be "problematic" or a drain on its resources' (Whatford 1996: 18). Labour's White Paper rejects parental interviews except where used by church schools to establish religious or sectarian commitment. But other less visible and potentially even more unfair ways of establishing applicants' suitability include the use (notably by some grant-maintained schools) of application forms which bear little resemblance to the school's published criteria and which may include intrusive enquiries into family background. It may be significant that just over forty per cent of the heads of grant-maintained schools questioned by Cauldwell and Reid (1996) declined to comment on their admissions procedures, possibly indicating the significance of covert selection in the competition for those pupils most likely to sustain or improve a school's academic reputation.

CONCLUSION: PRIVATE AND PUBLIC INTERESTS

In the 1997 White Paper, the Labour Government promised to restore 'a better balance' between fairness and co-operation on one side and, on the other, educational diversity and the 'power of schools to decide their own affairs' (DfEE 1997, p. 66). During the preceding ten years, that balance had fallen heavily towards individual and institutional self-interest, so that the renewed emphasis on collective responsibility is very welcome. The decision to end the Assisted Places Scheme exemplifies that priority. In the election campaign, Labour's commitment to end it was neither softened nor tactically adjusted in response to predictable charges of 'class envy' and of denying opportunity to deserving individuals. On the issue of what to do with the surviving maintained grammar schools, however, objections to outright academic selection were modified by reference to those main themes in recent policy debate – the benefits of diversity, and the right of individual schools and 'their' parents and governors to take the critical decision.

'It cannot be right that good existing schools should be forcibly brought to an end, or that parents' freedom of choice should be so completely abolished'. That objection to enforced reorganization comes from the 1958 (Conservative) White Paper, *Secondary Education for All: a New Drive* (pp. 5–6). Something very like it appeared in Labour campaign speeches in constituencies with grammar schools, the assurance being given that 'if there is no desire among local parents for a change in admissions policies, there will be no ballot and no change'. This avoided the obvious question about which parents (and other 'stakeholders') have the right to be heard, and seemed an unfortunate residue of the previous Government's efforts to reduce decisions about selection to an aspect of school self-government. Preparing the way for the Conservatives' 1996 White Paper, Gillian Shephard had asserted the particular right of grant-maintained schools to 'make their own decisions about how they operate', and to 'develop the character they judge will best suit the needs of their pupils and communities without being told by anyone else what to do' (23 March 1996). In that White Paper itself, that right was extended to all secondary schools, with a further proposal that governing bodies should be required (not merely 'requested') to consider each year how selective they wished their school to be (DfEE 1996). They were not asked to consider possible effects on other schools, or on efficient and equitable provision in that 'community'; institutional self-interest was to be the only relevant frame of reference. As the following example illustrates, such a view is inadequate. The decision of one grant-maintained secondary school in Bromley to select 25 per cent of its entry by general academic ability led all neighbouring schools to announce their intention to select similarly up to fifteen per cent of their intakes from September 1997 (West et al. 1997: 12). One school's decision may force others to change direction unwillingly in order to keep up, and one school's decision to expand or become more selective or create a sixth form may create problems for neighbouring schools, which the previous Administration clearly regarded as a bracing challenge inescapable in a competitive market. A Government believing in collective responsibility is surely obliged to be much less cavalier about the right of one school to take a decision directly affecting the fortunes of others without more public discussion.

Part of that return to collective responsibility will be the promised national guidelines on admissions procedures. For reasons which include (especially) the spread of covert forms of selection, and the invidiously unequal processes of self-selection which these promote (Walford 1997), it is to be hoped that the 'fairer ways of offering school places' promised in the present White Paper will be sufficiently robust to debar much that is done currently and will replace the present fragmentation with a consistent, transparent and fair system along lines recently outlined by West et al. (1997). But the more far-reaching proposition that comprehensive schools should be different but equal is one which the new Government may be declaring too easily in the context of that polarizing of ethos, reputation and intake which we outlined earlier. Warnings against a two-tiered system of chosen and unchosen schools have been given repeatedly as the quasi-market has taken shape. Energetic support for specialized schools, even with supporting reference to an appropriate division of labour within a 'family' of neighbouring schools, carries the danger of relegating to a residual category those which do wish or feel unable to follow that path. The danger was vividly illustrated in the 1993 Parent's Charter, in which every kind of secondary school was mentioned except the LEA-maintained comprehensives which most pupils still attended. 'Selection of children for unequal provision' has been the dominant principle on which English secondary education has been organized (Pring and Walford 1997, p. 3). Having previously appeared to accept uniformity as the consequence of pursuing equality, Labour is now beginning to 'link its traditional concern with equality with a new recognition of diversity' (Barber 1997, p. 175). In this New Order, it may indeed be more constructive to accept the desirability of diversity and concentrate on equity of access than to oppose policies which produce schools which are not 'fully' comprehensive in the old manner (Hirsch 1997, p. 160). But the successful fostering of specialization and diversity within a broader commitment to comprehensive secondary education requires serious attention to be given to ways of preventing differences becoming inequalities. To that extent at least, the Labour Government should recognize that the quest to raise standards for all cannot sensibly be divorced from issues of structure.

3 Educational Reforms, Gender and Families
Miriam David

My research on families and education, a form of feminist critical policy analysis, linking empirical studies with broader policy questions and issues, is the subject of this chapter. Given the recent election of a New Labour government and its commitment to 'Education, education, education', this research evidence becomes significant. Mothers' perspectives on their involvements in their children's education are explored in the context of recent educational reforms towards marketization and privatization of education and the wider social and familial changes which have influenced more general cultural shifts, including that towards parental involvement. My aim is to illustrate and elaborate mothers' understandings of the various changes; they are aware of the increasing inequities created by education reforms which are often at odds with the impact of cultural changes. Moreover, there is a dissonance between the discourse of educational reform and the practices of families in which mothers bear the burden.

New Labour's relevant policy proposals introduced since May 1997 include the White Paper *Excellence in Schools* covering homework policies, parent–school contracts, evening curfews, the raising of educational standards and the reduction of class sizes in primary schools; the scheme for *Welfare to Work*, specifically targeted on lone parents/mothers and assuming their desire for paid work to help with children's upbringing; the Dearing Report on *Higher Education in the Learning Society* (23 July 1997) and the government's immediate response which aims to expand educational opportunities to a wider public, including building upon the growth in mature women/mother students and those from poor and/or working class homes/families. All of these policy developments focus on families' relations to education from the perspective of officials and institutions rather than the families themselves. My evidence suggests a different reading of policy developments and the gendering of family work in relation to schools and education.

Education reforms and social policies remain high on the public agenda in many if not most advanced industrial societies, since education is seen as critical for economic competitiveness (Chubb and Moe

1990; Ball 1994; Whitty et al. 1996, 1997). In the last two decades the discourse of educational reform has essentially focused on marketization and privatization to create the conditions for more competition within education in order to improve educational standards – on what have sometimes been referred to as either neo-liberal or neo-conservative reforms (Apple 1997; Dale 1993). Moreover, parents have been targeted as the main consumers, customers or users of education, most able to decide on the best education for their children (David 1993; David et al. 1994; West 1994). Thus conditions have been created for parents to be able to choose within and between schools at transitions to and from primary school to ensure that their children receive the most appropriate education. By contrast, educational professionals and bureaucrats have been afforded much reduced roles within educational decision making. Indeed, educational reforms have also removed not only educational bureaucracy but also local government decision making, in favour of decisions at the local school level (Gewirtz, Ball and Bowe 1995). The school has indeed been afforded far more autonomy to make decisions and to raise and spend its own resources in the context of wider national guidelines on the curriculum and staffing. The whole panoply of the governance of education has been increasingly privatized and elements also marketized. This has given rise to an enormous growth in both strategic and critical research into aspects of education marketization (Fitz et al. 1995, Whitty 1996–7; Ball et al. 1995; Glatter et al. 1995).

At the same time, moreover, there has been a growing emphasis and expansion of education within the wider marketplace, including the growth and availability of educational technology and aids to learning, not only in formal educational institutions. Despite this explosion of information technology and educational materials, parents have still been seen as the main arbiters of such goods and services. Indeed, they have increasingly been expected to manage the ever more complex processes of their children's learning. Social democratic discourses have increasingly emphasized home–school relations, including quasi-legal contracts, homework policies and parental participation in school management, especially as parent governors (David 1993; Deem et al. 1995). Parental involvement has become increasingly part of a normative discourse about education where once it was largely the domain of professionals and educational bureaucrats.This, too, has given rise to a tremendous growth in strategic and critical research into aspects of parental participation or involvement in education (David 1993; Hughes et al. 1994; Wolfendale and Topping 1996).

Mostly, these two research fields have remained separate and relatively insulated from each other, fitting into different academic discourses, and both being immune to feminist critiques, let alone gender analysis. This paper is an attempt to bring together these two areas of research and to show the critical role that women, as mothers, play in both fields of endeavour, despite their invisibility or genderlessness in most of the scholarship and research. This paper also grows out of a wider and international feminist critique of such issues (see 'Discourse: studies in the cultural politics of education', special issue *Feminist Perspectives on the Marketisation of Education* edited by Epstein and Kenway, December 1996).

Moreover, the argument is that changes in girls' formal educational achievements may contribute to the growing emphasis, in the public policy arena, of women's roles as parents exclusively rather than as involved in the labour market – an entirely different market again. For instance, a recent BBC television programme (Panorama) raised a public debate about the effects of mothers' employment on children's educational achievements. This illustrated a growing 'neo-conservative backlash' against social, familial, economic and neo-liberal policy changes. The unpublished study most cited on the programme, by Margaret O'Brien, looked at mothers' employment – full-time, part-time, or lack of it – on children's educational performance at the end of secondary schooling. It was argued that mothers' full-time employment had a negative effect on children's, especially boys', achievements in the General Certificate of Secondary Education (GCSE). O'Brien did not investigate the whole range of maternal occupational and educational involvements in children's upbringing. Instead she studied the impact of maternal employment on children at the end of compulsory schooling, an age that is rare in the literature of parental involvement – where it is more usual to consider early childhood and primary schooling. It is interesting that she assumes what we have been trying to explore, that is mothers' differential involvements, which are normally occluded. As Orbach argued in *The Guardian* (16 March 1997) that kind of research feeds into the normative discourse about mothers' work being to care for and be preoccupied with children.

My research studies are presented first, followed by a discussion and interpretation of the various evidence and methodologies. In particular, I want to turn upside down the two research fields of parental choice and educational markets, and parental involvement in education, and focus on parental (or, rather, maternal) perspectives on current reforms and policies, illustrating the now normative discourses about choice and involvement, and how they are understood and interpreted by families in various social and familial positions or locations. The general issue is to consider the evidence from recent policy-relevant research about the relations between mothers and schools/education, and to show parents' differential involvements and especially mothers' perspectives and concerns, particularly at key moments, such as the transitions to primary schooling and from primary to secondary school. I do not want to argue simplistic one-way forms of causality between children's educational performance or achievements (however defined which itself is difficult) and mothers' types of involvement in education or employment (equally difficult to define).

RESEARCH ON PARENTAL CHOICE AND INVOLVEMENT IN EDUCATION

My overall aim is to apply a gendered focus or feminist analysis to the work on parental choice and involvement in education, which has been singularly absent from all the research studies on neo-liberal and neo-conservative reforms, especially on parental choice, and from those on neo-social democratic developments on parental involvement at home or school. Moreover, these two fields are not generally brought together but are treated as relatively separate areas of research, in part at least because one refers mainly to secondary and the other to early childhood and primary education.

Most recent research on parental choice of school and market forces in education has been critical analysis or evaluation of policy and its implementation from the point of view of education, and especially secondary education, (e.g. Whitty et al. 1994, 1995, 1996, 1997; Gewirtz, Ball and Bowe 1995; Woods, Glatter and Bagley 1996, and, in the USA, Chubb and Moe 1992; Crowson, Boyd and Mawhinney 1996; Witte 1996), rather than from the point of view of families, which is my feminist focus. The best recent survey of studies of choice of school across the nations remains that of Donald Hirsch, commissioned by the OECD (OECD, 1994). There has been a plethora of research on different aspects of educational markets in Britain, often in relation to the concerns particularly felt in North America or Australia and New Zealand, best summarized by Geoff Whitty (Whitty 1996–7). Steven Ball's work is at its richest in its theoretical rather than methodological but he has also, with colleagues, considered issues to do with types of 'choosers' and their effects upon the children. (Ball 1994; Gewirtz, Ball and Bowe

1995) Diane Reay has reanalysed some of their work and documented the role of mothers (Reay 1997)

Similarly, but separately, research on parental involvement tends to be from an educational or (nursery or primary) school vantage point rather than that of families, whether parents and/or children (Tizard et al. 1988; Edwards and Redfern 1988; Hughes,Wikley and Nash 1994; Hughes et al. in Bernstein and Brannen 1996; Merrtens 1995; Wolfendale and Topping 1996; Macbeth 1995. For the USA: Lareau 1989). Again, much of it ignores gender, although here there have been rather more feminist critiques, the best of which remains that of Valerie Walkerdine and Helen Lucey (1989). Together with colleagues I have begun to develop both theoretical and empirical qualitative studies of these issues (David, Edwards, Hughes and Ribbens 1993; David, Davies, Edwards, Reay and Standing 1996; David, Davies, Edwards, Reay and Standing 1997). Separately they, too, have developed their own feminist analyses and critiques (Edwards 1993; Ribbens 1994; Reay 1995; 1996; 1997; Standing 1997).

A feminist analysis would suggest both that it is important to consider issues from the point of view of families as much as education, and these two areas of policy and associated research are not discrete because of mothers' central and critical involvement in children's upbringing and education, whether in early childhood, primary or secondary school. Thus what is meant by involvement – as a preoccupation, if not an occupation – in children's care and education and the implications of educational reforms or policy change are also of concern. I will also look at parental expectations of educational achievements. I have also recently conducted some collaborative research separately on gender equality in educational performance and achievements, at the end of secondary schooling (both GCSE and 'A' levels and vocational qualifications), with Dr Madeleine Arnot and Professor Gaby Weiner, funded by the Equal Opportunities Commission (EOC, 1996). This has led to our speculations about the reasons for the changing 'gender gaps' in educational performances and in particular for girls' educational achievements by contrasts with what has become known as the 'most disturbing problem in education' – the under-achievements of white working class boys (Woodhead 1996). A book is forthcoming on these broad issues (Arnot, David and Weiner 1998, forthcoming). As far as I know, no research in Britain has been done on the relations between mothers' involvements and children's educational achievements, particularly not on examination performance for boys and girls at the end of secondary school.

A LONE MOTHER'S VOICE ON RECENT EDUCATIONAL
REFORMS

I will start with an example of our evidence. This quotation is drawn
from the second recent study of parental choice, involvement and
expectations of achievement in children's education: it is from a mother
in an answer to a question about issues involved in the processes of
choice of a secondary school for her son in year six in a state primary
school, the year of transition to secondary education in Britain. She was
a working-class lone mother living in an inner-city housing estate in
south London and one of the parents of 120 children, attending either
state or private primary schools and about to transfer to secondary
school, whom we interviewed:

*I wanted him at Riverway (GM boys' school) because I knew there'd be
something at the end for him ... And because it's just down the road it
would have took him five minutes to walk there in the morning. And
that was another consideration. And what else? It's just a brilliant
school for boys. It's a brilliant school but at the interview it was terrible
– they annihilated us at the interview. They made us, they made me feel
two inches. They belittled us ... I thought to myself, 'You pigs, look at
you, you can treat us how you want because you've got the pick' ... and
they refused us and it was horrible. It was so horrible ... We only got
one offer out of five ... And that was the last school on my list ... And
when we've needed help when our children were consistently refused
schools we couldn't, we didn't get the support we needed. I mean,
mothers whose kids were refused schools have gone to [the primary
head teacher] in desperation and she's said, '... I can't help you' ... I
was so wound up about this secondary transfer business I was going to
go on the telly, on that 'Your Shout' ... It's like [the City Technology
college down the road] – all the kids that went there, their parents had
money. D'you know that? We've done our own survey ... Because a lot
of the mothers, we went for the same schools ... And we found all the
kids that was accepted [there], their parents had money or were
involved in some kind of authority thing – like they had been councillors
or were previous parent governors from schools ... [And] I mean, if
you didn't have a posh voice when you rung [the exclusive private
school], they didn't have the courtesy to say goodbye when you put the
phone down ... the thing is, these schools, they treat you like shit
because they can have the pick of our kids basically. That is what I think*

and everybody thinks that. (Working-class lone mother living in an inner city housing estate.)

CRITICAL ISSUES IN MATERNAL INVOLVEMENTS AND INVESTMENTS IN EDUCATIONAL TRANSITIONS

This mother's passionate views and clear understanding of the impacts of educational reforms from her point of view illustrate many aspects of the kinds of evidence that we have assembled:

- that it is almost invariably mothers who are involved in the processes of choosing schools
- that it is almost invariably mothers who do what we have called the 'leg work' of finding out information, including academic performance/results, about the different options of schools available
- that there are strong 'support networks' of parents/mothers who discuss secondary schools and their preferences
- that lone mother families may, in certain circumstances, involve fathers in the choice processes in ways that compare and contrast with two-parent households
- that it is mothers that deal with the school and teachers/head teacher
- that working-class families focus on two of the three 'P's – proximity and pleasant feel, rather than (academic) performance – of the school they would choose
- that parents of sons tend to prefer co-educational rather than single-sex schools, which is what parents of daughters (in London at least) tend to prefer
- that the recent educational reforms, especially on parental choice of school, do not necessarily achieve their ostensible aims of allowing a 'free and equal' choice of secondary school
- that schools – whether state or private – rather than families are the final arbiters (parental choice versus chosen parents) and may make selections that may have discriminatory effects on particular types/ classes of family
- that families with financial resources are able to involve themselves in education and choices not available to poor and/or lone parent/ mother families
- that certain kinds of families, especially from the middle classes and with children in state schools, seem to be involved in being parent governors for their children's sake.

MOTHER'S INTUITION? CHOOSING SECONDARY SCHOOLS

I want now to consider in more depth our two studies and the general findings which confirm this passionate but crystal clear voice of this lone mother. The first study was based on a sample of seventy families in two inner London boroughs (one in the north and one in the south) in the immediate aftermath of the Education Reform Act (ERA), 1988 (David, West and Ribbens 1994). These parents all had children in year six, the final year of state primary school. We wanted to look at whether family and social changes – in terms of structures and processes – had any bearing on/relationship to the apparently current changes in school choice processes, as laid down in the ERA. These particular reforms have been seen as part of the beginnings of neo-liberal policy developments in that they have allowed for the creation of quasi-markets in education, with grant-maintained schools (GMS) and city technology colleges (CTCs) and the increase in public information about schools' performance and examination results on which parents were expected to make decisions (Ball 1994; Le Grand and Bartlett 1993). We wanted to convey both a statistical and illustrative picture of the processes of choice amongst families in London, where we knew there was enormous variety in terms of ethnicity, race and class as well as new forms of family structure, from lone-parent families – whether single, separated or divorced – to two-parent families, whether 'natural' or reconstituted/ blended, and containing step-parents and/or siblings and/or wider kin.

Our main conclusions from this study were that, as noted above, and as might have been predicted from much feminist work on families and childcare (e.g. New and David 1985) but never previously related to educational studies, *mothers* were invariably involved in the processes of choosing (secondary) school, whatever their social or family circumstances, and even race or ethnicity. Mothers did what we called the 'leg work' in seeking out the information, visiting schools and talking to other mothers and educators about the options and possibilities. In other words, it is, in fact, mothers' work in terms of their investment of time and energy in the processes, rather than based upon their intuition. The title of the book was taken from an article in the *Independent*, commenting on the processes of choice when we were writing the book, where the journalists acknowledged the fact that mothers rather than fathers were primarily involved – but they did not acknowledge how these mothers invested greater amounts of time and energy on what we would consider to be a form of 'work', and certainly a major preoccupation if not an occupation. More recently, Carol Vincent and Stephen

Ball claimed that parents claimed that they learnt about secondary schools on the 'grapevine' (September 1996). We would argue that there is something more systematic than a grapevine in operation: that there are clear social networks amongst groups of mothers.

However, although mothers were invariably involved, children and fathers/guardians were also involved in some cases and conditions. The involvement of children, whom we also questioned, depended upon their social class position. In this case we obtained a rough estimation of social class based upon the fathers' occupation where fathers were present, and the mothers' occupation in the case of lone-parent families. In other words, in working-class families children were more likely to be the main or joint chooser than in middle-class families. In these former families, the decision was more likely to be based upon a notion of a child's happiness, and therefore issues about friendships and the local neighbourhood school came up more often for working-class than middle-class children.

The three 'P's – pleasant feel, proximity, and performance – were the main mix of reasons amongst all the families, but proximity was more usual for working-class families. Middle-class families took a different view and were more concerned about the 'performance and pleasant feel'. Moreover, there were differences between the families in their choices for boys and girls, with a majority of parents of daughters opting for single-sex schools, and even parents of sons saying that they would have opted for girls' schools if they had had a daughter, whereas for boys it was more usually mixed schools whatever the social class, race or ethnicity.

Fathers were also involved in the choices in certain circumstances: interestingly, we found that lone-mother families (over a third of our sample in this study) often involved fathers explicitly or deliberately, since they were absent from the household. Such involvemtent had to be more explicit than in two-parent households, where there was often a clear sexual division of labour, with mothers having domestic and child-care responsibilities and fathers having (particularly) economic respons-ibilities outside the home. This motivated us to look more fully at family processes, not only of choice but of involvement of different family members at different stages. In particular, we wanted to explore Bernstein's notions (1990) of the new pedagogies of the new middle-classes more thoroughly. We were also interested in further exploration of our finding that the overwhelming majority of our families, whether middle-class or working-class, lone- or two-parent families, and of what-ever ethnicity, had great expectations for their children's educational achievements or attainments, prospects and futures. And given that our study suggested that choice processes were embedded in wider family processes and in the wider social processes creating more social and economic diversity, we wanted to follow through a range of findings:

> Overall, our two studies have provided considerable insight into the processes involved in choosing secondary schools and issues that parents and their children take into account. It is evident that families do not take these issues lightly but invest considerable amounts of time and energy into thinking about education and particular schools. However, we have found it hard to disentangle the ways in which families go about this from the broader ways in which families live their lives and give consideration to living in constrained circumstances. Inevitably for some families thinking about particular schools is a luxury that they are unable to afford. For others it is so important that it cannot be left to the vagaries of circumstance or constraints of time and money. The difference between families, in those who find it hard to give it consideration and those who would not abrogate the responsibility, has more to do with the ways in which they are now positioned with respect to the educational marketplace than their own wishes and desires. Diversity and choice in education has indeed created and exacerbated social and family diversity. (David, West and Ribbens 1994, pp. 145–6)

Given the multifaceted nature of the processes involved in families and school choices, we therefore bid, successfully, to the Economic and Social Research Council (ESRC) to conduct a much wider-ranging study of parental choice, involvement and expectations of achievement in education. This three-year study was completed and reported in October 1996 and published (West, David, Noden, Edge and Davies 1997). It was much wider and more extensive than the Leverhulme study although exploring similar themes of parents' differential involvement in the processes of choice of education, both at school and at home, for their children. Again, we wanted to provide a statistical picture and illustrative examples.

MOTHERS' INVOLVEMENTS AND INVESTMENTS IN TRANSITIONS TO AND FROM PRIMARY SCHOOL

This time we took *two* samples of families in London boroughs (north and south of the Thames), both in inner and outer London, and from twenty different schools. One sample was of families whose children were again in their final year of primary school (year six in state schools) and about to transfer to secondary schools (120 families); this was called the *'transfer'* sample. The other sample was of families of children who were in the first year (year one) or reception class of primary schools (111 families), or the *'reception'* sample.

As we wished to look more broadly at class and family dynamics and the changing context of more educational choice and diversity – as developed in subsequent legislation to the ERA, such as the Education Act, 1992 – we not only selected families whose children were in state schools but those whose children attended (fee-paying) private (preparatory) schools (Ball 1994; David 1993; Fitz, Halpin and Power 1993; Whitty, Edwards and Gewirtz 1993). In the event about thirty per cent of the 'transfer' sample and almost a quarter (23 per cent) of the 'reception' sample had children in private schools. As a result of this kind of sampling and the inclusion of private schools especially, we achieved samples that were even more biased towards the middle classes than our previous study. For example, based upon fathers' occupation (and mothers' occupation if available in lone mother families), 57 per cent of the 'transfer' group were in 'professional' (middle class) occupations and only 43 per cent in 'non-professional' (or working class) occupations, whilst the 'reception class' had a more even distribution with 52 per cent in professional and 48 per cent in non-professional occupations. Moreover, we had fewer lone-mother households and ethnic minority families. Indeed, there were *no* lone mother families in the private schools about to transfer to secondary school and only one in the reception class of private schools, but almost a quarter of 'transfer' families were lone parents of state school children and twenty per cent of reception class families in state schools were lone parents. Instead, we had a sample skewed to the upper middle class in the transfer group, and it even contained *boys* who were aged twelve or thirteen (levels seven or eight), since transfer to elite public schools (boarding) for boys is at thirteen, not eleven. The result was that this 'transfer' sample had 52.5 per cent of boys and only 47.5 per cent of girls. The 'reception' sample was more equitable with 49 per cent of boys and 51 per cent of girls. Ethnicity was not as varied as in our previous study, with only 23 per cent of 'non-white' ethnic groups in the reception sample and almost a third (31 per cent) in the 'transfer' sample.

Some of our main conclusions about involvements and investments in children's education and 'choices' of school are as follows. Mothers are again invariably involved in choosing (primary and secondary) schools for their children, whether at transfer or reception class stage, whatever the circumstances and contexts and however complex and multifaceted the processes. Again, it is largely mothers' work, especially in terms of investments of time and energy. Mothers were even *more* involved at the reception stage (95 per cent as opposed to ninety per cent for 'transfer' families) and took the main responsibility in seventy per cent of instances, whilst it was only 41 per cent for the 'transfer' group. The transfer group were also asked to recall who had taken the main responsibility at the reception stage and this confirmed mothers' apparent greater involvement in the early stages of education.

Fathers and children are involved in the choice processes in certain contexts and circumstances. Fathers were only involved in the decision-making process for 41 per cent of the reception class children (but children themselves not at all) and took the main responsibility in only three per cent of cases, whereas they were involved in the transfer process in over three quarters of decisions (78 per cent). For over half of children living with lone mothers (53 per cent) (all attending state schools), (absent) fathers again contributed to the choice of secondary school, confirming our previous finding. However, this involvement was significantly associated with the child's own input into the process and fathers and children together contributed. Overall, parents said that one in five of the transfer group of children 'made the final choice', but it was often from a shortlist presented by parents or choosing between the offers of schools. Fathers were often involved jointly with the mothers in the choice processes for the transfer group in private schools and middle class families in state schools, contrasting markedly here with our previous findings of a clear sexual division of responsiblity, and fleshing out Bernstein's notion of the new pedagogy of the middle classes (Bernstein, 1990). Indeed, fathers and mothers were far more often jointly involved in the interviews (in 23 per cent) than had previously been the case, highlighting interest and involvement especially from families who had already chosen private primary schools.

The reasons for the particular choice of school, whether at reception or transfer, were remarkably similar across the samples but somewhat more complex than in the previous study, in view of their range and given that we tried to tap into a 'hierarchy' of factors ranging from essential to important. This time, rather than the 3Ps, the most outstanding and 'essential' reason overall was the '*child's happiness*', although the meaning of this notion was clearly variable and dependent upon different conceptions of child development and family relations (Coldron and Boulton 1991). For example, one mother with a son at an independent primary school explained that the school, which had been *chosen before the son's birth*, had been selected because it offered a tried and tested route to the prestigious 'public' school which the boy's father and grandfather had attended. The two most important factors in her choice were, however, that her son be happy and that the school suit his needs. In this case, the child's happiness and needs did not arise from his individual characteristics but from his parents' plans for his future. In contrast, many state-school parents appeared to operate with a notion of happiness more rooted in the present. For example, one mother explained her top priority in choosing a school was that *'Mario's happy there. He is important to me ... I don't like to see him upset.'* The mothers of reception class children in private schools had deliberately chosen the school for its small class sizes and to prepare the child for transfer to secondary school, whereas some state school mothers had deliberately chosen the state primary school for its ethnic mix.

Implicitly rather than explicitly single-sex education was a key factor in choice of school,especially for private education, since many of the private pre- and/or preparatory and secondary schools were single-sex. This then certainly showed markedly in the schools chosen, although it was rarely referred to as what we called 'an essential factor'. Parents of girls were significantly more likely, however, to identify a single-sex school as their first choice secondary school than were parents of boys (86 per cent vs 65 per cent). Excluding families using private primary schools (who were more likely to apply to private secondary schools among which there were few co-educational schools), we find an even more marked preference for girls' than boys' schools (86 per cent vs 48 per cent) with working-class families significantly more likely than middle-class to cite single-sex intake as a significant factor (25 per cent vs 3 per cent). Thus parents perceived boys as a threat to girls' (and even each other's) education and identified the potentially negative effect of working class boys' behaviour on girls in the classroom; one mother suggested that girls were generally better off without *'boys' horrible habits'*.

Most interestingly, reasons for choice of school were not at all related to parental aspirations for the child in question. Parents almost universally wanted their children to receive education beyond the age of sixteen and to go on to higher education, yet again corroborating previous research. Children with fathers in professional occupations were however expected to pass 'A' levels significantly more often than were other children (93 per cent vs 78 per cent) and, conversely, children of non-professional fathers were more likely to be expected to gain vocational qualifications (49 per cent vs 17 per cent) but there were no clear differences in parents' employment aspirations for their children.

The ways in which parents chose, and were chosen by, secondary schools indicate different market segments, including one segment of private secondary schools, a second of selective state secondary schools, a third of Catholic state schools and a fourth of comprehensive schools (LeGrand and Bartlett 1993). When we examined which children were offered places at their parents' first choice schools a surprisingly consistent picture of about two-thirds emerged; while 74 per cent of middle-class children were successful, 68 per cent of working-class children were also successful across all the private and state school families; excluding the private primary school families, 77 per cent of middle-class compared to 66 per cent of working-class families were successful. However, this masks the systematic differences in patterns of applications to schools with different characteristics and the secondary schools children subsequently attended.

First the private school sector, as a segment, is neither homogeneous nor hermetically sealed. Of the 21 families from two of the four private preparatory schools in our study, only one child went on to a state secondary school: a girl with learning difficulties whose parents felt that a comprehensive school would be better able to cater for her needs. For all the other parents, applying to a London comprehensive school was simply inconceivable, as were the relatively accessible state grammar schools in neighbouring boroughs; as one mother put it,

> *fortunately we have the choice – we can afford to send them to private schools. If we couldn't, I think we would have moved out of London.*

The other two private primary schools were relatively cheaper, with three of the sixteen children from working-class families, and were located in outer London with several selective state secondary schools. Many of these parents used the private school for 'tactical' reasons to enhance the chances of their children passing entrance examinations for the local academically selectively maintained schools. One mother explained that her son would only have gone on to a private secondary school if he had not been offered a place at a state grammar school. Ultimately three of these children went on to comprehensive schools, six to selective state schools and the rest (not necessarily their first choice) to private schools.

The most distinctive group of parents with children at state primary schools were Roman Catholic; all thirteen (the majority working class) identified an RC affiliated school, which also was GMS, as their first choice and were subsequently offered a place. For the majority of parents who identified a GM school as their first choice it was not GM status but religious affiliation which was key.This was not the case for the parents of children at Church of England primary schools, where only about half identified a CE secondary school as their first choice. Amongst the other families, it was academic performance, as identified through the government's league tables, which proved the most significant differentiating characteristic. Overall, middle-class families identified first choice schools averaging over half (53 per cent) with five or more good (A–C) passes at GCSE, whilst working-class parents chose those averaging forty per cent. Thus, while middle-class children were only marginally more likely to be offered places at first choice schools than working-class children, they significantly were more likely to go on to a relatively 'better performing' school. However, this could not be explained by middle-class parents' preference for selective schools, nor by a tendency for different social classes to live in different areas.

Differences between families' financial resources, especially for school transport, and covert selection and social exclusion by the schools provided the main reasons. Middle-class children were more likely first to identify relative distant schools as their first choice and subsequently attend them. The importance of money in determining which schools were in fact available to any particular family was made particularly clear at Princess Road primary school in an inner-city area. The school was close to a mainline railway station and therefore children could quickly reach a suburban secondary school about fifteen miles away. This school had been undersubscribed in recent years and had performed poorly in the league tables but relatively better than the more local neighbourhood schools. It had thus become popular with parents at Princess Road. The schools' relationship had been institutionalized by an organized group school visit for year six pupils. Several families applied and some of these middle-class children went on to attend the school. However, one working-class lone mother explained that she had applied to that school for her son and had been offered a place there but simply could not afford the rail fare. In effect, by requiring schools to accept applications up to their physical capacity, families with the financial means and willingness to travel have been enabled to escape from unattractive local schools – a strategy that appears only to work for middle-class 'resourceful' families.

Middle-class children who were unsuccessful in obtaining a place at their parents' first choice of school subsequently attended higher-scoring schools than their successful middle-class counterparts, whilst the converse was true for the working-class children. Risk-taking, in terms of applying to schools at which an offer is uncertain, may be a productive strategy for middle-class families but appears counter-productive for the working class. Evidence of admissions procedures which manifestly favoured middle-class applicants was found at several schools – including, for example, some comprehensive schools which were former grammar schools admitting the children of ex-pupils in preference to local children, while others used interviews to select their intake – and there was occasional evidence of blatant class bias. Working-class and/or lone mother families may learn from this to be less ambitious, given the operation of apparent covert selection and the importance of finances (for transport at the very least) to get to distant schools.

Mothers' involvement at home and at school is so extensive as to be virtually universal, whether at the reception or transfer stage, such that it could be considered to be normative. Indeed, educational activities at home such as reading, drawing, writing and listening to stories, singing, cooking and baking are widespread for reception-class children, with mothers being centrally involved, whether the child goes to a state or a private primary school. Fathers' involvement at home is however confined to helping their young child with educational computer games, which they do far more frequently than mothers. A similar pattern emerged for the transfer sample, although fathers also helped children here with mathematics more frequently than did mothers.

Among the reception sample, parents sending their children to private primary schools appeared less concerned with the educational progress of their children prior to admission to school. This may be because private schools are more usually associated with less parental involvement and more professional autonomy. For instance, there were clear differences in both the reception and transfer samples in terms of school policies on parental involvement at school; opportunities to help in class were particularly rare in private schools. There is, however, an apparent imperative to be available to help in children's education. As one mother put it:

Parents now want involvement and it's encouraged. The norm is to encourage and ask why not if not...

Mothers often felt obliged to explain that they could not offer to help in class as they worked but, interestingly, there was no relationship between mothers' employment status and helping in class. Negotiating the provision of help appears a complex process relating to perceived needs, opportunities, invitations and the absence of obstacles such as other childcare responsibilities.

The most common form of educational involvement at schools, for both the reception and the transfer samples, was attending open evenings and discussing the child's progress with class teachers, followed by help on school trips. Few parents were involved in aspects of school management, such as governing bodies and PTAs, both of which were *less* frequent for parents of children in private primary schools. By contrast, the private schools tended to set homework for children from a relatively early age and enlisted parents' support in ensuring its completion. Taking this together with the absence of parental involvement in the classroom at private schools, private schools seem to take greater control over the educational process than their state school counterparts. Indeed only one of the state schools operated a formal homework timetable (as did all the private schools) but they may have operated PACT programmes (Parents and Children and Teachers) and expected children to complete work left unfinished, including reading at home. However, many parents chose extra educational help out of school for their children, particularly at the point of transfer to secondary school, in the form of private tutors or coaches. This was relatively common and crossed both class and private/state school lines.

In sum, there are different notions of involvement over differing kinds of education for different groups of parents. However, the key issue is that mothers are invariably involved, whatever their social and/ or familial circumstances and whatever the issue. They have, and take, the main responsibility for all aspects of childcare, including education, whether they are lone mothers, working class or middle class, employed or at home; investing resources and time, just as the official and normative discourses would have us believe. However, what is interesting and significant from this study is that these patterns of responsibility, as sole or joint responsibilities, vary in terms of social class and relations with fathers, whether absent or at home. Some, largely middle-class, fathers' involvement in choice processes is greater than in the previous study, which is largely to do with the private school families but also covers some of the state school families; those whom Bernstein (1990), for instance, has called the 'new middle classes'. Thus fathers' involvement in choice processes is considerable at transfer to secondary school, including absent fathers of lone-mother households. For some middle-class fathers of private school children, this may have to do with their necessary investment of financial resources (although, in common with most social researchers, we did not ask about finances – but this could constitute a new research study). However, as noted above, many working-class and/or lone-mother families would have made different secondary school choices had they had the necessary financial resources or not been excluded from certain schools on the grounds of social class. Evaluations of types of school and views of types of education wanted may not always have the same effect; it depends upon financial and social circumstances.

Turning to wider questions of involvement – not only in choice processes, whether of primary or secondary school, state or private, but also in children's education at home and at school – there is considerable diversity related to the ways in which parents, and mothers especially, think about education, but it is almost universal for mothers to concern themselves with children's education at home. Patterns of parental involvement at school, vary amongst families and are to some extent dependent upon the type of (private or state) school chosen. There are major differences in policies (especially on homework or school involvement) between the private and the state schools, which had surprised some families and disappointed a number of mothers. This was equally true for those mothers who had selected private schools and those who had perforce sent their children to state schools. The key point here, however, is that choices of school entail not only differences in prior involvement but have implications for subsequent involvements and activities, illustrating very different patterns of education and expectations about school, from both families and the schools themselves.

Finally, again we have found that the overwhelming majority of our families have great expectations for their children's educational future; they hope that their children will proceed on to higher education. Whether this is a realistic expectation is another matter. But it may have to do with mothers' changing roles, desires and expectations, whether middle-class or working-class, and with higher levels of achieved education for themselves. From my various studies, including that conducted for the EOC (Arnot et al. 1996), I would speculate that mothers' involvement in education, both personally and on behalf of their children, has led to the improvements in girls' education and achievements that we now witness. This may therefore begin to account for the rising educational aspirations and expectations for the next generation that the above two research studies have found. The evidence for the EOC, in brief, shows a closing of the gender gap in educational performance and achievements, especially at GCSE and in 'A' levels, with girls outperforming boys in some key subjects. More-over, some of this has been achieved in single-sex girls' schools rather than coeducational schools, which may also account for our finding of parents' preference for single-sex schools for their daughters above all and the anxiety felt about working-class boys. This anxiety has in any event become part of an official public agenda, orchestrated by Chris Woodhead, Her Majesty's Chief Inspector, and Head of Ofsted (*The Times*, March 1996). So the question of mothers' involvement in employ-ment having negative effects on children's educational perform-ance appears unlikely in the face of this evidence. Indeed, given that O'Brien's study was of a cross-section rather than a cohort of children going through secondary schools, it is not clear what kinds of occu-pational involvement and their length had the effects of limiting chil-dren's, especially boys', educational performance. Our study would seem to indicate that mothers cared passionately, as evinced by our initial quotation, about their sons' as much as their daughters' edu-cation, and that they wanted the very best that they could get for their children. The so-called crisis of working class boys' underachieve-ment, as raised, may have more to do with the resources available to particular inner city schools than to patterns of maternal involvement in education and/or employment, given our evidence of almost universal involvement, investment and interest in education at home and at school.

Methodologically, we are at a crossroads in our understanding of social class, given mothers' changing educational and occupational activities and involvements and more global socio-economic changes. Some general issues arise from this research which link to the wider changes in women's lives and how we research them. Together with colleagues, I have been giving some consideration to these questions, too, in an effort to grapple with more reflexive academic feminist accounts.

> Within the individualistic, competitive ethos of higher education, owning up to being a mother seems almost like a confession of weak-ness, a limitation which might detract from intellectual productivity. The choices we need to make about our children's education on a daily basis often seem to intrude on, and subtract from, our work as aca-demics. Discourses around parental involvement in education cast everything that mothers do as enhancing or holding back children's educational progress. There are problems here...of how to ask mothers about this without conjuring up mothers' feelings and their

own judgements about it. And our own feelings as researchers on mothering are inevitably implicated. We need therefore to give consideration...and foreground particular issues to do with evaluative discourses and judgements in order to make sense of their complexity. It is clear that we cannot step outside of these discourses entirely, but we can bring them out in order to locate, understand and research them. Not to do so continues the process of denial or occlusion of the complexities. (David, Davies, Edwards, Reay and Standing 1996, p. 220)

CONCLUSIONS

In conclusion, public agendas about education and educational reform, whether New Labour, neo-liberal or neo-conservative, foreground parents but do not explicitly focus on gender issues; nor does the related research on either parental choice or involvement in education. However, if we apply an explicitly feminist focus and analysis of families' views and voices on these educational policies, we find, as I hope I have clearly shown, that mothers are critical and centrally involved in their children's education both at home and at school, and particularly at key moments of transition, such as the choices about transitions to primary and secondary school. However, whether other family members are involved depends upon the mothers and their social and familial circumstances, such that mothers in middle-class families, with children in either state or private schools, may involve fathers, as may lone mothers from more working-class circumstances. It is, however, mothers that are key to their children's education; and increasingly they are opting for single-sex secondary education, particularly for their daughters. However, the resources that they may have available limit the extent to which they may be successful in achieving their aims and aspirations for their children. Discourses about mothering in relation to education/schools in various contexts are also now high on the public agenda, especially in relation to children's educational achievements. However, they remain a normative discourse with very little substantive evidence to confirm that mothers' work involvements prejudice boys' achievements. Indeed, one could assert more readily that mothers have contributed positively to the improvements in girls' educational achievements and the closing of the gender gap in educational performance, for which they should be praised, not blamed. Furthermore, mothers continue to aspire for higher educational opportunities for their sons and daughters, despite the increasing social diversity in economic life generally and globally. These aspirations are now being giving official legitimation with the variety of New Labour policies – although they do not give explicit recognition to mothers' voices, which remain occluded.

4 School Effectiveness, School Improvement and Contemporary Educational Policies

David Reynolds

The last twenty years have seen the arrival of school effectiveness and school improvement research and practice to a position of central influence upon the educational policies being pursued within England and Wales. The new Labour Government's White Paper *Excellence in Education* shows the influence of the effectiveness and improvement paradigm on virtually every page, from the espousal of a 'pressure and support' philosophy (Fullan 1991), to the adoption of a 'valued added' perspective on assessing levels of school achievement (Goldstein 1995) and to belief in the value of development planning (Hargreaves and Hopkins 1991).

The enthusiasm for utilizing effectiveness and improvement knowledge is not just in evidence amongst those in the political and policy-making sphere. There is also a substantial growth in teachers' and head teachers' enthusiasm for use of the knowledge base, reflected in an expansion in the members and activities of the Higher Education/School networks that are organized from centres at the Institute of Education in London, the University of Bath, the University of Nottingham, the University of Newcastle and the National Foundation for Educational Research, to name but a few of the locations.

This contemporary popularity of the knowledge bases has, though, been accompanied by an increasing wave of criticism concerning the quality, applicability and utility of effectiveness and improvement knowledge. Much of this criticism seems a continuation of the highly positive conventional academic enterprise in which a thesis is exposed to its antithesis. Many academics seem to believe genuinely that the very centrality of the effectiveness and improvement discourse within the political and policy-making spheres makes the evaluation of its quality of even greater importance than it would be for material that is not so central to the policy discourse.

Many of the criticisms seem rather wide of the mark, however. Thus criticisms of school effectiveness research for its limited range of outcome measures (Hamilton 1996) seem difficult to square with the multiple outcomes now axiomatic within the world's effectiveness research enterprise (Teddlie and Reynolds 1998; Reynolds 1996). Criticisms concerning the simplicity of the knowledge base (Hamilton 1996; Elliott 1997) are difficult to square with the contextually specific, theoretically modelled versions of the effectiveness and improvement paradigms that now represent the disciplinary cutting edge (Gray et al. 1996; Reynolds et al. 1996; Stoll and Fink 1996).

However, there may be more validity to a third set of criticisms which suggest that the effectiveness and improvement community may have lost some of its critical faculties with regard to the policies of the present and the past government (Hamilton 1996; Elliott 1997). It is important not to overstate the point: there have been numerous attacks made upon government policies by those within the discipline who have seen these policies as departing from what would be suggested by school effectiveness research (see review in Sammons and Reynolds 1997).

It may be, though, that criticism has been muted by the closeness of many in the school effectiveness and improvement communities to government politicians and civil service administrators. Increasingly, these administrators share the same platforms and symposium presentations as the researchers. Publications also now come from policy-makers, practitioners and researchers together. Professional bodies and indeed governmental Task Forces and advisory committees show all three groups working together, seemingly productively.

There is of course much to support the utility of such close relationships between researchers and policy-makers, particularly since it is exactly these kinds of relationships that have been historically suggested as necessary to improve the rather poor levels of take-up of educational research within the policy-making 'sphere'. However, such close relationships can only be profitable when all sides enter them in a spirit of mutual honesty as well as in a mutual desire for harmonious working relationships that can improve the outcomes of education for the benefit of children.

This chapter therefore hopefully takes this spirit of mutual honesty further by evaluating the nature of the linkage between government policies and the effectiveness and improvement knowledge and research enterprise. We noted above the extent to which the effectiveness knowledge base has been utilized by the government to provide intellectual foundations for its policies in education. However, it is clear that school effectiveness and school improvement knowledge may possess findings and approaches which support somewhat alternative visions of educational policies to those which have been generated by the present government, and by the past government for that matter. In order to improve the quality of the policies being pursued, and in order to answer those critics who have seen effectiveness and improvement as supine to governmental interests, some reflexivity and self-criticism seems much to be needed.

THE GENERATION OF THE SCHOOL EFFECTIVENESS KNOWLEDGE BASE, 1967 TO 1997

Detailed reviews of the school effectiveness research literature, the history of the field and the 'leading edge' issues that are now widely recognized as such in the field are available elsewhere (Teddlie and Reynolds 1998; Reynolds et al. 1996; Reynolds et al. 1994; Reynolds and Cuttance 1992; Bosker and Scheerens 1997). What we propose to do here is to present a severely truncated description of the intellectual foundations on which the White Paper has been built.

Early school effectiveness research work came mostly from a medical environment, with Power (1967, 1972) showing differences in delinquency rates between schools and Gath (1977) showing differences in child guidance referral rates. Early work by Reynolds and associates (1976, 1982) into the characteristics of the learning environments of apparently differently effective secondary schools was followed by the work of Rutter et al. (1979) into differences between schools measured on the outcomes of academic achievement, delinquency, attendance and levels of behavioural problems, utilizing this time a cohort design that involved the matching of individual pupil data at intake to school and at age sixteen. Subsequent work in the 1980s included:

1 'Value-added' comparisons of educational authorities on their academic outcomes (Department of Education and Science 1983, 1984; Gray, Jesson and Jones 1984; Woodhouse and Goldstein 1988; Gray and Jesson 1987; Willms 1987);
2 Comparisons of 'selective' school systems with comprehensive or 'all ability' systems (Steedman 1980, 1983; Gray et al. 1983; Reynolds et al. 1987);
3 Work into the scientific properties of school effects, such as size (Gray, Jesson and Jones 1986; Gray 1981, 1982), the differential

effectiveness of different academic sub-units or departments (Fitz-Gibbon 1985; Fitz-Gibbon, Tymms and Hazelwood 1989; Willms and Cuttance 1985), contextual or 'balance' effects (Willms 1985, 1986, 1987) and the differential effectiveness of schools upon pupils of different characteristics (Nuttall et al. 1989; Aitkin and Longford 1986).

Towards the end of the 1980s, two landmark studies appeared concerning school effectiveness in primary schools (Mortimore et al. 1988) and in secondary schools (Smith and Tomlinson 1989). The Mortimore study was notable for the wide range of outcomes on which schools were assessed (including mathematics, reading, writing, attendance, behaviour and attitudes to school), for the collection of a wide range of data upon school processes and, for the first time in British school effectiveness research, for a focus upon classroom processes.

A study by Smith and Tomlinson (1989) is notable for the large differences shown in academic effectiveness between schools: for certain groups of pupils, the variation in examination results between similar individuals in different schools amounts to up to a quarter of the total variation in examination results. The study is also notable for the substantial variation that it reported for results in different school subjects, reflecting the influence of different school departments: out of eighteen schools, the school that was positioned 'first' on mathematics attainment, for example, was 'fifteenth' in English achievement (after allowance had been made for intake quality).

Ongoing work in England and Wales now remains partially situated within the same intellectual traditions and at the same intellectual cutting edges as in the 1980s, notably in the areas of:

1 Stability over time of school effects (Goldstein et al. 1993; Gray et al. 1995; Thomas, Sammons and Mortimore 1995);
2 Consistency of school effects on different outcomes – for example, in terms of different subjects or different outcome domains such as cognitive/affective (Goldstein et al. 1993; Sammons, Nuttall and Cuttance 1993, Thomas, Sammons and Mortimore 1995);
3 Differential effects of schools for different groups of students (for example, of different ethnic or socio-economic backgrounds or with different levels of prior attainment) (Jesson and Gray 1991; Goldstein et al. 1993; Sammons, Nuttall and Cuttance 1993);
4 The relative continuity of the effects of school sectors over time (Goldstein 1995; Sammons et al. 1995);

5 The existence or size of school effects (Daly 1991; Gray, Jesson and Sime 1990; Thomas and Mortimore 1994), where in most studies eight per cent to twelve per cent of the total variance in pupil achievement is attributable to educational influences. There are strong suggestions that the size of primary school effects may be greater than those of secondary schools (Sammons et al. 1993, 1995);

6 Departmental differences in educational effectiveness (Fitz-Gibbon 1985, 1992).

Additional recent foci of interest have included:

1 Work at the school effectiveness/special educational needs inter-face, studying how schools vary in their definitions, labelling practices and teacher/pupil interactions with such children (Brown et al. 1996);

2 Work on conceptualising the nature of the school and classroom processes within ineffective schools (Reynolds 1991; Reynolds 1996), where it is argued there are on view a number of 'pathologies' which make it inadvisable to study these schools using only the factors that have been shown to be present within effective institutions.

3 Work on the potential 'context specificity' of effective schools' characteristics internationally, as in the International School Effectiveness Research Project (ISERP), a nine nation study that involves schools in the United Kingdom, the United States, the Netherlands, Canada, Taiwan, Hong Kong, Norway, Australia and the Republic of Ireland (Reynolds et al. 1994). Reynolds and Farrell (1996) have also reviewed the international literature on this topic.

School effectiveness research has identified the following factors as potentially important in creating effectiveness:

• The nature of the leadership provided by the head teacher, with more effective schools having better head/deputy head relations, and having a management style and structure that involves heads setting goals, establishing directions and possessing that most popular of contemporary management terms, a 'mission', *but* having also an active involvement of staff in planning the means to achieve school goals through some decision making. The effective school has a balance, then, in its management between vertical push and horizontal pull, between laterality or diffusion, and centralization. Indeed, it possesses a balance between managerialism and collegiality that is ensured by having elements of both present at the same time.

- Academic push or academic 'press', involving high expectations of what pupils can achieve, utilizing strategies that ensure large amounts of learning time (such as well-managed lesson transitions), utilizing homework to expand learning time and to involve parents, and entering a high proportion of pupils for public examinations to ensure they remain 'hooked' in their final years.
- Parental involvement, both to ensure the participation of significant others in children's lives in the rewarding of achievement and effort, and also to ensure that in cases of difficulty the parents will, if it is appropriate to do so, support the school against the child.
- Pupil involvement, both in the learning situation within the classroom (though here the involvement needs to be within a firm and organized structure) and within the school in societies, sports teams, leadership positions, representative positions, and the like.
- Organizational control of pupils, which is in turn generated by cohesion, constancy and consistency within the school. Organizational cohesion is likely to be enhanced by both planning and co-ordination of school activities, and by a degree of ownership of the school by the staff itself, to be generated by a good flow of information and by procedures that involve staff in the organization. Organizational consistency across lessons in the same subjects, across different subjects in the same years and across different years in the pupil learning experiences they offer is clearly likely to be facilitated by development planning and by those forms of professional development which involve utilizing members of staff as 'buddies' to each other, in which observation of each other's practice ensures that the range of individual practice is made clearer to organizational members, to be acted upon.

THE DISCOURSE CONCERNING 'SCHOOLING'

Having studied the school effectiveness knowledge base as above, it is clear that it resonates with much of the contemporary educational discourse that is associated with 'New Labour', as it did to a lesser degree with the discourse of the previous Conservative administration. Some of the specific school effectiveness 'process factors' such as the head teacher are indeed currently the focus of active intervention (through the introduction of new professional qualifications, for example).

Others – homework and academic press, for instance – resonate through the contemporary educational discourse in general.

In many ways, the White Paper proposes the further intensification of the large number of educational policies which have utilized 'the school' as the unit of policy implementation and change. The Conservative government's Education Acts of 1981, 1986 and 1988 began this process with the publication of school results, changes to school governance, the introduction of market-based policies to reward or punish schools in accordance with their popularity in terms of parental choice and the freeing of schools from outside local education authority control (see reviews in Hargreaves and Reynolds 1989; Ball 1990). Additionally, the school was to be the focus for improvement by means of use of development planning (Hargreaves and Hopkins 1990), target setting and the use of value added comparative data to inform planning (Fitz-Gibbon 1996).

The contemporary discourse is firmly, therefore, about 'the school' and the White Paper proposes further intensification of these historical pre-existing policies and pressures that are designed to maximize the leverage upon the level of the school, particularly including an enhanced role for local education authorities in maximizing school quality by means of pressure and support.

However, the discourse about schooling so prevalent in the United Kingdom may not be about the factor that school effectiveness research shows to be most important, namely teaching. In the United States, Australia and the Netherlands, for example, the national discourse concerns teaching *and* schooling, a reflection of their historical concerns with teacher effectiveness and instructional effectiveness probably. In the United Kingdom, the concern has been the school only.

What factors may be responsible for this? Firstly, there is a particularly British view that teaching is an 'art', not a science, and that therefore it is personal factors and qualities, often idiosyncratic and difficult to influence by educational policies, which are the key factors. It goes without saying that such a view – linked no doubt to those other quaint British beliefs about 'gifted amateurs', 'muddling through' and indeed to the whole problem of the two cultures and Britain's placing of education within the humanities tradition – is not heard within other countries, probably because it is clearly wrong and probably also because it is recognized as condemning societies where it is prevalent to having only those small number of excellent teachers who inherit the 'art', rather than the larger number who could acquire the applied science of a teaching methodology.

Secondly, there is a belief in Britain that we do not need a discourse about teaching because teaching is such a simple 'technology' that it does not need elaboration.

Thirdly, we have been held back in Britain from a discourse about teachers and teaching by our unwillingness to confront the issue of inter-teacher variation. School effectiveness research when it began had to struggle against a widespread unwillingness to permit school-against-school comparisons, a situation potentiated by the frankly evasive and opaque prose of Her Majesty's Inspectorate. Although a knowledge of which individuals and indeed Departments are effective is an essential building block of our educational knowledge on 'good practice', the fact that effective teachers have to be studied in contrast to ineffective teachers has clearly been politically and interpersonally difficult to handle.

Fourthly, school effectiveness researchers have themselves been partially responsible for this state of affairs, since because critics of schools said 'schools make no difference', researchers celebrated the school level, not the classroom level, in their attempted rebuttals.

This is not an exhaustive list of reasons: the absence of any British tradition in the fields of 'Learning and Instruction' within educational psychology is also important, as has been the focus upon the *goals* of education within British educational discourse rather than the *means* that have been the focus in most of our industrial competitors. The tendency of some in the discipline of school effectiveness in the United Kingdom to waste their time playing politics has also not helped (the successful American teacher effectiveness community has been notable for *not* playing politics, for sticking to its knitting and for consequently generating what is probably the world's most robust knowledge base).

Our British unwillingness to address issues to do with teaching has been shown to be costly by a number of recent events. Firstly, continued Ofsted reports have shown a very wide variation in teacher behaviours, competence and in consequent outcomes, although it must be stated that these judgements rest more on an experiential than on a research-orientated knowledge base. Secondly, British school effectiveness research has increasingly been showing that the range of variation *within* schools dwarfs the range of variation between schools (Fitz-Gibbon 1996) and that the influence of the teacher and of the learning level considerably exceeds that of the school. Indeed, the more one looks at the relative effects of schools as against teachers, the more one is given plausible explanations for why so many of our educational reforms have not thus far been successful. We have, by intervening with the school level rather than with the learning level, been 'pulling levers' that have small effects on their own and which may not have generated any 'ripple through' to affect the key level of the classroom.

Thirdly, the cost of our inability to address issues concerning teaching and the learning level has been shown by those countries which do have the knowledge base intervening productively in children's lives in ways unknown to us. Bob Slavin's (1996) *Success For All*, a literacy programme of awesome power which generates cohorts of children in which few possess reading ages below their chronological age, was based soundly on teacher effectiveness research, as is the highly successful *Dutch School Improvement Project* (Reynolds et al. 1996).

If we were to look at research into teachers and the teacher effectiveness field outside Britain, we see emerging international consensus on the importance of the following factors (Slavin 1996; Creemers 1994):

1 The Quality of Teaching, involving:

- clarity of presentation
- management of the learning environment
- a restricted range of goals
- structuring of curriculum content
- questioning skills.

2 The Appropriateness of Task, involving:

- good match between task/ability
- appropriate grouping strategies.

3 The Incentives Used, involving:

- high expectations
- reward-based control
- appropriate feedback.

4 Time Use, involving:

- maximized learning time
- lesson pace
- minimal class management.

5 Opportunity to Learn, involving:

- maximized curriculum coverage.

Indeed, it could reasonably be claimed that we have in the area of teacher effectiveness a technology of good practice that is every way as valid as that on the more currently fashionable area of schooling.

It is of course possible to argue that there *are* proposals to impact more directly upon the classroom or learning level in the White Paper, namely the provision of information to teachers concerning effective teaching practices in the area of literacy proposed for implementation in all primary schools from 1998 and the new 'standards' required of those wishing to acquire Qualified Teacher Status (QTS).

Nevertheless, the clear message of the White Paper is that it is to be the school, not the classroom, that is to be the focus of policy intervention. One needs to ask whether, given the evidence of school effectiveness research internationally, this is only necessary rather than sufficient to secure major and fundamental change in educational outcomes.

THE DRIVERS OF SCHOOL IMPROVEMENT

If it is true that school effectiveness research would argue for a different policy direction to be followed which recognizes the salience of the classroom rather than the rather 'school-obsessed' way proposed in the White Paper, then a second area of possible mis-match between effectiveness research evidence and proposed educational policies relates to the proposed 'driver' of school improvement, the Local Education Authority (LEA). In the White Paper, LEAs are themselves to be required to produce educational development plans, and are to require the production of such plans with associated targets from all their schools. There is, of course, an extensive literature about the value of target setting and development planning of these kinds, both from the United Kingdom and abroad (see surveys in Reynolds et al. 1996).

However, existing evidence suggests that LEAs may not have historically been a very powerful determinant of the achievement outcomes from schools, with only quite small differences in achievement levels remaining between LEAs after one has isolated the effects of background factors (Gray, Jesson and Jones 1984). Whilst it is possible that LEA influence might be enhanced and maximized by the kind of policies proposed in the White Paper, it is important to note that this maximization of LEA influence does not appear to have happened historically.

As well as the LEA being a 'driver' or initiator of change, it is also the intention that there is to be greater transfer of knowledge between schools that will come as a result of their having access to a much wider range of performance data. However, a number of factors may weaken the power and potency of this process, in particular the existence of the market pressures of parental competition that may make schools possessing good practice reluctant to transfer it to schools that have less than good practice or the possible inability of school personnel to easily pick up good practice when it is offered to them.

Interestingly, the one area of schools where there is huge variation and where the persons who are routinely managing that variation are in close professional contact is at the Departmental level within secondary schools (Fitz-Gibbon 1996) and the year level within primary schools (Mortimore et al. 1988). Within-school Departmental variation (value added) within an average group of schools is likely to dwarf by a factor of two or three times the variation in mean school performance, school versus school, yet this variation has not been historically routinely used as an 'engine' or 'driver' concerning good practice to improve schools.

Put simply, the White Paper proposes the use of an LEA 'driver' that may have little influence and a school-to-school-level driver that may be difficult to operate. The large *within*-school (rather than *between*-school) variation that could have been a very powerful driver (given the huge variation) is not mentioned or utilized as a source of possible improvement, probably (as we noted earlier) owing to the historic difficulties of the British educational system in recognizing within-school variation in the first place.

The advantages of utilizing a within-school driver such as the Departmental level is as follows:

- The Departmental level in a secondary school or 'year' level in a primary school is closer to the classroom level than is the school level, opening up the possibility of an intervention generating greater change in the learning level;
- Whilst not every school is an effective school, every school has within itself some practice that is relatively more effective than some other practice. Many schools will have within themselves practice that is absolutely effective, across all schools. Every school can therefore work on its own internal conditions;
- Focusing on building upon the variation 'within' schools may be a way of permitting greater levels of competence to emerge at the school level, since it is possible that the absence of strategic thinking

at school level in many parts of the educational system is related to the overload of pressures amongst head teachers, who are having referred to them problems which should be dealt with by the day-to-day operation of the middle management system of Departmental heads, year heads, subject co-ordinators and the like;

- Within-school units of policy intervention such as years or subjects are smaller and therefore potentially more malleable than those at 'whole school' level;

- Teachers in general, and those teachers in less effective settings in particular (Stoll and Myers 1997; Reynolds 1991; Reynolds 1996), may be more influenced by classroom-based policies that are close to their focal concerns of teaching and curriculum, rather than by the policies that are 'managerial' and orientated to the school level.

A 'LITTLE ENGLAND AND WALES' MENTALITY

Any concern about the prospects of the new government's educational policies improving the situation within the United Kingdom is magnified by the realization that the White Paper is rather ethnocentric. In its desire to move to a situation where the present 'leading edge' schools are joined by the great majority of other schools, the focus is upon utilizing the within-Britain variation as a kind of educational learning experience. The possibility that Britain may benefit from a systematic assessment of educational policies from outside our geographic boundaries is not one that is explored systematically, even though the Appendices to the White Paper contain data that shows a poor United Kingdom performance in some skill areas.

The attempt to look for educational solutions from 'within' rather than 'without', as it were, is of course a marked contrast to the educational philosophies increasingly in evidence in other countries. The 'America 2000' goals in the United States were based upon an extensive discussion and analysis of American performance in basic skills taken from international surveys like those of the International Assessment of Educational Performance (Reynolds and Farrell 1996), and included considerable material on what it was that other, high-scoring countries appeared to be doing in their educational practice (Stringfield, Ross and Smith 1996). The design of some of the much vaunted educational systems of the Pacific Rim, such as that of Japan, which appear to perform very well in all existing international achievement surveys, was indeed partially based in their pre-school or kindergarten phase upon Hungarian models, through the modelling of practice following a series of visits of Japanese educational policy-makers and politicians to Hungary in the early 1970s.

Interestingly, the Pacific Rim societies themselves are currently fascinated by the need to take account of best practice from around the world, and are currently interested in learning about what could be called 'progressive' methods which involve a focus on new, affective outcomes, an enhanced role for learners in determining their learning situation and the possibilities of children's collaborative learning in groups within lessons being expanded as a proportion of lesson time, thereby generating competencies in group-related skills (Reynolds 1997). All this stands as a stark contrast to the rather ethnocentric tendencies of the White Paper, and indeed as a contrast to the quite frequent use of overseas examples of good practice in the speeches of David Blunkett in the two years leading up to the 1997 election.

The absence of non-British sources of policy proposals may be very costly indeed for the prospects of British educational advance. Firstly, there is now a considerable volume of evidence to show that the British system of education is not performing well by comparison with others, with a very poor performance in mathematics, average performance in literacy, and above-average performance only in science (Reynolds and Farrell 1996). Whilst it is highly likely that some of these differences between countries reflect the influence of social, economic and cultural factors which are operating both to enhance achievement and to make the 'mission' of the schools easier in other countries (in the societies of the Pacific Rim, for example), the British performance is worse than those countries with similar economic, social and cultural backgrounds, suggesting indeed that it is the educational system of other societies that is more effective than that of England and Wales. There are also hints that other countries may have a more 'reliable' system in the sense of having schools and teachers who are more similar, without the range of quality that is seen in British educational settings (Creemers and Reynolds 1996).

By averting our eyes from what these other educational systems do, we may have impoverished the policies against which it is proposed that our schools should 'benchmark', since even the best of British educational practice, particularly in areas where we may have severe problems such as the primary age phase, may not be as effective as what might routinely exist in other societies. What policies might these societies have to show us?

At system level, some of them (such as those of the Pacific Rim) could show us a prevalent belief that all children can learn, and that there is no need for any trailing edge of low-performing pupils. We might be able to see teacher training that focuses upon giving all teachers the 'technologies of practice' that they need as foundations for their future professional development, a marked contrast to the British emphasis upon teachers being enabled to discover their own foundations of professional knowledge.

At school level, one might see frequent testing of students (again in Pacific Rim societies), undertaken in order to give high-quality information on how pupils are doing so that they can be re-taught if necessary. One might also see, in Switzerland for example, the use of children's textbooks that are nationally provided and designed by groups of experienced teachers to prevent the necessity of individual teachers having to provide their own individually constructed material.

At classroom level, one might see (in many societies, including those of the Pacific Rim and some in Europe such as Switzerland) whole-class interactive teaching, in which the teacher instructs the class for 80–90 per cent of the time whilst at the same time heavily involving students in the lessons through frequent questioning, permitting children to shout out the right answers and permitting students who have finished work to peer-tutor others.

Whilst the importance of looking at other cultures is still occasionally a theme in the speeches of Labour ministers after the election, and whilst in fairness David Blunkett's enthusiasm for learning from other societies remains undimmed, the absence of rigorous proposals for cross-cultural learning within the White Paper remains a factor that is likely to impoverish its policy prescriptions.

THE TRANSMISSION OF KNOWLEDGE TO PRACTITIONERS

One of the most important distinctions between the present government's proposals and past educational policy pronouncements is that, in future, serious attempts will be made to ensure that best practice in the areas of teaching methods, school organization and educational arrangements in general will be passed on to all personnel in the educational system, rather than the latter being encouraged to 'discover their own' practice in their particular working contexts. Past practice in teacher's professional development was often premised upon the importance of ensuring that the long-term professional development of teachers was safeguarded by letting them 'own' the practice of professional develop-ment, yet it is likely that these practices might have generated high levels of professional development for 'leading edge' practitioners but low levels of development for those in the professional 'trailing edge', leading to the variability in the quality of practice shown by many international surveys (Reynolds and Farrell 1996).

The present government's intention is to focus pre-service training upon the provision of 'foundations' in terms of enhanced subject know-ledge and teaching skills, and also to ensure that specific bodies of know-ledge relating to skills in the areas of literacy and numeracy are also provided through use of in-service training days. However, the diffi-culties of ensuring that this knowledge base actually gets picked up by practitioners may be intense. Tymms (1995) notes the two forms of knowledge transmission that have existed historically as 'cultural' diffusion and 'demic' diffusion, the one typified by the process of knowledge trans-mission that takes place when scientific ideas are put forward in a scientific paper or book, and the other typified by the process of intellectual apprenticeship that takes place when one learns from a person the 'craft knowledge' that accrues to that individual by virtue of their experience.

If, as seems highly likely, the existing British teaching force may have been trained in the 'apprenticeship' or 'cultural diffusion' mode, the pro-fession may find the 'demic diffusion' mode particularly difficult to take advantage of as utilized within the new post-White Paper arrangements for the giving of 'best practice'. Tymms (1996) notes the possibility that teachers may behave as did those medieval villagers who starved them-selves to death rather than adopt the new agricultural techniques that were bringing prosperity to villages close by, but which had not been brought to them in ways that permitted them to take them up.

If this analysis is correct, the transmission of 'good practice', after decades of permitting the invention of practice, will have to pay atten-tion to the presenting culture of the teaching profession, their prior training and socialization, and their definitions of which knowledge bases are appropriate and useful for them. Given our knowledge of teacher cultures, it seems likely that the presentation of knowledge in the areas of effective teaching and schooling practices should have the following characteristics:

- It should be concerned with teacher focal concerns (such as teaching and curriculum) rather than with issues to do with the more remote managerial level of the school;

- It should be related to 'real life' situations by frequent use of examples of persons and practice to make the knowledge 'real' in the eyes of teachers;
- It should be delivered by those, such as excellent head teachers and teachers, who have authenticity in teachers' eyes;
- It should appeal to teachers' sense of morality and moral purpose (Fullan 1991) as well as to their emotions.

Educational knowledge, then, might at the moment need to be more like the knowledge bases of cooking, for example, than that of applied or pure science, with its utilization of the rational empirical paradigm. Ideas about Chinese and Indian cuisine have been in existence for many hundreds of years, and the 'rational' excellence of these culinary traditions long recognized. However, it took the arrival of Chinese and Indian persons in the United Kingdom to spread the 'technology', which had not been widely taken up before.

If education is similar, it will take considerably more than the contemporary throwing of the ideas about effective practices at the teaching profession to ensure the take-up of the practices. It seems doubtful if the White Paper recognizes this fully.

CONCLUSIONS

We have outlined in this chapter a range of doubts as to the extent to which the existing range of educational policies being pursued are likely to achieve their goals. In determining these policies, there is no doubt that school effectiveness and school improvement knowledge has played a crucial role, since the influence of the paradigm is in evidence as a determinant of the new policies.

However, much of the knowledge base appears to have been ignored in the shaping of the new policies, particularly in the areas of the importance of the teaching and learning level, the relative historical unimportance of the local authority in determining achievement levels, the absence of within-school variation as a possible driver of achievement, and the absence of any focus upon educational systems 'overseas'.

To report these conclusions is not to disavow, or to negate, what 'New Labour' is following as its educational policies. All of the latter are no doubt absolutely *necessary* to the achievement of the goals of an enhanced 'quantity' of educational achievement and an enhanced 'equality of educational opportunity' in its distribution. All of the present policies are not, however, likely to be *sufficient* for the achievement of these ends. One hopes that the recently established relationship between 'New Labour' and the effectiveness and improvement communities will permit the telling of these truths.

5 Race, Nation and Education: New Labour and the New Racism

David Gillborn

> The 'other' is never outside or beyond us; it emerges forcefully, within cultural discourse, when we *think* we speak most intimately and indigenously 'between ourselves' (Bhabha 1990, reprinted 1994, p. 309 original emphasis).

It is cruelly ironic that in the European Year against Racism and Xenophobia (1997) the British general election was fought between two main parties each vying to be the more patriotic, the more secure in its nationalist credentials. Benedict Anderson's influential analysis of nations as 'imagined communities' highlights in dramatic fashion the myth-making that constitutes *the nation* as a powerful symbolic device, serving at once to secure and reproduce particular interests while silencing discordant voices and rendering numerous groups as the marginalized 'Other' (Anderson 1983 and 1991). My argument here is that contemporary political discourses of *nation* and *national identity* do more than merely rehearse such images, invoking a particular imagined community as a licence for their chosen doctrines. Rather, they offer a new, and dangerous, twist in attempts to achieve what Homi Bhabha (1990) terms 'the impossible unity of the nation'. Specifically, the attempts to re-imagine a simple homogeneous Britain (secure in its historical and contemporary excellence, its humanity and a fundamental – *pseudo-biological* – separateness) promote a return to the assimilationist policies of the past, where minority interests, needs and experiences are removed from the public policy agenda, and emphasis is placed upon the need to *conform*. In education, the resulting policies penalize institutions serving ethnically diverse student populations and threaten further to entrench current inequalities of opportunity (Gillborn 1997; Tomlinson 1997).

The chapter takes the following form. First, I offer a brief consideration of 'the new racism' as a distinctive characteristic of Thatcherite politics. Second, I provide an analysis of the new racist content of Labour appeals to 'the nation', its history and supposed character. Third, I chart the policy consequences of such constructions, especially insofar as they threaten to extend existing ethnic inequalities of opportunity through the adoption of colour-blind approaches to issues of selection and pedagogy. Finally, I reflect briefly on how these strands might represent a form of new assimilationist politics – a politics where the 'normality' of white middle-class perspectives, experiences and needs is assumed, while ethnic minority interests and distinctiveness are obliterated beneath an individualist discourse that holds students, their parents and communities to blame for failure.

THE NEW RACISM

As Kenneth Thompson has noted, during the late 1970s and the early 1980s a central strand in the New Right's emerging 'discursive ensemble' stressed a culturalist construction of the nation as a (threatened) haven for white (Christian) tradition and values (Thompson 1992, pp. 349–50). This position frequently drew on racial imagery and attacked the 'multiculturalism' that was supposed to have widely infiltrated social policy, not least in education. As Martin Barker (1981) has emphasized, however, this was not a simple restatement of old familiar racist themes. Indeed, Barker contrasts *'the new racism'* with previous pseudo-scientific conceptions.

Figure 1:   Characteristics of 'old' and 'new' racism

old racism (*pseudo-science*)	**new racism** (*pseudo-biological culturalism*)
race superiority	culture difference

Classic nineteenth-century *'scientific racism'* is commonly defined in relation to a dual focus: first, asserting the empirical existence of separate human races; second, a belief in the innate superiority of certain races over others. Such a view was, of course, central to Nazi atrocities earlier this century and although popular (folk) racisms often still draw on similar beliefs, these sentiments are not widely acceptable in mainstream political discourse. Nevertheless, Barker argues, racism has continued to play a central role in Thatcherite politics, adopting a 'new' form that stresses *culture* (rather than *colour*) and emphasizes *difference* (rather than claiming *superiority*):

> You do not need to think of yourself as superior – you do not even need to dislike or blame those who are so different from you – in order to say that the presence of these aliens constitutes a threat to our way of life (Barker 1981, p. 18).

This kind of perspective is not, of course, wholly new. Neither has it completely displaced cruder and more obviously 'racialized' discourses. Robert Miles, for example, argues that Barker 'ignores the imagery of the English working class, where more "classical" forms of racist expression abound' (1993, p. 73). Similarly, the mid-1990s witnessed a renewed confidence among psychometricians – scientific racism has once again attained a degree of public respectability. Despite, or more likely *because* of, the public furore concerning *The Bell Curve* (Herrnstein and Murray 1994), IQists have once again found their opinions sought by the media. They have taken advantage of the debates as an opportunity to reconstitute their work as 'hard science' (i.e. factual and value-free) that is now breaking its public silence after years of suppression by a politically correct conspiracy between media and liberal intellectuals (cf. *Wall Street Journal*, 13 December 1994, p. A18). Their messages are food and drink to commentators on the right, keen to justify yet more elitist reforms of public policy (e.g. Johnson 1994; Tooley 1995. For a critical review see Drew et al. 1995). These are vitally important developments, but they do not discredit Barker's analysis. Rather, they point to the need continually to interrogate discourses for their racialized content and/or consequences: a *de*racialized discourse can have no less racist consequences (Gillborn 1995; Reeves 1983; Troyna 1993). *The 'old' and 'new' racisms, therefore, are not exclusive nor competing discourses: they are, in fact, mutually supportive.*

New racism, therefore, is not a break with classical racist theories but an adaptation to new conditions and constraints: 'racism theorized out of the guts and made into commonsense' (Barker 1981, p. 23). In this way, nations are constituted according to a 'pseudo-biological cultural-ism' (ibid.) that asserts the inevitable and 'natural' distinctiveness of a nation's people and positions an antagonism to 'outsiders' as not only understandable, but as *instinctive* and *positive*.

Nations on this view are not built out of politics and economics, but out of human nature. It is in our biology, our instincts, to defend our way of life, traditions and customs against outsiders – not because they are inferior, but because they are part of different cultures. (Barker 1981, p. 24)

I now wish to examine how these strands can be identified in contemporary political narratives of the 'British' nation: first, in Tory pronouncements; second, in Tony Blair's analysis of the past, present and future as he reinvented his political party as '*New* Labour'. As we will see, there is little between the two positions.

THE NEW RACISM AND THATCHERITE NARRATIVES OF THE NATION

We have ceased to be a nation in retreat. We have instead a newfound confidence – born in the economic battles at home and tested and found true 8000 miles away . . . And so today we can rejoice at our success in the Falklands and take pride in the achievement of the men and women of our task force. But we do so, not as at some flickering of a flame which must soon be dead. No – we rejoice that Britain has rekindled that spirit which fired her for generations past and which today has begun to burn as brightly as before. Britain found herself again in the South Atlantic and will not look back from the victory she has won. (Margaret Thatcher, 3 July 1982)

There is no need here to spend long dissecting the various strands of Thatcherite narratives of the British nation and 'its' people. Nevertheless, it is useful to recall the strident tones adopted by Thatcher and to highlight a couple of particularly significant elements in her version of Great (again) Britain. The quotation above is especially apposite: it is drawn from a speech made shortly after Argentinian forces surrendered on the Falkland Islands/Malvinas and exemplifies key elements in Thatcherite versions of the nation.

First, there is a concern to assert a common bond between contemporary and historical events and people. There is at work here an 'intimation of simultaneity across homogeneous, empty time' (Anderson 1991, 145). There is projected a deeply rooted (pseudo-biological) commonality. 'Britain *found* herself again in the South Atlantic': it is more than an attempt to *emulate* some past glory, it is a *re*kindling of the *same* flame: *a lineage*.

Second, the triumphalist tone should be treated with seriousness. It is easy to scoff at such overtly militaristic (and colonialist) language, but this is more than simple jingoism. Britain as strong (militarily, if not always economically) and victorious (where it chooses to flex its armoured muscles) became a central component in Thatcherite attempts to re-imagine Britain as the same world power it had been in the past. Indeed, this same triumphalism is present in Thatcherite representations of Britain as a *moral* (not merely military and economic) power.

> the British character has done so much for democracy, for law, and done so much throughout the world, that if there is a fear that it might be swamped, people are going to react and be rather hostile to those coming in (Margaret Thatcher, *Daily Mail*, 31 January 1978, and quoted in Barker 1981, p. 15).

This, now infamous, quotation demonstrates vividly a sense of moral superiority and exemplifies how easily the construction of national distinctiveness becomes a justification for racist policy; in this case promoting greater controls over immigration from the Caribbean and Indian subcontinent.

Although its namesake has lost power, Thatcherism's closed and bigoted version of the nation (and the racism that lies at the heart of that concept) is alive and well, not just in the post-Thatcher Conservative Party, but in Tony Blair's 'New Labour'.

NEW LABOUR AND THE NEW RACISM

> I believe in Britain. It is a great country with a great history. The British people are a great people (Tony Blair, *Leader of the Opposition*. The first words of the 1997 Labour Party election manifesto)

Tony Blair's project to re-make the Labour Party has also addressed the need to re-make Britain:

> New Labour. New Britain.
> The party renewed. The country reborn.
> New Labour. New Britain.
> (Tony Blair, the final words of his speech to the 1995 Labour Party Conference, 3 October)

It is entirely predictable that Blair as leader of the main opposition party found much to criticize in the current state of the nation. Less predictable, and certainly more interesting, is the way that he addressed issues of social and national identity. Perhaps surprisingly, rather than advocating a break with a past characterized by massive inequalities and injustices, Blair's attempt to imagine a 'New Britain' traded directly on many of the same supposed glories and traits familiar as themes in Thatcherite narratives of the British nation and character.

> We enjoy a thousand material advantages over any previous generation; and yet we suffer a depth of insecurity and spiritual doubt they never knew...
> The generation that knocks on the door of a new millennium, frightened for our future and unsure of our soul.
> We live in a new age but in an old country.
> Britain won two World Wars.
> We had an Empire and formed a Commonwealth.
> We invented the sports the rest of the world now plays; gave the world some of the finest literature, art and poetry.
> We are proud of our history but its weight hangs heavy upon us.
> Why?
> Because it has left us for far too long defining ourselves as a nation, not by what unites us, but by what divides us.
> (Tony Blair. Speech to the 1995 Labour Party conference, 3 October)

Superficially, of course, there is a strong contrast between Thatcher's post-Falklands declaration of 'a newfound confidence' and Blair's portrait (more than a decade later) of a national identity crisis. Certainly parts of the script have changed, but the essential (and essentializing) plot remains the same. The Britain of the past is defined in terms of a world-shaping military, colonial and civilizing influence – a history 'we are proud of' and which played a crucial symbolic role throughout his speech. Blair also signalled his intention to wrap himself in the Union Flag, rather than the more traditional red one:

> We are patriots. This is the patriotic party. (ibid, p. 17)

Most significantly, Britain and the British are defined as insiders ('we') who 'had an Empire', 'invented' games and 'gave' to the world wonderful art and literature; *the discourse positions the 'Empire' and 'Commonwealth' as possessions; defines their people as outside the British nation; and, in all major respects, as of lesser importance.* This same version of Britain was revisited a year on:

> ... consider a thousand years of British history and what it tells us.
> The first parliament of the World; the Industrial Revolution – ahead of its time; an Empire, the largest the World has ever known, relinquished in peace.
> The invention of virtually every scientific device of the modern World.
> Two World Wars in which our country was bled dry, in which two generations perished, but which in the defeat of the most evil force ever let loose by man showed the most sustained example of bravery in human history.
> This is our nation.
> Our characteristics: common-sense, standing up for the underdog, fiercely independent.
> (Tony Blair. Speech to the 1996 Labour Party Conference, 1 October)

The key elements of Thatcher's post-Falklands address (the assertion of a national lineage; the triumphalist tone) are not only present, but taken to new extremes. British world-firsts play a key role (first Parliament; first to industrialize; first to invent ...), indeed, their deployment achieves a dramatic re-imagining of Britain as a benign civilizing force (rather than a controlling and exploitative colonizer). The triumphalist tone is remarkably unrestrained, but even more striking is the complete amnesia that is displayed when it comes to non-British contributions to human history (political, economic and artistic) 'The invention of virtually every scientific device of the modern World'.

So much for the scientific work of the Chinese empires, the irrigation systems of the ancient Egyptian peoples, the genius of Leonardo da Vinci or, more recently, the refugee scientists and others who worked on the development of the first atomic bomb. Indeed, as any school students fortunate enough to be introduced to antiracist curricula materials probably know, numerous other significant 'modern' inventions arise from work beyond British shores. Prime Minister Blair might be surprised to discover, for example, that blood transfusions (a not unimportant medical procedure) are possible because of the work of an African-American scientist (Charles Richard Drew) or that the automated traffic signal (a device so commonplace it seems strange even to think of it as an 'invention') was patented by Garrett A. Morgan (an African-American) in 1923. Further examples, though plentiful, would be tedious: the point is clear. The narration of Britain as the historic (and natural?) home to scientific discoveries and inventions is at best hugely overstated; at worst, such a position might even be thought bigoted. From the perspective of this paper, however, the same speech contains an even more revealing example of the strategic re-imagining of the nation's past: 'an Empire, the largest the World has ever known, relinquished in peace.'

First, we should note that the contemporary British state *still* has a number of colonies and 'dependencies': additionally, of course, there is ongoing political and armed struggle for independence within the boundaries of the United Kingdom itself (it is surprising how quickly we can forget bombs in English cities when the historic causes do not fit the present narrative). While 'Empire' may be too grand a word, therefore, Britain continues to maintain unequal and disputed colonial links with other states.

Second, the idea that the Empire was 'relinquished in peace' is absurd. Numerous independence movements have fought (and succeeded) in opposition to British rule. The War of American Independence; the struggles for self-determination in the Indian subcontinent, in parts of Africa and the Caribbean are among the best documented. Such struggles cost countless lives and were often met with fierce opposition from the colonial power. It was only after the Second World War that the rush to 'decolonize' gathered its greatest momentum, driven not by altruism but by new economic and geo-political realities.

Once again, therefore, this narrative of Britain serves to silence discordant voices. The idea that Britain effectively *gifted* colonies their freedom first serves to reinforce the myth of Britain as liberator and defender of freedom; and second, denies the very real political (and military) struggles that preceded the 'granting' of independence (as Britain would define it)/the 'winning' of freedom as the 'colonies' might express it.

In all of this, Blair remakes Thatcher's 'Britain' in all key respects. The nation is defined in pseudo-biological terms as a world leader in economic, military and humanitarian fields. Britain, therefore, is essentially defined as a nation of white insiders and colonial appendages. If New Labour's view of the nation is uncannily reminiscent of Thatcherite versions, what about their specific education policies? Surely here there is some clarity of distinction? These questions are addressed in the next section.

COLOUR-BLIND POLICIES: DIVISIVE CONSEQUENCES

Education is the effective way of ensuring equality of opportunity. Last September's OFSTED report on the achievements of ethnic minority pupils has focused the minds of those working in education (David Blunkett, *Shadow Education Secretary*, February 1997, quoted in *The Runnymede Bulletin*, 1997)

In September 1996 the Office for Standards in Education (Ofsted) published a document which, albeit briefly, punctured the deafening silence that had grown in policy-making circles around issues such as racism and equal opportunities (Gillborn and Gipps 1996). In writing that review, my colleague Caroline Gipps and I did not wish merely to summarize a body of academic research but sought also to address policy-makers (at national, local and school levels). We presented clear evidence that silence on race issues was contributing to the persistence of injustice. We concluded that a decade's research, plus our own survey of new data from a range of LEAs, indicated that:

- the education system is still scarred by racism;
- significant inequalities of opportunity persist;
- in some areas the situation is getting worse, not better.

Despite these continuing injustices, very many young people from ethnic minority backgrounds *do* succeed in the education system. Unfortunately, the best evidence to date suggests that such successes are often won despite the system rather than because of it. Too many young people of ethnic minority background find their aspirations frustrated by a system that places additional barriers in their path. A failure to consider ethnic diversity has been one of the most striking and consistent features of all recent education reforms. It has allowed existing inequalities to persist while creating the conditions for further discrimination and exclusion in a system that adopts a 'colour-blind' rhetoric but frequently behaves in ways that systematically disadvantage minority students.

As I have noted, race equality was not an issue in the general election campaign of 1997. Indeed, a detailed analysis of Labour's policy documents at the time reveals a total silence on racism. The most dramatic example of this was to be found in Labour's own policy and promotional materials. A visit to Labour's site on the Internet allowed visitors to search not only the election Manifesto but also several other key policy documents. A search for the word 'tax' produced 57 separate 'hits'. That is, 57 separate references to 'tax' in the manifesto and related sources. A search for 'racism' produced no hits: according to the party's own inter-active database, therefore, at the time of their election victory there was no reference to 'racism' in Labour's electoral and other key policy documents.

A lack of action on racial equality was highlighted, by the head of the Commission for Racial Equality (CRE), shortly into Labour's first term back in power. In its main story of the day, *The Guardian* reported criticisms by Sir Herman Ouseley under the headline 'Blacks "losing out in Blair's new Britain"' (22 July 1997, p. 1). Ouseley was reported as attacking many aspects of the Government's policies but as praising the DfEE 'for its work on black underachievement' (ibid.). This may have been prompted by the Government's first White Paper, *Excellence in Schools* (DfEE 1997), published earlier that month (just 67 days after the election). The document finally broke with years of de-racialized discourse on education by including discrete references to racial inequalities in exclusion (DfEE 1997, p. 57) and promising that under Labour 'Schools will be taking practical steps to raise ethnic minority pupils' achievements and promote racial harmony' (DfEE 1997, p. 6). The latter quotation is how the document summarises two paragraphs specifically devoted to 'Ethnic minority pupils' (DfEE 1997, pp. 34–35). Amounting to less than a side of text (in an 80-page document) this is a pitifully small section: nevertheless, it *is* a start. The document commits the DfEE to continuing the 'task force' on ethnic minority students, which was set up by the Tories following publication of the Ofsted review (including Sir Herman as a member). The section further promises to consult on ethnic monitoring and to provide guidance on 'tackling racial harassment and stereotyping' (DfEE 1997, p. 35). Unfortunately, there is no evidence that this commitment to race equality has had any effect on the rest of the proposals in the document: the curriculum, teacher education, testing and selection – all are discussed in familiar colour-blind terms. In fact, the latter is especially worrying since the Government's proposals threaten further to entrench existing racial inequalities of opportunity. The question of selection, and the underlying assumptions it exposes, illustrate clearly the continued danger of colour-blind policies. A swift side-reference to ethnic diversity is not enough, an awareness of racism must inform policy across the board.

Selection in schools

> To those who say where is Labour's passion for social justice, I say
> education is social justice. Education is liberty. Education is oppor-
> tunity (Tony Blair, April 1997, quoted in the *Times Educational
> Supplement*, 18 April 1997, p. 6).

In making good its commitment to social justice, New Labour has
much to do. Many young people from working-class and ethnic minority
backgrounds, despite their own commitment to education, experience
schooling as unjust. For them schooling is a constraining process, dominated by an externally imposed curriculum that is frequently ethnocentric. Education can be a liberation, but often the reality is a daily grind
shaped by forces of selection that (whatever the official rationale) work
to close down opportunities and remake existing inequalities. Selection,
however, has been an area where Labour have been swift to act. Indeed,
even *before* their election victory, the party won amendments to an education bill so that the first Education Act of 1997 (and the last of Major's
government) was stripped of all sections granting greater freedom for
schools to select by ability at the point of entry (*Times Educational
Supplement*, 21 March 1997, p. 6). Here at least Labour delivered without equivocation. The story on selection, however, goes further than
debates about a return to the eleven-plus.

> No return to the 11-plus. The comprehensive system will stay, mod-
> ernised for today's world, taking account of children's different abil-
> ities but not setting them apart (Tony Blair. Speech to the 1996
> Labour Party Conference, quoted in the *Times Educational Supple-
> ment*, 4 October 1996, p. 4).

In fact, *setting* children apart is exactly what Labour intend:

> There should be no return to the 11-plus. It divides children into
> successes and failures at far too early an age. We must modernize
> comprehensive schools. *Children are not all of the same ability, nor
> do they learn at the same speed.* That means 'setting' children in
> classes to maximize progress, for the benefit of high-fliers and
> slower learners alike (Labour Party Manifesto 1997, p. 7, emphasis
> added).

We favour all-in schooling which identifies the *distinct abilities* of individual pupils and organizes them in classes to maximize their progress in individual subjects (Labour Party Manifesto 1997, pp. 3–4: emphasis added).

Support for the wider use of 'setting by ability' has been an emerging part of Labour's education policy for some time: it was mentioned by Tony Blair in a speech at the Institute of Education in the summer of 1995 and became a stronger commitment a year later when he announced that 'In Government we will start from a general presumption in favour of grouping by ability and attainment'. Predictably, the White Paper *Excellence in Schools* has much to say on the subject. Interestingly, the document explicitly attacks any attempt to view internal selection as a denial of equal opportunity:

> The demands for equality and increased opportunity in the 1950s and 1960s led to the introduction of comprehensive schools. All-in secondary schooling rightly became the normal pattern, but the search for equality of opportunity in some cases became a tendency to uniformity. The idea that all children had the same rights to develop their abilities led too easily to the doctrine that all had the same ability. The pursuit of excellence was too often equated with elitism (DfEE 1997, p. 11).

Labour is committed, therefore, to an extension in the use of selection *within* schools. This is justified with reference to a belief first, that children have 'distinct abilities'; and second, that they learn at different speeds. These views carry a lot of common-sense power and echo exactly the kind of thinking that underpinned the 1943 Norwood Committee's view that there were different 'types' of student – a view that ultimately found expression in the selective tripartite system of the post-war period. Although Tony Blair is against such an overtly selective system, his assumptions about 'ability' and natural differences embody just such an approach. Any suggestion that such significant differences do not exist is dismissed as doctrinaire.

The wisdom of Labour's commitment to 'setting' and other forms of internal selection can be questioned both conceptually and practically. First, despite Labour's certainty regarding children's different abilities, there is no clear consensus on the scientific status of such a view. There is no need here to review the historical misuses to which IQ tests have been put in the name of natural selection and the protection of racial/ ethnic/intellectual purity (see Gould 1981; Kamin 1974, 1995). Despite

recent attempts to revive a crude (and racist) version of 'intelligence' as
fixed and genetically based (Herrnstein and Murray 1994), even mainstream psychometricians now reject any simple notion of intelligence as
a fixed and generalized potential (Sternberg 1996). And yet this, essentially, is what Labour's policy on setting claims: that children have
fundamentally different intellectual capabilities – so different that education should separate them and deal with them differently. Although
New Labour would (presumably) accept in principle that early test
scores are highly likely to reflect differences in class background, English language fluency and other *social* (as opposed to genetic) factors, in
practice their policy threatens to add further weight to processes that
take such measures as proxies for some hidden, deeper 'ability'. Such
views are highly contested in Western academia, and rejected in several
non-Western education systems, but they are fundamental to Labour's
support for setting.

   In addition to the conceptual criticisms of its underlying assumptions,
Labour's support for setting should also be questioned on more practical grounds. Grouping pupils by ability is frequently justified in terms
of supporting the higher achievements of 'more able' students, but
research evidence on this is not conclusive. Somewhat more firmly based
are fears that such selection replicates and further entrenches existing
social divisions based on social class and ethnic differences (Gipps and
Murphy 1994; Hallam and Toutounji 1996; Hatcher 1997; Slavin 1990,
1996). Specifically, once pupils are placed in a 'set' there is relatively little chance of their being moved. Placement in a low set usually means:

- less access to high status knowledge – *low sets often follow restricted
  curricula*;
- access is denied to the highest qualifications – *those in low sets may be
  entered for examinations 'tiered' at such a level that a GCSE higher
  grade pass (A*–C) is simply not permitted for students on that paper*;
- lower teacher expectations;
- increased disillusionment among students.

These problems are associated with grouping by ability regardless of
ethnicity: there is even more cause for concern when we consider
research specifically concerned with the placement of ethnic minority
students.

   Students of South Asian ethnic background may be additionally disadvantaged by teachers' misreading of *language* issues, as if they reflected
deeper-seated *learning* problems (CRE 1992; Troyna 1991; Troyna and
Siraj-Blatchford 1993). Alternatively, there is considerable evidence

that teachers' tend to view African-Caribbean students as likely to be disruptive or to present other disciplinary problems (e.g. Connolly 1994; Figueroa 1991; Gillborn 1990; Mac an Ghaill 1988; Mirza 1992; Sewell 1997; Wright 1986). Such stereotypes can lead to placement in lower sets even where black students have equal (or superior) test scores to more highly placed white peers (Wright 1986).

The research evidence on setting and ethnic origin, therefore, suggests that setting can unnecessarily disadvantage students of ethnic minority background. If the new government is unaware of this research it should do some homework: not only was it summarized in the review published by Ofsted in 1996, but a special report by the Commission for Racial Equality criticized exactly these assumptions as early as 1992:

> The purpose of this report is to alert schools to the need to re-examine critically and radically what so many of them take for granted; namely, that pupils are "naturally" selected and streamed by their own intrinsic abilities and merits . . . unless schools monitor their performance and their policies rigorously, in all areas and by ethnic origin, many ethnic minority children may continue to be quite unfairly 'set to fail' (Commission for Racial Equality, 1992, p. 44).

> schools (through the adoption of various selection and setting procedures) may play an active, though unintended, role in the creation of conflict with African Caribbean pupils, thereby reducing black young people's opportunity to achieve (Gillborn and Gipps 1996, p. 56).

The evidence on selection and ethnic minority students clearly demonstrates the need for policy-makers to abandon the colour-blind approach that has dominated recent education reforms. The Labour government is free to assert that such an approach will operate to 'the benefit of high-fliers and slower learners alike' (Labour Party Manifesto 1997, p. 7) but there is no convincing evidence for this: on the contrary, there is well-founded evidence that such a policy will have a detrimental effect on ethnic minority students. The absence of 'racial' signifiers from the policy is no guarantee that the policy will not have differential, racist effects: 'colour-blind' language can disguise 'colour-specific' consequences.

The immediate outlook for race equality, therefore, would seem to suggest little hope for significant change in the short term: Labour's discursive construction of the nation and its most vaunted education policies signify a failure to break with assumptions and practices that have already proven to operate to the disadvantage of many ethnic minority groups. The long-term forecast may be even gloomier: so far as race, racism and ethnicity are concerned, there is a convergence in Labour and Conservative policy discourse that may foreshadow a new phase of ethnic assimilationism.

RACISM, 'BRITISHNESS' AND THE NEW ASSIMILATIONISM

the ideas of 'race' and 'nation', as in a kaleidoscope, merge into one another in varying patterns, each simultaneously highlighting and obscuring the other (Miles 1993, p. 76).

There is no need to revisit the long established analyses of the vital role that racism has played in the definition of Britishness, both at the national and popular levels. Paul Gilroy's (1987) exploration of the 'ethnic absolutism' that operated through the dialectics of nation and culture in the 1980s has continued relevance. More recent work has revealed the complex, but still clear, racist connotations that 'Britishness' retains for many young people, including white teenagers as well as their 'minority' peers (cf. Back 1996; Hewitt 1996; Modood et al. 1994).

But the current situation has more importance than a simple re-telling of an old familiar story. We risk oversimplifying the situation (and underestimating the scale of the problem) if we simply interpret as short-lived expedience Tony Blair's statements on the nature of Britain and the British. Paul Gilroy has charted the historic difficulties of Labour politicians and socialist intellectuals as they attempted to engage with nationalist sentiment without simply re-making the authoritarian and racist versions celebrated by the right (Gilroy 1987, especially Chapter 2). As I have already noted, it would appear from Blair's recent speeches to his party's national conference that such problems are a thing of the past: he has no difficulty in re-articulating (for a New Labour Britain) exactly the kind of authoritarian, mythical Britain familiar in Thatcherite rhetoric. This development threatens important consequences, particularly in relation to the positioning of race inequalities in future policy debates.

As we have seen, 'racial' and other inequalities continue to feature in New Labour agendas; however, it is their deployment that is significant. The Education White Paper, for example, includes a section solely concerned with minority students, but in so doing seems to suggest that all other issues are devoid of any special importance so far as race equality is concerned. Similarly, the role of race inequality in Blair's speeches is revealing:

> You can be tough on crime and tough on prejudice too.
> In any young country the talents of all are allowed to flourish.
> There should be no discrimination on grounds of disability, gender, age, sexuality or race. In its place, tolerance and respect. And I say to the Tories: those who play politics with race or immigration betray the decent values of any civilized society (Tony Blair. Speech to the 1995 Labour Party conference).

The speech makes no direct reference to 'racism', but calls instead for 'tolerance and respect'. By counterpoising 'tolerance and respect' against 'prejudice' and 'discrimination', Blair effectively equates racism with the most obvious and crude actions of individuals – nowhere is it presented as a feature of structures or institutions. Additionally, Blair's use of 'race' in this context is an example of what Barry Troyna (1994, after Mary O'Brien 1984) terms *'commatization'*; offering a perfunctory mention among a list of other worthy issues (disability – *comma* – gender – *comma* – age – *comma* – sexuality) all of which are then immediately relegated back to the sidelines. The only separate mention for 'race' comes as part of an attack on the Conservative Party for playing politics regarding immigration: interesting that even here the then Leader of the Opposition felt no compulsion to set out an alternative to Tory policies and practices.

So, current inequalities of opportunity feature in Labour's rhetoric but seem to impinge little on its policies: the same can be said of the Tories. Early in the general election year, Prime Minister Major addressed similar territory and accepted, albeit somewhat grudgingly, that inequalities of opportunity exist. Though he seemed loath to name them, his language drew attention to regional, class and racialized inequalities:

> I don't wish to paint a picture of utopia. There is much still to be done. I don't pretend that the prospects for the young black man in Brixton is yet as open to talent as it is to the young white man in the Home Counties. It clearly isn't (Major 1997, p. 6).

Although even this admission came as a surprise to some, Major's solution was less encouraging. First, he advocated 'tolerance' and 'civility' as the way forward:

'Oh,' says smart, knowing opinion. 'Is that all? Tolerance? What a banal commonplace, little thing'. Yes, indeed. It is so banal, so commonplace this tolerance, that it is Alpha and Omega. It is so little a thing that if it disappears, men die.

If you disbelieve me look at Srebrenica. That's a warning of what happens when people no longer tolerate other religions or values or races. Tolerance had disappeared. Civility vanished.

Civility goes far beyond politeness. It's a breakwater against first thoughts and worst instincts. It inhibits anger, pulls away from prejudice. Civil people acknowledge other people – they respect their cultures and traditions (ibid., p. 4).

Tony Blair and his Prime Ministerial predecessor were agreed, therefore, on *tolerance* as the key to progress. This is fortunate because, earlier in the same speech, Major identified tolerance as a fundamental 'British' trait – again, 'racial' divides are deliberately downplayed while simultaneously constructing 'the British people' as white/non-minorities:

Many decent people feared racial tension – that there'd be riots, killings and endemic hatred, a trench war between dark and light-skinned peoples... But the great trench war between the races never happened. Why is it those fears were so wrong? I believe it was thanks to the fundamental goodwill and decency of the British people (ibid., p. 3).

At the time of the 1997 general election, therefore, both Labour and Conservative Parties pinned their hopes for greater equality of opportunity on *tolerance*. The significance of the word will not be lost on students of 'race' and ethnicity in Britain: the same word featured centrally in a speech in 1966 by the then Labour Home Secretary Roy Jenkins. The speech advocated 'not a flattening process of assimilation but equal opportunity, accompanied by cultural diversity, in an atmosphere of mutual tolerance' (quoted by Mullard 1982: 125). The speech is often cited as a key turning point in British 'race relations', marking a move away from assimilationist policies and toward more liberal notions of integration and cultural diversity. As Chris Mullard has demonstrated, however, this change was largely illusory. Although Jenkins's speech was significant in acknowledging that inequalities of opportunity existed, the thrust of policies remained unchanged:

cultural diversity is tolerable so long as it neither impedes progress to political integration nor explicitly challenges the cultural assumptions of our Anglo-centric society. That is to say the political imperative of assimilation in this model is no longer, as construed in the early sixties, dependent upon complete cultural subjugation: the means to the ends have slightly changed, but the ends remain the same (Mullard 1982, pp. 126–7).

The convergence of contemporary political opinion behind a well-worn notion such as 'tolerance' is significant. The word performs the same function now as in 1966: it allows the commatization of racist inequalities while pursuing social policies that not only ignore the diverse needs and experiences of minority groups, but threaten further to institutionalize existing inequalities. For John Major, the key to the future was simple: *more colour-blind policies*:

Few things would inflame racial tension more than trying to bias systems in favour of one colour – a reverse discrimination that fuels resentment. An artificial bias would damage the harmony we treasure. Equality under the law – yes; equality of opportunity and reward – yes. These promote harmony. Policy must be colour-blind – it must just tackle disadvantage. Faced by British citizens, whatever their background might be (Major 1997, p. 7).

And what does this look like in education? More of the same market policies:

But how do you achieve equality of opportunity?
It begins with education. Over the last few years we've opened up our schools so parents – and taxpayers – can see how well they're performing. That hasn't always made comfortable reading. Too often bad schools are found where we need good schools the most – in areas where education is a life line of hope ... Testing children on the basic skills, and giving parents the results. Inspecting schools on a regular basis. And, when it's really necessary, closing down failing schools. ... Specialist schools, grant-maintained schools, city technology colleges and – yes, if parents want them – grammar schools. This is the choice we're opening up (ibid. pp. 7–8).

Where the Tories were taking this policy line is clear – a return to the assimilationism of the 1960s and the early 1970s. John Major sought explicitly to reduce race (a factor strongly related to structural inequalities) to a mere surface characteristic – '*complexion*':

> If the man in the same office, cursing the same computer when it goes down, following the same football team, grumbling about the same cafe menu, has a different complexion, then it's just about the only thing different about him. His job, his family, his hopes, his fears, his allegiances, his experiences are often otherwise all the same. Life is lived, people join in, people belong. Darkness, lightness – that's a difference losing significance with every day crossed off the calendar (ibid., p. 6).

Notwithstanding the gendered nature of the perspective, its assimilationist thrust is clear: cultural diversity is to be tolerated, but the ideal scenario is one where 'race' and ethnicity are reduced to superficial and empty categories denoting 'dark and light-skinned peoples' (ibid., p. 3). It is a mark of how far race and ethnicity had been removed from public debate that Darcus Howe (one of the most prominent of black cultural critics) was moved to describe Major's speech as 'an historical moment': 'I have never in my 35 years in this country heard a leading political figure speak so positively and openly on the question of race' (Howe 1997).

The colour-(and culture-) blind future of education policy under the Tories was certain. Given Labour's acceptance of Tory employment law and the bulk of previous education reforms, one could be forgiven for imagining that in that development we could also perceive something of the future under New Labour. Certainly, the new Government's prescriptions for education have to date been overwhelmingly colour-blind. Despite an occasional reference to ethnic diversity, the lessons of decades of research and bitter experience have yet to be learnt. The new Prime Minister has put his personal weight behind policies that (whilst largely de-racialized – hardly ever addressing race explicitly) threaten to heighten the existing ethnic inequalities of achievement: selection provides a critical case study. Although Blair has set his party against selection at the point of entry to school, even before its election, he had committed a Labour Government to extend selection within schools via setting. I have noted that research in the UK and North America overwhelmingly suggests that such strategies operate to the disadvantage of ethnic minority students. There is no good reason to suppose that such approaches will not have similar effects in the future.

CONCLUSIONS

As Stuart Hall has noted, the assertion of some pseudo-biological fixity, an inevitable distinctiveness, is a central characteristic of ethnicity and nationalism.

> It [ethnicity] is not one thing; it is almost always contradictory, its meanings are always contested, it is always to some degree sliding to encompass new meanings in new conjunctures, it can always be differently articulated to different political positions, it is nothing in itself except in terms of the other discourses with which it can be articulated and with which it is strategically deployed. *It presents itself as a natural given, a kind of inscription in the bones – if we look hard enough in the genetic structure itself – which protects us against the open-endedness and the contingency of historical change and the variability of cultural production* (Hall 1993, UEL videotape, emphasis added).

In contemporary discourses of the British nation we see all the familiar racist sub-texts of previous attempts to imagine into being a heroic, liberating and homogeneous nation space. In this chapter I have specifically focused on developments in Labour's adoption of patriotism as a deliberate strategy. It could be argued that Tony Blair merely fell into the trap of Thatcherite imagery, unwittingly repeating her popular authoritarianism without realising its racialized nature. In his presentation of Britain as a triumphant, biocultural homogeneity, he has polished and added to its racialized form. Prime Minister Blair's version of Britain is no less problematic than that offered by his predecessors. Shortly before his electoral defeat, the previous incumbent of that office outlined his plans for a colour-blind future: one of de-racialized policy discourse, with racialized outcomes. Unfortunately, there is no convincing evidence that the current PM is any more able to imagine a Britain that is not as racially exclusive as any of its previous incarnations.

But there is more at stake here than Blairite rhetoric: this is more than a Labour politician simply assuming rightist language in order to get elected. Contemporary political imaginings of the British nation reassert a direct relation between nation and ethnos. It is a formula within which racism and inequality can be commatized while supposedly colour-blind policies have particular and predictable outcomes. The new racism that disfigures much contemporary policy threatens a return to the assimilationist politics of the past with all that entails for increased surveillance, social control and exclusion (see, for example,

Vincent and Tomlinson 1997). The new assimilationism, as we could call it, differs from previous versions in several respects, not least its adoption of the language of inclusivity; positing a multicultural Britain where everybody can share in prosperity. The discourse does not overtly position ethnic minority communities and cultures as a threat: rather, by deracializing policy, and asserting individual responsibilities and duties, the scene is set for the further pathologization of minorities if and when they emerge as less 'able' (that is, given least opportunity) to participate in the brave new Britain crafted by New Labour. The simple fact is that on average minority youth do not start on an equal footing: quite apart from the racism they face in school, in the economy and on the streets, they are disproportionately likely to be in families near or below the official poverty line (Modood et al. 1997). These constraints must be addressed in any policy claiming to offer an equal chance for all. At present, however, attention to 'ethnic minority' issues is limited to discrete initiatives. The main policy drives continue to adopt a deracialized approach, assuming a simple, homogeneous (and exclusionary) vision of the nation and its interests. The gross inequalities that scar contemporary education will continue while ever a critical understanding of racism is absent from the thinking that informs central policy making.

ACKNOWLEDGEMENTS

This chapter has been influenced by conversations, debates and arguments with many people. Among the most important individuals were Michael Apple, Stephen Ball, James A. Banks, Georgina Emmanuel, Samidha Garg, Dorn Gillborn, Jagdish Gundara, Richard Hatcher, Gillian Klein, Jane Lane, Richard Majors, Heidi Mirza, Tariq Modood, Sally Tomlinson, Carol Vincent, Gaby Weiner, Geoff Whitty and Deborah Youdell. Of course, I take full responsibility for the views expressed in the chapter.

6 Beyond the Bell Curve: New Policies for the National Curriculum

Bob Moon

I want to argue that outmoded conceptions of the human mind and intelligence underpin too much of recent educational policy making. This problem is particularly acute in relation to schooling, but many of the assumptions spill over into attitudes towards higher and, especially, adult education. The problems created by these flawed perceptions influence decision making across the political spectrum. The political manifestos published by both the major parties, in probably the last election of the century, demonstrate an almost identical lack of awareness of what one of our leading educational thinkers, Jerome Bruner, has called 'the cognitive revolution' (Bruner 1996).

There is, however, a new government. And it was under the previous government, particularly in the period 1987 to 1997, that policy became increasingly directed away from any recognition of the significance of this new and more optimistic understanding of human potential. If the rhetoric of the new Labour commitment to opportunity and standards is to be realized, then no time can be lost in joining a debate that has been, de facto, taboo for more than a decade.

Let me begin by explaining what I estimate to be the central tenets of Bruner's revolution. First there is the now widespread acceptance that the conception of intelligence that emerged in the early years of the twentieth century has only limited relevance to the organization of schooling, teaching and learning. Equally importantly, ideas about the measuring and testing of this intelligence have come to be seen as of very limited use. Secondly, there is the now sound body of knowledge that our capacity to learn is crucially determined by the opportunities we have to actively engage around any task; through verbalizing, practising and exploring in a socially interactive way. In saying that, I am suggesting much more than a pedagogic strategy. Theories about how our intelligence works reach into every corner of human activity, schooling more than most. Acceptance of new ideas about the extraordinary workings of the human mind require a change in the culture and organization of schooling. Educational policy-makers too play a crucial role in this process.

I want first to explore these two developments in more detail, pointing out the relevance for policy. I then want to turn to the direction that policy could take if a stronger consensus around such ideas can be built. The story of schooling in the twentieth century, in fact from the origins of national school systems, has been dominated by social stratification. This is an oft-told tale, but the persistence of the process into the pores of classroom activity is less appreciated. We need to look at the story again to make the links with policy today.

In 1868 a Royal Commission, chaired by Lord Taunton, reported on the way secondary schooling might develop:

> we shall call these the Third, the Second, and the First Graded education respectively... It is obvious that these distinctions correspond roughly, but by no means exactly, to the gradations of society.
> *First Grade*: This class appears to have no wish to displace the classics from their present position in the forefront of English education.
> *Second Grade*: though most of these parents would probably consent to give a higher place to Latin, they would only do so on condition that it did not exclude a very thorough knowledge of important modern subjects, and they would hardly give Greek any place at all.
> *Third Grade*: belongs to a class distinctly lower in the scale... The need of this class is described briefly by Canon Moseley to be 'very good reading, very good writing, very good arithmetic' (Schools Inquiry Royal Commission, The Taunton Report, 1868, pp. 15–21).

A hundred years on, in 1938, the publication of the Spens Report established the template from which the Education Act would be drafted:

> Intellectual development during childhood appears to progress as if it were governed by a single central factor, usually known as 'general intelligence, which may be broadly described as innate all round ability'. It appears to enter into everything which the child attempts to think, or say, or do, and seems on the whole to be the most important factor in determining his work in the classroom. Our psychological witnesses assured us that it can be measured approximately by means of intelligence tests... The average child is said to attain the effective limit of development in general intelligence between the ages of 16 and 18... Since the ratio of each child's mental age to his chronological

age remains approximately the same, while his chronological age increases, the mental differences between one child an another will grow larger and larger and will reach a maximum during adolescence. It is accordingly evident that different children from the age of 11, if justice is to be done to their varying capacities, require types of education varying in certain important respects (Spens Report on Secondary Education, 1938, pp. 357–81).

The conceptualization of differentiated types of schooling is almost identical. The rationale, however, had changed. At least for the Taunton commission the self-evident nature of class represented an overt justification for a hierarchy of schools. A century later psychometrics were advanced as providing a scientific explanation for precisely the same formulation. The story continues. A leaked internal Conservative Party memorandum in 1994 asserted:

> While ABC1s can conceptualize, C2s and Ds often cannot. They can relate only to things they can see and feel. They absorb their information and often views from television and tabloids. We have to talk to them in a way they understand (leaked Tory Party election proposals by former minister John Maples, reprinted in the *Financial Times*, 21 November 1994, p. 10).

The relationship between nineteenth-century social structures and the assumptions of twentieth-century psychometrics has been extensively explored. In a series of publications since the early 1950s Brian Simon, for example, has relentlessly questioned the normative basis of the psychology that came to have such a hold on popular, as well as professional, opinion (Simon 1978).

The heyday of mental testing, as far as the English and Welsh school systems is concerned, was the 1950s, with the IQ test determining secondary school selection. The obvious unfairness and regional inequalities led eventually to a more unified provision. The need, however, to 'categorize' and 'sort' remained deeply ingrained in school culture. The three classes of the nineteenth century, and the three types of school of 1944, have been transformed into an individual typology: the able, the average, and the 'low' ability. This last group retitled over the last decade as the one out of five pupils who have special needs. As an aside it is worth pointing out that no other country in Europe places twenty per cent of pupils in this category. All the statistical equipment associated with the development of mental testing is now harnessed to standardizing the design of national tests. Whilst the centre and left are quick to condemn the linking of ethnicity and the bell curve as the Herrnstein and Murray (1994) controversy showed (Jacoby and Glauberman 1995) there is a great reluctance to open any debate around wider implications.

It is important to be clear about why we should be concerned about the way standardization is so pervasive in the school system. First, as the reference to class indicates, it continues to sustain deep social divisions within the school system. The lower down the socioeconomic scale, the lower the test score. Successive failures to do anything about this, despite some heroic efforts in the more socially conscious 1960s and 1970s, has even had the effect of pushing the issue off the agenda completely.

Secondly, our understanding of the human brain and how our mind works has grown significantly. We know, for example, that there is a geography of the brain. Neurological studies repeatedly show how an accident may incapacitate one type of activity, but not necessarily all. Antonio Damario (1994) illustrates this brilliantly in his account of the story of Phineas P. Gage, a construction engineer in mid-nineteenth-century New England, who lost a part of his brain in an extraordinary blasting accident.

Howard Gardner's concept of multiple intelligences is also now widely known, with references beginning to appear in new Labour speeches on education. The significance, however, remains misunderstood. If the plurality of intelligences is accepted then all sorts of consequences follow. The structure of curriculum, modes of assessment and public reporting of comparative data concerning schools and districts are all drawn into question.

Thirdly, the incompatibility between the aims of most schools and the normative categorizing of intelligence and ability can be quickly shown. Most schools proclaim the importance of developing the whole person. Scholastic performance is important, but so are other types of abilities: the creative, aesthetic, interpersonal, practical and physical, to name just a few. None of us, whatever our educational record, would claim strength across all these dimensions. School labels and system labels, however, fail to differentiate. The attempt, in the 1980s, to introduce records of achievement acknowledging the wider spread of student talent soon fizzled out in the face of national curriculum levels and tests.

There are social, scientific and philosophical reasons, therefore, for questioning the dominance of the bell curve in school and curriculum organization. One of the difficulties, however, is that normative systems make for tidy affairs – and bureaucracies throughout the western world have exploited the apparent orderliness of intelligence testing through-out this century. The American military, for example, introduced the blanket testing of all recruits as early as 1917:

> If the army is to be efficient it is evident that the work which requires most brains must be given to men with brains. We can easily imagine what would become of an army if all the men in it who were fit to com-mand were set to digging the trenches, and if those fit only to dig trenches were made its officers. Plainly if the army machine is to work smoothly and efficiently it is as important to fit the job to the man as to fit the ammunition to the gun (Chapman 1988, p. 68).

Even then the contradiction between test scores and real perform-ance was causing concern:

> The value of these examinations is almost always overrated or under-rated. Generally speaking, the officer of long Regular Army experi-ence rejects them as being valueless and his opinion is very apt to be at once adopted by any young officer who learns it. The new officer, if left to himself, accepts the results of this examination as final and con-clusive and gives to the matter an unjustified value that often leads to his disappointment (Chapman 1988, p. 69).

Whilst many politicians and educational administrators, once joined in debate, can perceive deterministic categorization of pupils as prob-lematic, the policy options that open up are few. Labour, for example, frustrated at the inability of the system to promote any significant level of social mobility, has turned towards school improvement as the new panacea. Improvement, at present, however, remains constrained within the normative systems of measurement. Numbers of A–C grades at GCSE, for example, has achieved a dominance in secondary education that outweighs all other factors (a sort of crypto-grammar school sym-bol). Reading ages, again assessed by standardized, normative statistical techniques, represent a similar problem, as do all the national tests.

I will return to the sort of policy implications later. For now, however, I want to look at a second aspect of the cognitive revolution: the all-pervading understanding that, for real learning to take place, pupils, indi-vidually or in groups, need rich participatory opportunities to construct understanding and meaning. Here the debate with politicians and administrators becomes more difficult, particularly in the English con-text. Any ideas of pedagogies that imply a move away from ordered and teacher-led classrooms now strikes horror into politicians of all persuasions. The myth that 'sixties'-style, group-based discovery learning sold a generation or more short has been repeated so often that it has, particularly in the media, become accepted common knowledge. Labour's adoption of traditionalist rhetoric about classrooms is a recognition of this political reality.

The cognitive revolution, however, is in one sense all about structure, although of a sort significantly different in kind than expressed through tidy rows of desks. The new perspectives on learning grow from new understandings of the way the brain and mind work. Arguing for a more active, socially interactive role for learners is not to take up sides in the polarized, and perhaps now tired, debates surrounding child-or class-centred teaching and learning. It does, however, imply a pedagogy that goes beyond imitation, copying, even apprenticeship, and beyond the inactive presentation of purely propositional knowledge. In this argument, I am following Bruner again:

> The child no less than the adult is seen as capable of thinking about her own thinking, and of correcting her ideas and notions through reflection – by 'going meta', as it is sometimes called. The child, in a word, is seen as an epistemologist as well as a learner... No less than the adult, the child is thought of as holding more or less coherent 'theories' not only about the world but her own mind and how it works. These naive theories are brought into congruence with those of parents and teachers not through imitation, not through didactic instruction, but by discourse, collaboration, and negotiation... It is not simply that this mutalist view is 'child-centred' (a not very meaningful term at best) but it is much less patronizing toward the child's mind (Bruner 1996, p. 57).

The old-style idea of mental types created a paternalism every bit as powerful as that shown towards class. The idea that all children, to use Bruner's phrase, have the capacity for 'going meta' is at the heart of the new approaches to classroom and school organization.

In an important sense the cognitive revolution is confirming our intuition about good teaching. There was nothing soft about the child-centred way in which Socrates established mathematical understanding in the slave boy. The questions posed, the structuring and scaffolding of learning, knowing the extent of the boy's learning and how far, in that dialogue, he could go are at the heart of the pedagogic process. The jealously guarded and expensive Oxbridge tutorial system is another example. Laurence Stenhouse always thought that his Humanities Curriculum project methodology, with its implicit understanding of the significance of interpretative dialogue, would eventually find a time and place to prosper.

The difficulty is that the social organization of school today mitigates against this sort of teaching and learning. The curriculum tends to be a one-chance event: miss an idea, miss a page, and the patterns begin to disappear. But we all know, however elegant a curriculum, that engagement with learning becomes messy. National curriculum testers do not like that, but it is a reality. All of us, when we really learn something, progress in fits and starts. Periods of rapid progress are followed by interludes of stagnation. I am immensely grateful that, as I came to grapple with information technology in recent years, preordained moments of testing were not part of my curriculum. The school curriculum, however, goes lock step. The idea that any individual mind will conveniently follow the route set out by the intrepid and not always, as we know to our cost, successful designers of the subjects of the national curriculum is absurd. But the tests presuppose this. The structure of the curriculum and the progress of an individual learner are nearly always conflated. Deviations from such means are always problematic for education systems. Herbert Kliebard (1996) has movingly shown how frontier schools in Wisconsin, offering a highly differentiated curriculum responsive to individual needs, were obliged to introduce standardized curriculum regulations. 'Once this now bureaucratic structure began to take hold,' he suggests, 'it generated its own dynamic, and with that development, far-reaching pedagogical practices consistent with the new organizational structure were reinforced and extended' (Kliebard 1996, p. 139). These structures, he suggests, assume a life and meaning of their own through which children process rather than learn.

There is an uncanny resonance between the Wisconsin story and, on a much broader front, the massification of testing in England in the 1990s. Parallels could, and have, been drawn with the ubiquitous late nineteenth-century 'payment by results' regime of Robert Lowe. In one sense the motivation behind this is more than bureaucratic order. The standards crusade is important in terms of individual opportunity and national well-being. The danger, however, is that the politically simple message about raising standards can hide the question of whether the standards are the right ones in the first place. And the measures of standards, in the quest for simplicity and comprehensibility, may in fact become so massaged that they fail to describe in any significant way that which it is assumed they do. If you compound this with the now well-known way in which certain symbols, for all sorts of cultural and sociological reasons, gain legitimacy far beyond their real worth, then an educationally and politically volatile situation is highly likely to develop.

England is unique in having created a political and policy cocktail around curriculum and testing legislation. The opposition of teachers of English to crude forms of testing effectively led to the downfall of the last but one Conservative Secretary of State. The political imperative to be seen to be active is only manageable if the policy instruments have professional and technical credibility. In too many aspects of the national curriculum neither have been achieved.

A Labour government with a commitment to inclusivity and opportunity, as well as acknowledging the creativity that comes from 'differences', has a particular challenge. The ambition to raise standards has, to a significant extent, to focus on those without the social and economic advantages of the majority. For the less fortunate, however, a triple whammy of policy hits hard. First, the curriculum itself, however broadly conceived, represents a value system at odds with the daily experience of many children. If anything this was made more acute by the breadth of the primary and secondary national curriculum and some of the decisions about what knowledge was of most worth. Some of the programmes developed in the early 1980s that sought relevance were also squeezed out by the rapacious time demands of a ten-subject curriculum. At the secondary level perhaps the most striking casualties were the vocational and vocationally-oriented courses introduced across the country as part of the technical and vocational (TVEI) initiatives in schools.

Pointing to the well-established link between values, culture and curriculum is not necessarily to imply adoption of a relativist position. But it is an impediment for some children. Art appreciation in the primary school and compulsory Shakespeare in secondary schools are fine, but teaching and testing regimes have to acknowledge that some children come advantaged to such learning.

Secondly, for many children the national curriculum is a 'one chance' experience. Teachers need to 'cover' the syllabus. An orderly didactic approach has a place. Yet real understanding is nowhere near so linear or sequential as the national curriculum orders suggest. In many areas children, in addition to their experiences in school, are supported by a range of outside enriched resources, personally through their parents and materially in the form of the wide range of books and multi-media artefacts. The discourse created, sometimes the remediations required, are far less accessible to the economically disadvantaged child of the inner city.

Thirdly, as I have already discussed, the labels of the normative test-ing system create their own dynamic, with all that means for self-esteem.

Let me pause a moment on self-esteem before trying to sketch out some of the policy implications of my argument. How we feel about our-selves is crucial to learning. One aspect of the development of mind is our capacity for intersubjectivity – recognizing how others perceive what we are doing, and how they acknowledge what I feel and all the complex spirals of understanding that goes with that. I want to give a final quote from Bruner to show the link between self-esteem and the cognitive revolution:

> How self-esteem is experienced (or how it is expressed) varies, of course, with the way of one's culture ... Only two things can be said for certain and in general; the management of self-esteem is never simple and never settled, and its state is affected powerfully by the availability of supports provided from outside. These supports are hardly mysterious or exotic. They include such homely resorts as a second chance, honour for a good if unsuccessful try, but above all the chance for discourse that permits one to find out how or why things didn't work out as planned. It is no secret that school is often rough on children's self-esteem, and we are beginning to know something about their vulnerability in this area. (Bruner 1996, p. 37)

A policy for improved standards involves bolstering self-esteem. The very children who need this most are those most cast down by the relent-less application of standardized judgements and normative symbols. As the testing system stands, just under half of those at seven, eleven, fourteen and then at GCSE will feel they have failed to do as well as the majority. The long-proved link between social status and achievement will ensure that, despite a significant and even increasing number of crossovers, those on either side of the bell curve of achievement will stay roughly in the same camp. And that is as it has been for most of this century.

Policy options for governments or opposition have become increas-ingly constrained by the political rhetoric about standards. A few years back the so-called gold standard of 'A' level was perhaps the most cher-ished symbol that had to be held on to. The cousin qualification of 'O' level was dispensed with under the stewardship of the Conservative minister, Keith Joseph, in the early part of the 1980s. In the period fol-lowing the 1988 Education Reform Act a range of new tests have come into play, and any suggestion of their unreliability or irrelevance puts the virility of government on the line. Does any room for manoeuvre remain? I want to indicate five broad policy directions that go beyond the particular politics of the late 1990s. My thesis is that moves in this direction are inevitable – and better the nettle is grasped now if a new momentum for curriculum reform and improved standards is to be achieved.

First, there is plenty of anecdotal evidence, as well as empirical findings (Campbell and Neill 1994, for example), that the national curriculum, even as revised, prescribes too many subjects in an overly detailed way. This is true at the primary level, where the amount of time spent teaching literacy and numeracy appears to have fallen as teachers attempt to cover the demands of the other subjects. At secondary level, curriculum overcrowding remains an obstacle to providing teaching and learning to exploit the full range of intelligences that children can display. Vocational learning remains marginal. Evidence from the USA (Shulman 1992) is increasingly suggesting that children learn more if they are taught less. The demands of 'coverage' often militate against the sort of learning that really ensures things stick. The opportunity to revisit, revise, look at things from different angles and perspectives, read about it, try things out, verbalize, all the multiple strategies that those within the cognitive revolution see as so important, need time to be developed.

The problem in England is that the national curriculum essentially used the old 'O' level and 'A' level as benchmarks or starting points. In every subject development group the need to ensure pupils reached traditional sixteen-plus and eighteen-plus took the whole population in tow. And this links to standards.

Let me give an example. What ought to be the standard expected of someone who could communicate at a minimal level in a modern foreign language? As it stands at the moment, only a minority of students attain the A–C old 'O' level grade and a smaller percentage again pass 'A' level. Many would argue, however, that to communicate in another language, even to the degree of joining in discussions at an academic conference, requires a confident, and that term is important, ability to use the language at a significantly lower level. Real understanding and use of the content of the first secondary year's course books might achieve this. It shows how influenced the curriculum is by traditional standardization that we have to argue for raising standards by teaching less. It is a policy option, however, to uncouple sixteen-plus and eighteen-plus from the design of the national curriculum. This would involve setting realistic objectives for the majority of the school population and creating new national standards that everyone seeks to achieve. Subsequent progress would be based on achieving the national standard but would follow a different sort of route, perhaps to a new-style examination at eighteen.

Creating new national standards across a significantly limited curriculum would almost certainly raise standards with more time for the majority to achieve and flexible curriculum opportunities for others to make faster progress. The argument here is for multiple ladders of achievement, rather than the uniform standardization of the test score leading to examination grades.

My second proposal is one that Peter Mortimore and I suggested nearly a decade ago (Moon and Mortimore 1989). Abolish the sixteen-plus GCSE examination as it stands. The UK stands alone in Europe and throughout most of the world in continuing with an expensive, subject-by-subject sixteen-plus 'leaving' examination. GCSE represented a moment in time and though some of the innovations introduced help improve teaching and learning at the secondary level, it is now anachronistic and far too expensive. Some schools spend almost as much per year on paying GCSE entry fees as is spent on the books and resources for teaching the school as a whole. It is time-consuming and, across the 14–18-year-old curriculum, it severely dents the amount of teaching time available. In the UK most fifteen-year-olds effectively stop work in February or March in order to take examinations in May or June. More than a term's teaching is lost – which is not the experience of secondary school pupils in other countries. Reinstating that teaching time would improve standards.

My third proposal follows from this. The enormous savings from taking out GCSE could then be reinvested into a fourteen-plus curriculum through to eighteen, assessed through teacher continuous assessment and some criterion-related tests (taken at any age) and leading through to a more comprehensive profile of achievement at 18. The form and nature of any core could be argued about, but some diversity would be necessary. It is a key to the success of the secondary school system that courses for fourteen- and fifteen-year-olds are developed that motivate all young people. GCSE does not do that, as the huge drop-out rates show.

Fourthly, if across the pre-school to eighteen curriculum there is a more realistic but restricted core, space opens up for a range of locally-based, school-based activities. Schools should be judged on the range of variety of opportunities they provide. Perhaps one of the most dispiriting features of the last decade has been the unwillingness of teachers and schools to 'risk', as they saw it, national curriculum progress by allowing time for other activities. Innovation and experiment as words have almost disappeared from the teaching lexicon.

The best moments of learning often come at unexpected times, outside the bureaucratic, predictable and standardized regime in which far too many schools feel they are working. A sense of exploration unfettered by time limits and age-related tests must be brought back into the curriculum if schools are to contribute significantly to developing articulate, confident and flexible young people. The design of the curriculum and the structures of any measurement of progress must go beyond the world of percentages if we are to boost the self-image, improve standards, and develop positive attitudes towards a future where lifelong learning is taken for granted in the social culture of the times.

To achieve a new sense of innovation and experimentation a final point needs to be made. Curriculum policy in England is far too centralized. Recent in origin, it lacks any of the checks and balances that formally centrally controlled systems display. Across the channel in France we find the archetypal concept of central control. But look at it in practice and you find a healthy corpus of consultative mechanisms for bringing a range of interest groups into the change process. The immature English model, driven initially by authoritarian Secretaries of State, displays all the worst characteristics of overly centralist systems. Decisions made by a few are required to be rapidly implemented by the many. The few are subject to the vagaries of media manipulation and Whitehall politicizing. Respect for evidence grows weak. Others have described just how chaotic the national curriculum building process was (Taylor 1995; Barber 1997). But re-establishing a balance between central prescription and the energy and creativity that more localized decisions can make is crucial. It is not restoring the old order. New forms of accountability in curriculum policy are here to stay and government has a crucial role in this. Relentlessly trying to hammer half a million teachers and more than twenty thousand schools into line is failing. The inspiration to find the solutions to the problems facing the educational system must go beyond government. The changing social, economic and technological environment present challenges that require the involvement of everyone within the education service and to achieve this some devolution of responsibilities is absolutely crucial.

These proposals are located within the English context as the last decade of the century draws to a close. Underlying all this, however, is the quest to open up the education *system* to new forms of creativity and opportunity. The normative quest for standardization has gone too far. Ironically, the strategies being adopted have more in common with the closing years of the last century than at any time since the 1950s. Thinking the unthinkable, as a fashionable policy option, in education is almost wholly a question of looking back. England is not unique in this, but the particular brew of Thatcherism and some new Labour beliefs is closing down the vision of the more optimistic of the human capacity to learn and understand, to theorize and create, visions that the revolution in our understanding of cognition has done so much to promote. The story is, as I suggested at the outset of this chapter, an old one. John Dewey, writing in the first years of this century, was very clear about the responsibilities that policy-makers bear in education. Word for word the analysis holds good for today:

> It is easy to fall into the habit of regarding the mechanics of school organization and administration as something comparatively external and indifferent to educational purposes and ideals. We think of the grouping of children in classes, the arrangement of grades, the machinery by which the course of study is made out and laid down, the method by which it is carried into effect, the system of selecting teachers and assigning them to their work, of paying and promoting them, as, in a way, matters of mere practical convenience and expediency. We forget that it is precisely such things as these that really control the whole system, even on its distinctively educational side. No matter what is the accepted precept and theory, no matter what the legislation of the school board or the mandate of the school superintendent, the reality of education is found in the personal and face-to-face contact of teacher and child. The conditions that underlie and regulate this contact dominate the educational situation (Dewey 1901).

7 Educational Assessment in an Era of Reform

Roger Murphy and John Wilmut

Until the second half of the 1970s educational assessment attracted relatively little attention. There was a general consensus that teachers were responsible for teaching and assessment in the classroom, and that examining boards provided external certification. In contrast, assessment practices and outcomes are now matters of public debate. There appear to be three major factors (which are not unique to the United Kingdom) which have brought about this change.

First, far larger numbers of students are being brought within the processes of monitoring and selection, to which assessment is central. This is a result of the widening of access to education, including the creation of the CSE examination in the 1960s, the raising of the school-leaving age in the 1970s, and the more recent creation of a common examination at sixteen, increased access to post-sixteen qualifications and a greatly expanded Further and Higher Education sector. Elsewhere in the world there has been considerable widening of access to educational provision in newly independent countries, and increased demands as populations have grown.

Secondly, governments have become more concerned about the value of their investments in education and training, and now wish to monitor outputs much more carefully. The concern has been fuelled by the need for increased international competitiveness, leading to a greater demand for the specification of required educational outputs, and the establishment of mechanisms to assess student performance and attainment. The third factor is a matter of practical expediency: standards can be levered up and curriculum changes effected more quickly by changing assessment demands than by changing inputs to the education system.

Thus, educational assessments, tests and examinations have been a major focus in debates about education in the UK and elsewhere during the last twenty years. Murphy and Torrance (1987), Broadfoot (1996), Gipps (1994), Black (1998) and others have reviewed in detail various aspects of the way in which this has occurred, and the pressures which have resulted. It has clearly become necessary to ensure that assessment is of the highest quality, and seen to be so, so that there has been a drive to improve the way in which assessments are conducted, to clarify the function which they perform in communicating information about educational changes in individuals, schools and larger groupings, and – perhaps most significantly of all – to understand the influence which they have upon the curriculum experiences of learners.

An illustration of the way in which assessment is clearly seen as a powerful influence when it comes to understanding the forces that shape education policy and practice can be seen in Nuttall's (1984) analysis of the changes that led up to the launch of the GCSE examination in the late 1980s. The paper lays out a very clear analysis of the way in which the move to that particular assessment system was linked very closely to curriculum debates and the desire of central government to take a much more interventionist stance in relation to the curriculum experienced by pupils in UK schools.

> The DES has taken upon itself a much more overt role in steering examination reforms and giving themselves rights (unprecedented since 1945) over the approval of the detailed content of examination syllabuses and schemes of examination, since it is the DES that have the final say over national criteria. Having failed in their attempts to control or influence markedly the curriculum through documents like *A Framework for the School Curriculum* they can succeed by another route, at least for the curriculum of secondary schools (Nuttall 1984, p. 174).

From the early 1980s the notion of assessment-led curriculum change became commonplace, and the scene was set for the subsequent battles over the introduction of a national curriculum, covering four stages of schooling from five to sixteen, with attainment targets, four layers of assessment arrangements linked to the four key stages of schooling, and school performance tables (Murphy 1987 and 1989). These are issues to which we will return during this chapter as we present an overview of educational assessment changes and the way in which they have contributed to the formation and implementation of educational policy.

We wish also to reflect upon what is known about educational assessment at the end of the twentieth century. Do we, for example, have at our disposal methods of assessment, techniques of analysing assessment data, or insights into how assessment can be employed most effectively, which will allow us to plan the use of assessment in education in a more sophisticated and successful way than could have occurred fifty years ago, when 'O' level and 'A' level examinations were first introduced? Wood's (1991) overview of research into tests and examinations, commissioned by the University of Cambridge Local Examinations Syndicate, is an excellent summary of a burgeoning literature on various aspects of assessment. The task undertaken in that volume already needs to be repeated, and another parallel volume could easily extend to a similar length, pulling together the huge amount of research and development work on other aspects of assessment which has occurred during the 1990s. The development and implementation of key stage assessments for all children following the national curriculum in state schools in the UK has created something of an assessment industry, with test developers, educational evaluators and researchers keen to understand the impact of these assessment changes on pupils' learning experiences, teaching styles and effectiveness, and on school effectiveness and improvement. In parallel with that, developments in vocational education and training have produced new competence-driven assessment models, along with work-based observation and portfolio assessments, which have in turn opened up new dimensions in assessment and accreditation methods.

There is far too much new and interesting work on assessment for us to summarize it in any complete way with this chapter. Wolf (1995), Torrance (1995), Broadfoot (1996), Gipps (1994), Gipps and Murphy (1994), Murphy and Broadfoot (1995), and Goldstein and Lewis (1996) between them lay out many aspects of those developments, relating them to specialist concerns such as equity, social change, the rise of competence-based assessments, authentic assessment, and the technical aspects of setting and analysing assessments. Ultimately, however, this is not simply a matter of an improved understanding of the techniques of assessment and their effects; it is much more fundamentally a matter of understanding and debating different philosophies of assessment. In many societies, and over many decades or centuries, assessment has moved from being a powerful and mysterious set of controls, kept under wraps by a ruling elite to be used for their own imperialist purposes, to becoming something that is owned much more extensively by all those who participate in education and learning. Thus at the heart of debates about assessment is the need to address philosophical questions, such as: What is assessment for? Who controls it and determines the rules under which it will operate? What rights do those being assessed have to be given information about the procedures being used to assess them, and the outcomes of those procedures?

THE TENSIONS

The three factors which have resulted in the increased interest in assessment worldwide have not all pulled in the same direction, and have resulted in a very messy environment within which changes in assessment structures and methods may take place, and within which an assessment agenda for the 21st century might be established. Most notably, the focus on assessment as a means of monitoring and managing education, and as a process of selection, has often been at the expense of the use of assessment as an essential input to the conduct of teaching and learning. Piper and McGaw (1992) have suggested that the tensions surface in three cross-purposes identified by, and common to, many education systems.

The first cross-purpose is between attainment and learning. The assessment of attainment is likely to be concerned with competition and selection, particularly in relation to careers and employment, while assessment for learning is concerned with individual development and personal improvement. The second is between accuracy and adequacy, and is the age-old debate about whether the primary demand is for reliable assessment or for valid assessment. The third cross-purpose is linked to the second, and is between inclusive and exclusive assessment. To what extent should assessment encompass all aspects of student learning? What is included is frequently what is easiest to assess: assessment methods which may be used for the widest range of skills (such as oral performance, in dance, and in many craft areas) are time-consuming, expensive, and not amenable to simple quality control procedures. Written tests, on the other hand, are cheap to operate and easy to control, but have limited scope. However, what they assess can rapidly become what is valued in the curriculum.

Thus, governments tend to be more supportive of externally set assessments, and to focus on standards of performance in those areas where assessments can most easily be made. Assessments made by teachers are widely felt to be less dependable and insufficient resources have generally been put into procedures (such as agreement trialling) which would enhance their quality.

One of the most significant attempts in the UK to synthesize the various demands on assessment process was made by the committee responsible for the construction of assessment procedures for the national curriculum in England and Wales, the Task Group on Assessment and Testing (DES 1988). Sadly, many of their aspirations were not achieved as a more bureaucratic and simplistic model emerged in the implementation phases (Daugherty 1995). Gipps (1994) has suggested that two assessment paradigms can co-exist; one is strongly focused on assessment for learning, is classroom- and teacher-based, and recognizes and exploits the involvement of the assessor with the student being assessed. The other is more formal, is test- or examination-based, and may lead to performance tables, school comparisons and standards monitoring by government agencies. The difficulty, as with the operation of national curriculum testing, is one of status, and where the resources go. Moreover, it is once again evident that the importance attached to test or examination results (either for individuals or for institutions) ensures that they will have a disproportionate influence on the curriculum and on what students and teachers perceive to be important aspects of learning.

NEW PHILOSOPHIES OF ASSESSMENT

An analysis of assessment developments in the UK reveals greater shifts in the way people think about assessment and how they use it than in the technical attributes of assessment systems. Educational assessment always has been and always will remain a complex process, because collecting good evidence from learners about their learning, and evaluating it, is never easy. Multiple choice testing, which appeared to present a major advance in assessment technology thirty years ago, now sits alongside many other assessment methods and is seen to have its own set of strengths and weaknesses. Current advances in the availability and potential of information technology may open up further possibilities in on-line individually tailored assessment systems, whereby students being assessed interact with a workstation, which is programmed to set them assessment tasks in a way that is responsive to their own response patterns to previous items. Developments like this will not, however, really change the nature of the more fundamental underlying questions about assessment:

- What is educational assessment being used for?
- Who decides on the ground rules for any assessment system (methods, criteria, results, etc.)?
- What is the contribution of the person being assessed, and what are his or her rights to information about the assessment procedures and its outcomes?
- How does educational assessment best serve the needs of different stakeholders – students, teachers, policy-makers, other interested parties?

There are, of course, no simple answers to such questions. What is notable, however, is the extent to which they are now being asked. As a consequence it is now much more usual for people to consider the form-ative uses of assessment to feed into and enhance learning processes, as well as considering the summative processes of certification, grading and (in many instances) selection. The once simple view of educational assessment – that it is solely about labelling students with crude and fairly meaningless grades or marks – is no longer widely accepted (Murphy and Joyes 1997). As a result, even in formal national curriculum testing, there is an acknowledgement that this has several purposes (including one which is primarily diagnostic) and marked scripts and mark break-downs are returned to schools for analysis and use. Furthermore, Black and Wiliam (1998) have pulled together evidence to demonstrate the powerful effect that formative assessment can have on improving stu-dent learning. The conclusion of their review is that those searching to find ways of increasing the standard of pupil learning should look at improved formative assessment as one of the most effective strategies around.

Alongside this, in many cases assessment systems have become far less reductionist, allowing opportunities for assessments to be recorded as prose statements as, for example, within profiles and records of achievement. Assessment thinking has in many respects broken free from the shackles of psychometric theory (Gipps 1994), allowing edu-cators to treat assessment results as rich qualitative data, full of complex meanings and amenable to different types of interpretation, rather than being seen as simple numerical judgements on some obscure scale. This liberation of educational assessment from its former stance as a poor distant relative of the powerful dynasty of psychometrics is a very signi-ficant milestone, which opens up a world of opportunity for those who wish to take assessment developments in new directions, and Gipps has explored this shift of paradigm in some depth.

Assessment is not an exact science, and we must stop presenting it as such. This is of course a part of the post-modern condition – a suspension of belief in the absolute status of 'scientific' knowledge (Gipps 1993; Torrance 1993). The modernist stance suggests that it is possible to be a disinterested observer, while the post-modernist stance indicates that such detachment is not possible: we are social beings who construe the world according to our values and perceptions. The constructivist paradigm does not accept that reality is fixed and inde-pendent of the observer; rather, reality is constructed by the observer and thus there are multiple constructions of reality. This paradigm would then deny the existence of such a thing as a 'true score' (Gipps 1994, p. 167).

New post-modern educational assessment is more fluid, regarding the results of assessments as evidence amenable to different interpretations by different individuals. Such evidence is crucially also seen as evidence derived from a particular context, and context is of course an extremely important influencing factor in understanding any aspect of human behaviour or performance. Educational assessment experts (e.g. Nuttall 1987) have followed developmental psychologists (e.g. Donaldson 1978) in highlighting the powerful influence that context has on educational performance. Nuttall summed up this issue in the following way:

> The conclusion is inescapable: the way in which the task is presented, the presenter, and the perceived significance of the task to the student – factors which might be termed the 'context' of the task...can all have a major effect on the performance of the person presented with the task. Assessment (like learning) is highly context-specific and one generalizes at one's peril (Nuttall 1987, p. 115).

As we have seen in our analysis of trends in educational assessment, this question of contextualization of assessment procedures, and the need to interpret assessment evidence and results in relation to the context(s) within which they have been derived, has emerged as a major factor in relation to moves towards competence-based assessment systems in the 1980s and 1990s.

AUTHENTIC ASSESSMENT AND KEY SKILLS

The term 'authentic assessment' has been coined to describe the approaches to assessment which seek to reflect more accurately the diversity of learning, at the point at which it occurs, than is possible with external, written or fixed response tests (Torrance 1995). A most important aspect of this concept is the resulting empowerment of the student, so that aspects of authentic assessment are closely related to processes of review and evaluation, by the student, of his or her own achievement, the planning of future learning and the setting of targets. These are familiar undertakings in the areas of recording achievement and action planning, on which a great deal of work has been done over the last few years. In turn, this approach relates closely to the promotion of concepts of lifelong learning, and the development of descriptions of skills which the individual requires in order to be able to manage his or her learning or, in other words, to be autonomous as a learner.

From the government's and employers' perspectives the development of learner autonomy is an important strand in creating a more flexible and responsive employment market. It is argued that individuals must be able to adapt to more rapidly changing employment demands, with some capacity to transfer existing skills to new contexts and to learn new skills without excessive amounts of support (Oates 1996). The emphasis therefore shifts to the development of skills which underpin a wide range of activity; these have been called core or key skills, and it has now become a matter of considerable interest to see whether students and potential employees possess these skills at an acceptable level at various stages of the education and training systems (Murphy et al. 1997).

Although there is no absolute agreement about which skills are essential, it is widely accepted that the capacity to communicate in various ways, the abilities to use number and to be able to work with others, the capacity to think critically and to review and evaluate are all pretty important. It is also generally accepted that these skills must be learned and used in one or more contexts, so that attempts to assess them must also be contextualized. Unfortunately, once these skills become required for a qualification, for which formal (perhaps external) assessment mechanisms are required, their role in enabling and supporting learning in all contexts may be more limited. However, the skills have been increasingly seen as an essential aspect of the drive for higher educational standards, and this has led to a government decision to launch a national stand-alone key skills qualification from September 2000.

COMPETENCE-BASED ASSESSMENT

One of the most recent and most significant developments in assessment in the UK has been the emergence of competence-based assessment (Wolf 1995). This is not unique to this country, with parallel developments in many other parts of the world, often fuelled by the need for new approaches to vocational education and training. Here competence may be viewed as a deep cognitive structure; we are able to distinguish someone who is competent in doing a task in, say, a workplace setting from someone who is not, normally without relating this to a single skill or piece of knowledge. Competence in a particular setting is a complex matter, and decisions can be made about whether a person is competent or not by observing one or more relevant performances (Wood and Power 1987). A basis for judging the adequacy of such performances may be required, and this may be linked to the perceptions of what constitutes competence in the task. In most approaches to this type of assessment the basis for judgement will be a series of performance criteria, usually backed up by some statements which either define the range of contexts in which the performances are to be observed or the specific skills and knowledge which have to be used. These are a set of outcome statements, since they define what a person has to be able to do, rather than the learning processes which enable competence to be acquired.

In the UK first NVQs and then GNVQs have been defined in this way. In the former qualification the outcome statements were devised by industry-specific bodies, relating the statements to known tasks and required competencies. For GNVQs the statements relate to broad vocational areas. In passing, it is important to note the considerable overlap between the requirements in some GNVQs and in syllabuses for some parallel 'A' and 'AS' level examinations. Examples would be in science and business studies, where the traditional distinction between academic and vocational qualifications is fairly meaningless. The attempt to implement the Dearing post-sixteen qualifications report (Dearing 1996) has been built upon the ambition to break down the very unhelpful divide that has existed in the UK in relation to both academic and vocational education and training and their largely separate qualification systems.

In discussing competence-based assessment it is important to distinguish the concept from its implementations. Both NVQs and GNVQs have had their critics in the educational world and from a workplace perspective. There have been questions about their validity and about their effectiveness in contrast to more traditional methods of acquiring a qualification. There have also been questions about their purpose, particularly in the case of GNVQ, and its role in providing an alternative pathway to higher education. But there have also been difficulties with the design and conduct of assessment, and these have tended to overshadow some of the more fundamental issues. Both NVQ and GNVQ qualifications have used wholly or mostly internal assessment, judging evidence against the performance criteria, and questions have been raised about the reliability of these judgements, and about the extent to which quality assurance and control systems have ensured comparability of judgements from assessor to assessor and centre to centre (Murphy et al. 1995). Difficult issues, concerning the sufficiency of evidence and its authenticity, the use of simulated tasks where real ones cannot be conducted, and the need for written tests of knowledge to be used, created a pressure which first caused the specification of the outcome statements to become more detailed and complex (in an effort to achieve absolute clarity for the assessor) and now a move towards both qualifications having a higher level of externally devised and managed assessment, and tighter moderation procedures.

NVQs and GNVQs have provided qualifications for many who could not previously acquire them. In particular there is ample evidence of the success of GNVQ in providing for students whose approaches to learning were not satisfied by 'A' levels, and who have benefited from the explicit and open requirements of the qualification, the opportunities to take a greater control over their learning and the freedom to generate evidence of competence in their own ways. In NVQs there are many individuals for whom the qualification, and its achievement in a workplace setting, generating evidence from tasks which they do on a daily basis, has been a lifeline. At the same time there has been a real danger that the difficulties in managing two very complex and expensive qualifications, and the failure of many students to complete them, will tend to overshadow their benefits, and that they will be undermined by adverse publicity.

TEACHERS AS ASSESSORS

Teachers in schools and colleges have always worked at some disadvantage as assessors. Those undertaking assessment in workplace situations have faced similar (though not identical) problems. Teachers have rarely learned about assessment as part of their initial training and systematic professional development in assessment techniques and issues has been limited. In this respect workplace supervisors and other assessors, working in vocational areas have been better served by the TDLB units, though these have only recently become a compulsory requirement for all assessors.

Assessors in schools, colleges and workplaces have relatively limited control over the construction of what are seen to be 'important' assessment processes. Their role in relation to examinations and tests has been a subordinate one and there is a widespread perception that assessments which they devise, or over which they have direct control, are not to be relied upon. In the matter of the management of coursework, teachers have limited opportunities for creative inputs to the assessment process; the era of teacher-devised and managed assessment within CSE (and, to a lesser extent, GCE) examinations has now ended with the phasing out of all Mode 3 schemes.

Teachers have limited opportunities for self-help in the matter of assessment. They are provided with some excellent support and guidance materials, particularly in relation to national curriculum assessment, but many use these in isolation, and have few opportunities to test their understanding and judgement with their peers. The problem is particularly acute in primary schools and in small departments in some secondary schools and smaller colleges, where there is no provision for standardization meetings or agreement trialling. The LEAs, which in the past had a capacity to provide liaison of this sort (although they did not always do so), now have very limited resources indeed, and many do not support teacher assessment activity in any way.

Teachers and workplace supervisors, acting as assessors in externally driven systems (such as the national curriculum, for GCSE and 'A' level coursework, in GNVQs or NVQs), have often found workloads excessive. This problem has been more evident in recent years where the complexity of assessment against multiple output statements has made heavy demands. These statements have emerged as a result of the pressure to define, as precisely as possible, the performances expected at the conclusion of a programme of study, and governments have often driven forward with these without making sufficient resources available and without providing for professional development. More seriously, there has often not been a sufficient guarantee that workable quality assurance and control systems could be operated, and one of the features of the most recent development work has been a greater consideration of the complexities, costs and workability of moderation and verification systems.

However, moves towards greater amounts of external assessment in, for example, NVQ and GNVQ and key skills, discussed in three important recent reports (Capey 1995; Dearing 1996; Beaumont 1996), continue to weaken the role of teachers as assessors, and to bring these qualifications closer in approach to GCSE and 'A' level examinations and to national curriculum assessment.

CHANGING ASSESSMENT STRUCTURES

There is a widespread and justified belief amongst teachers and assessors that the assessment goalposts have not stopped moving since about

1985, since when GCSE, National Curriculum Assessment, GNVQ, NVQ, the National Record of Achievement and many other initiatives have come on stream and each been revised at least once. Government has often moved into new structures prematurely, with small amounts of consultation and little or no research, and revisions have followed, again often without sufficient exploration of the causes of the problems which have been encountered. To some extent this disreputable period of development has ended; more care is now being taken, there is more research being funded, and a wider spectrum of people is being consulted. There is, however, still a belief that perceived problems with the education system will be solved just by restructuring some aspect of the assessment and qualifications system. Whilst there may be some truth in this, there are considerable dangers, some of which we have already noted.

CONCLUSION

Perhaps the biggest steps that have been made can be summarized as follows. Firstly, educational assessment is a complex activity which can never be undertaken without facing major challenges related to accuracy, dependability and impact on learning. Secondly, a natural consequence of this is that decisions about how educational assessment is to be undertaken are likely to be highly political. Powerful interests are invested in arguments for carrying out assessments in particular ways. For this reason assessment reforms need to be made hand in hand with curricular reforms, in relation to clearly defined ideals for lifelong learning.

As we move into the 21st century it is right that we continue to have high expectations for improving both opportunities for and achievements in human learning. Part of the story of the past has been of poor educational provision, at times ensuring the position of a privileged elite, and at times using idiosyncratic assessment procedures to make sure that the definition of what counted as acceptable learning was kept within very restricted boundaries.

A movement towards a more inclusive approach to encouraging all members of our society to engage in meaningful and purposeful learning and personal development must involve a more enlightened approach to educational assessment and the certification of many different types of learning. The development of a wider range of assessment methods, and a more flexible view of where and when assessment can occur and who is best placed to carry it out, both open up new opportunities to make assessment more effective, more relevant, and more supportive of wider lifelong learning ambitions.

We do now know a great deal about the potential and the shortcomings of different approaches to assessment. This knowledge is now more readily available to a wide range of stakeholders and the interests of a few can no longer be secured by pretending that assessment is some kind of obscure science based upon secret knowledge, which was the preserve of a small band of assessment experts. Now that 'the genie is out of the bottle' we can start to build learning and assessment opportunities which promote rather than inhibit widespread improvements in the lifelong learning of all in our society.

8 Challenging Tripartism: Class and Inequality in Post-Compulsory Education Policy

Denis Gleeson

In the past decade, patterns of participation in further education (or post-compulsory education) have changed dramatically, increasing from thirty per cent in the early 1980s to seventy per cent plus in 1994–5 (FEFC 1996). In 1994–5, three million students were enrolled in further education (2.2 million of whom were in provision funded by the FEFC), of which ten per cent were GNVQ, eight per cent NVQ, ten per cent GCSE and eighteen per cent 'A' and 'AS' level students. At present seventy per cent of sixteen- and seventeen-year-olds are in full-time post-sixteen education, most of them in FE colleges rather than schools, with eight per cent in part-time education. Additional to this, government assumptions imply an increase in student numbers over the period 1994–1999 of twenty per cent, and a 5.5 per cent growth in the full-time equivalent number of adults in further education in the same period (FEFC 1996). At the same time it is acknowledged by the FEFC that institutions funded by the Council will need to make efficiency savings of at least five per cent each year in the period 1996–1999. Thus, in order to meet fiscal targets, colleges will be expected to finance capital and other programmes through private finance initiatives at a time when their finances are severely overstretched. Within these constraints, three developments are likely to take place in FE colleges, as primary providers of post-compulsory education development in the next three years:

- closer integration of institutions with business, commerce and industrial networks, including TECs;
- increased investment in staff development, linked with investment in new technology and technologies of learning associated with increased numbers of students and shortfall in staff;
- further reduction in average levels of funding with implications for staffing, management and professionalization.

129

Essentially, the main funding method demands on the one hand that institutions maximize recruitment and retain students on courses which enable them to achieve a range of qualifications. On the other, on a declining funding base, it demands a new 'flexibility' in relation to learning and provision which encompasses wider student participation, following different modes of study in a variety of contexts. Going to college and studentship is increasingly taking on a different meaning linked with new technologies of management, learning and age participation.

Expansion in a sector which now commands £3 billion of public funds can be explained in various ways, as a substitute for employment, through to improved GCSE results, raised pupil expectations and better careers advice. From a voluntaristic system catering mainly for a minority of school-leavers destined for academic or trade training, the boom in staying on and returning has had two dramatic effects: first, in creating the foundations for universal post-sixteen provision and, second, in generating credential inflation to meet diverse demand. By far the biggest thrust has been in the tertiary domain (Green 1986) – from YOP to YTS, B/TEC, CEE, CPVE, TVEI, City Technology Colleges and Schools, G/NVQ and modern apprenticeship – suggesting a long line of initiatives in search of a policy solution. With 16–19 and adult student numbers growing in tandem, policy interest in post-compulsory education has never been as great, in terms of (i) its relationship with HE, economic growth and cost-effectiveness and (ii) its accommodation within the mainstream of state education policy.

A major problem facing this emerging sector is that neither policy element has been informed by research, and its growth is underpinned by successive, often contradictory, government initiatives. Recent retro-modern attempts to place a tripartite ordering on such haphazard development have had a tendency both to look back and to plan for an idealized 'Fordist' model of schooling and selection (Green and Rikowski 1995). According to Ainley (1996), this model and its accompanying tripartite divisions broke down after the long post-war boom in 1974 with the oil crisis, and with it the economic basis of full employment. In seeking to revive essentially tripartite principles the Dearing Report is criticized here for ignoring mistakes of the past which, under similar circumstances, failed to deliver the missing vocational 'middle ground' of English education. One is reminded here of Katz's (1965) observation that historic compromise is part of an English policy tradition which seeks to ' ... preserve the traditional and respond to the modern by avoiding the resolution of uncomfortable dilemmas ... their evasions of the essential confrontations have left Britain with unresolved and debilitating tensions' (Katz 1965).

If the tensions to which Katz refers underline a legacy of missed opportunities in the policy-making process, the reality is that they remain with us today, largely unaddressed. To avoid 'reinventing the wheel', it is important, as Reeder (1979) points out, to revisit this recurring debate, in order to address unchallenged policy assumptions which restrict a more enlightened vision of 14–19 education and beyond. An immediate priority, argues McCulloch (1991), is to revise Crowther's original notion (but to replace its tripartite connotations of three types of mind), with the 'rehabilitation of the practical', an issue which I return to later in the paper. Another, is to embrace a unified credit and modular approach, across GNVQ, 'A' Level and work-based (NVQ) provision, on lines advocated by the National Commission on Education (1995). It is to some of the policy-related issues associated with such debate that I first turn.

THE CHANGING POLICY FOCUS

Post-compulsory education and training has in the past decade attracted the interest of government, trade unions, employers' representatives, educationists and the increased participation of students themselves. Moreover, international monitoring of post-compulsory education by the OECD and the World Bank, in terms of assessing national economic growth and development, has raised global interest in post-school issues. In Britain recent interest has followed on from various influential Government White Papers (1991; 1994) which acknowledge that decades of failure to invest in post-compulsory education have left Britain with a vicious cycle of low skills, low wages and low productivity. At long last, partly driven by such argument, there appears to be an emerging consensus that post-sixteen education and training provision in England and Wales has not worked for a majority of school leavers, or in meeting the perceived needs of a better trained workforce. The view has emerged among previously sometimes antagonistic parties (the Conservatives, Trade Unions, the CBI, the Labour Party, the National Commission and various left and right 'think tanks') that nothing short of a 'skills revolution' is required to arrest Britain's downhill economic spiral.

In various and contradictory ways such apparent consensus has placed post-compulsory education at the centre of policy debate in Britain and elsewhere. Once marginally viewed as the Cinderella or handmaiden of British industry, further education has become an integral part of mainstream mass education. This has been influenced by a number of contradictory factors, ranging from the collapse of traditional youth and adult labour markets to the initiation of a centrally controlled, but locally generated, internal education market. Related factors such as improvements in GCSE and 'A' level results, the take-up of vocational qualifications and increased student participation rates, mean that post-sixteen education and training reform is seen as a matter of building on success. Despite the lack of enthusiasm for science and engineering, there are encouraging signs that more adults and young people are taking advantage of the broadening FE curriculum framework, with its emphasis on parity of esteem between academic and vocational qualifications, credit transfer, work-related training and improved higher education provision and access (FEFC 1996). Moreover, with general national vocational qualifications (G/NVQs) and Modern Apprenticeship) now on stream, there are signs that post-compulsory education is, at last, opening up the range of opportunities first envisaged by the Crowther Report (1959). From an all-time low of less than twenty per cent of school-leavers participating in full-time post-compulsory education in the 1960s and 1970s, there has been a steady increase, with more than seventy per cent of school-leavers now going on to some form of further education and training (Smithers and Robinson 1993).

Diverse influences at home and abroad, unemployment, the decline in manufacturing, changing technology and work organization, marketization and global factors, have meant that political interest in post-compulsory education has become a universal phenomenon. Such factors, increasingly associated with post-industrial change in society and production, have brought into question traditional distinctions between school, education and work, including those associated with academic and vocational education. Two other related factors have also placed post-compulsory education high on the political and policy agenda. The first concerns the transition from an elite to a mass system of further and higher education, which involves changing values, hierarchy and differentiation in the emerging new system. Here, policy issues to do with progression into higher education, course development, student recruitment and employment, organization and resource management, feature significantly. The second concerns the control of funding and costs, as unprecedented student numbers become absorbed into post-compulsory and higher education (Ainley 1994: Brown and Scase 1994). Not only has this attracted Treasury interest in further and higher education policy; it has also raised new questions concerning both the relationship between post-compulsory education, economic growth and efficiency, and how to categorize and differentiate institutions, qualifications and students in the emerging mass market. It is to both aspects of this equation that this chapter is addressed.

CATEGORIZATION AND DIFFERENTIATION

Viewed optimistically, the impact of market forces has radically altered the traditional base of post-sixteen compulsory education and training. Increasingly, the shift of resource towards the student challenges conventional patterns of course and institutional development, creating new pathways and patterns of provision. Despite worries about the fragmentation and diversification associated with the recent mass expansion of post-compulsory education and training, there is, according to Robertson (1994), a discernible policy thread running through the reform process which will hold it together. Evidence for this, Robertson argues, is reflected in an emerging credit culture which will allow students to 'trade' in the market place. Following on the introduction of G/NVQ, this policy has informed a systematic tripartite (re)ordering of an already expanding tertiary sector (Gleeson 1983; Green 1986). In seeking to place order on a previously chaotic qualifications jungle, the Dearing Report has tacitly endorsed successive government claims to have closed the long-standing division between high-status academic and low-status vocational courses. A key attraction here is the role G/NVQ plays as a parallel but equivalent route toward employment and higher education. The intention particularly with G/NVQ is that it will have equivalent status to 'A' levels, encouraging both staying on and upskilling, providing progression both to university and to work, and thereby bridging the historic academic–vocational divide. Two related questions arise: can G/NVQ fulfil these multi-functions, and whose interest and what economic purpose does this so called alternative route serve?

In addressing this question the lack of historical sensitivity in current debate needs to be noted, not least because, as McCulloch (1991) argues, it threatens to distort the reform process. Awareness, for example, of the historical antecedents underlying Dearing's proposals should at least enable future policy-makers to avoid 're-inventing the wheel'. This would seem important, given Crowther's recommendations for the absorption of an 'alternative route' within tripartite structures, more than three decades ago (Crowther Report 1959). In promoting GNVQ *today* as the alternative to an essentially fragmented academic route, polarization has been approved to the exclusion of integration between the two. On the one hand, rejection of the Higginson Report (DES 1988), which proposed radical changes to the long-established and repeatedly criticized 'A' levels, has legitimated continued pressure from right-wing groups for the retention of 'A' level essentially unchanged. On the other, government remains committed to the continued development of outcome-driven, essentially work-based NVQs as the central basis for its vocational training reforms. With the growing, if belated, recognition that these two radically different types of qualification did not add up to an appropriate post-sixteen provision, G/NVQ has taken on the appearance of a political solution, designed to satisfy the differential requirements of employers, labour markets, and post-compulsory education itself. Failure to respond to calls for a unified system of qualifications that cross the 14–19 age range has resulted in G/NVQ both meeting the needs of industry and responding to the pressure for increased participation. Although TVEI and subsequently the National Curriculum emphasized curriculum breadth and a technical/vocational perspective for all young people, the White Papers (ED/DES 1991, 1994, 1995) sought to establish a three-track system for academic and vocational programmes, and progression post-sixteen redrawn in Figure 1.

Figure 1:   Three Parallel Pathways in Post-sixteen Education and Training

Academic	GNVQ	NVQ	Equivalent job level
Post-graduate		Level 5	Professional, Middle management
Degree		Level 4	Higher technician, Junior management
A/AS level	GNVQ Advanced	Level 3	Technician, Advanced craft, Supervisor
GCSE (grade C or better)	GNVQ Intermediate	Level 2	Basic craft
	GNVQ Foundation	Level 1	Semi-skilled

While this chapter deals with various aspects of differentiation and its rationale in a primarily English (though not Scottish) context, it is worth remembering that most European educational systems also have or had tripartite divisions. These divisions, linked with legitimating notions of parity of esteem, are premised on a variety of distinct but parallel routes between academic, technical and vocational tracks, including alternancebased approaches. Though parity of esteem is not a new concept in the British context, it has hitherto had little positive influence on the ways in which the academic–vocational divide has been perceived in practice. Traditionally, the widespread 'common-sense' belief in tripartism is represented by the division of people into Plato's *men* of gold, bronze and iron. The history of its translation in English education in the twentieth century represents, according to Reeder (1979), a series of ill-fated attempts to reproduce these natural divisions in the education system, which others maintain reflects Britain's class structure and lack of competitiveness (Wiener 1981). This recurring policy theme also has its roots in the struggle between old humanists, industrial trainers and public educators which has characterized the history of state education in England and Wales (Williams 1965). Coffey (1992), for example, points to the way that a tripartite hierarchy of educational provision in Britain was explicitly linked to class divisions in the late nineteenth-century, where professional education in the public schools stressed leadership, with general education for the middle class and skilled working class in grammar schools and job-related training for the rest (if they were lucky) in elementary schools, where the emphasis was on 'obedience' rather than leadership. By the twentieth century, the divide between grammar schools and public schools had narrowed, at least in curricular terms, as the growing middle classes sought the same academic education as had developed originally for the sons of the aristocracy. Tripartism by then had become the division between academic, technical and practical routes. This is seen most clearly in the Norwood Report of 1943, which was the precursor to the 1944 Education Act and the political settle-ment that followed it, a central principle of which found expression in the British secondary tripartite system of grammar, technical and modern schools in the post-war period.

A belief in three clearly differentiated types of people is fundamental to one of the dominant ideological belief systems in British educational politics (and especially, although not exclusively, in the ruling Conser-vative elite), which Skilbeck (1976), following Williams (1965), called 'classical humanism'. Raymond Williams's notion of the English school curriculum as a compromise between the old humanists, the industrial trainers and the public educators might have led one to expect that the rise of the comprehensive movement and the subsequent expansion of Further Education would provide the ideal context in which to realize a public educator's model of the curriculum, at the expense of the old humanists and the industrial trainers (Whitty 1992). Such optimism was not to reckon with the combined class interests which underpinned classical humanism. For those whose views are close to this ideal such tripartism is seen as the 'natural order of things'. There are four logically separate but commonly conflated assumptions within this tripartite 'common-sense'. Firstly, that people fall naturally (socially and genetically) into three distinct types, academic, technical and practical. Secondly, that these are closely correlated with 'ability' as it is generally understood. Thus, the most able are naturally academic, the least able are practical and the technicians fall in the middle. The third assumption is that schooling and the curriculum should similarly be divided into different types of provision, to correspond to these different types of people and ability. The fourth assumption is that the opportunities and needs of the labour market also fall into the same neat divisions. None of these statements stands up to logical and empirical examination when taken in isolation let alone together, but such ideological beliefs are notoriously resistant to rational challenges. Not only do such beliefs live on but they have also become, in the 1990s, overlain with class, market, qualification and funding-led effects.

Though social class is not specifically referred to in the Norwood Report as the criteria for three types of learning, the allocation of pupils to three types of school corresponded to the perceived needs of a reconstructed post-war economy, which were closely associated with class, gender and occupational divisions. The critical determining factor of general intelligence testing for ability as the instrument of differentiation at eleven-plus, obscured the deeper relationship between social class and education – trenchantly observed by researchers in the 1950s and 1960s (Glass 1942; Floud and Halsey 1957; Crowther 1959; Douglas 1964; Jackson and Marsden 1962). Evidence of middle-class dominance in grammar education, for example, linked with convincing statistical data of class wastage from grammar schools, elicited evidence that tripartism both impeded equality of opportunity and the flexible skill requirements of an expanding economy (Halsey, Floud and Anderson 1961). For Bernstein, such research described (but did not explain) the deeper principles of social, economic and cultural control which gave rise to such inequality. At the centre of Bernstein's (1977) analysis of education is the role it plays in the cultural reproduction of class relations and its cultural transmission as the order of things, in what is learned in the classroom and workshop. Central to his argument is the way education constitutes a major influence in the structuring of experience and identity through the curriculum, the message systems of which are rooted in the wider society. The influence is not, however, mechanical but finds expression in the cultural reproduction of class relations, which significantly impact on levels of pupil achievement, expectation and life chances (Halsey 1988; Halsey, Heath and Ridge 1980). Bernstein illustrates the point with reference to the persistence of ideology and power in reproducing strongly held belief systems:

> How a society selects, classifies, distributes, transmits and evaluates the educational knowledge it considers to be public, reflects both the distribution of power and the principles of social control. From this point of view, differences within, and change in, the organisation, transmission and evaluation of educational knowledge should be a major area of social interest (Bernstein 1997).

The significance of Bernstein's analysis here is that it offers a way of critically examining the cultural and economic assumptions underlying 'common sense' theories of social difference. It also points to the strong boundary mechanisms which prevent redefining relations between subjects, themes and qualifications in the curriculum. In Bernstein's terms '... attempts to change degrees of insulation reveal the power relations on which the classification is based and which it reproduces' (Bernstein 1996). According to Frankel and Reeve's (1996) view, any study of further education which does not recognize the significance of such principles from school into FE and beyond would be incomplete. Their work points to the ways in which FE has historically served the educational career aspirations of distinct occupationally defined strata, essentially those in the lower professions, trades people and skilled workers. In institutional terms, FE came to be situated between the elementary and junior secondary schools, grammar and public schools and universities. Though FE today has evolved to become more diversified – to include a middle-class constituency, an emphasis on expanding its links with HE provision for adults and the unemployed – its curriculum traditions remain overlain by occupational imperatives, class and status divisions which differentiate academic ('A' level), vocational (GNVQ) and work-based (NVQ) routes. Although these divisions are not of FE's making, a further problem is that they are largely designed for the 16–19 age group, despite the fact that three-quarters of the sector's students are now adults. As Frankel and Reeves point out: '... many older adults and people not seeking employment are now excluded from a further education curriculum oriented to industry and the reskilling of the workforce. There is evidence that the further education curriculum is *juvenescent* and unadapted to the needs of adults'. This, plus the continuation of gendered provision in areas associated with childcare, nursing and secretarial studies (female) and construction, engineering, science and technology (male) suggests that class, race and gender divisions cannot be separated off from the curriculum and qualification base of FE (McCrae, McGuire and Ball 1996). As further education strives to meet increasingly diverse needs, which embrace service to the community, customers, consumers, local and national skill targets, there is evidence that a combination of markets, funding and tripartism is impeding its development and responsiveness. While a more unified approach to the curriculum and qualifications will not automatically overcome social and economic divisions within and outside FE, it will contribute toward a less fractured and inclusive FE environment.

THE MYTH OF TRIPARTISM

Once even a cursory examination is made of twentieth-century English educational history, there is a glaring paradox. Despite the dominance of this apparent tripartite perception, the middle strand of the three has always had a troubled and low key existence. Until the 1960s, the focus was on three types of schooling. The 'top' and 'bottom' of the system are well known: the grammar schools that developed out of the public school tradition and the various schools that evolved from the elementary school into the secondary modern schools of the 1950s and 1960s. Despite various attempts to develop technical high schools in the middle, less than five per cent of all secondary pupils attended such schools in this period, with less than half of all LEAs making nominal provision for such schools. A little over twenty per cent of all school leavers progressed into grammar schools of whom significant numbers of working-class pupils dropped out early, indicating a pattern of wastage bemoaned at the time by a cross-section of parliamentarians (Jackson and Marsden 1962). With the exception of ten per cent of school leavers entering apprenticeship or trade training, the vast majority of school leavers entered semi-skilled or dead-end jobs, mainly from the secondary modern sector (Roberts 1987). This latter cohort were not very visible because of the relative full employment and economic expansion in the 1960s: a period in which the warning signs of decline in demand for traditionally skilled labour became increasingly apparent. The oil crisis, the decline of manufacturing and rising unemployment from 1974 onwards further exposed the failure of tripartite divisions around social class lines which followed the 1944 Act, which aimed to reflect and reproduce expected skilled openings in society at the time.

Though Crowther (1959) anticipated this looming crisis with recommendations for innovative 14–18 post-school reform, the historical lessons of that period went unheeded. Attempts to explain such policy failure with reference to the loss of technical schools has become a convenient feature of contemporary historical folklore. In reality, it was policy and funding neglect rather than the loss of technical schools which accounts for the 'missing prong' of tripartism – with the *real* tripartite division operating between private schools, grammar schools and the rest. More recently, Whitty and others (1993) show how the technical school, the latest rebirth of the CTCs and Technology Schools, have largely repeated these earlier experiences. This line of argument, about the lack of a technical stream, which was first popularized by the Black Paper writers of the late 1960s and early 1970s, and later given credence by the then Labour prime minister, James Callaghan, in his Ruskin speech (1976), has influenced more than two decades of Conservative education reform in search of the missing 'middle ground' of English education.

Following comprehensivization in the 1960s and 1970s, and with the later exception of CTCs and technology schools, the focus largely changed from separate technical schools to technical curriculum provision. McCulloch (1989) argues that the initial conception of the TVEI was originally aimed at this middle group of 'technical' young people, though, as the initiative developed, the objective became one of providing vocational education for *all* – largely by teachers and LEAs *redefining* TVEI as a cross-curricular initiative at institutional level. GNVQ, following CPVE and TVEI, can be seen as the latest in a long series of attempts to establish this middle, technical higher vocational track, now seen as lying between 'A' levels and NVQs. McCulloch (1989) and Sanderson (1994) both demonstrate the dangers of attributing simplistic explanations for the failure of technical education in Britain, and both list a range of interrelated complex factors. As Gleeson and Hodkinson (1996) argue, this complexity can be explained by (i) an inevitable internal tension within classical humanist tripartism and (ii) conflicts between this widely held classical humanistic ideology and other deeply held but possibly less dominant educational ideologies within English society. The internal tensions in classical humanism arise because, in English society, very few people have naturally aspired to the technical route. As people strove for what Bourdieu (1984) called academic 'distinction', both technical schools and secondary modern schools began to ape the grammar school curriculum long before comprehensivization became the norm. At the same time, anxious aspiring parents wanted their offspring to attend grammar, not technical, schools if they passed the eleven-plus. In essence, middle-class families saw anything other than grammar (or public) school as inappropriate, seeing both technical and modern schools as for the working class. In this context, the upwardly mobile working class were also more likely to aspire to the academic grammar school route than to a technical career that kept them firmly below the class equivalent of the glass ceiling. This process was reinforced by the common system of taking young people with the best eleven-plus passes for the grammar schools, giving the technical high schools (where they existed) at eleven-plus or thirteen-plus those who were left (Jackson and Marsden 1962). Thus, a technician was identified not through a positive interest in or aptitude for technical studies, but simply as someone who was not judged capable of an academic career. This partly explains the lack of investment in technical schools, which were more expensive than grammar schools. In such an elitist system, the self-interest of the dominant groups suggests that most money and resources should be spent on the top level, not the middle, even though common sense suggests that technical education will, inevitably, be more expensive.

Late twentieth-century post-16 tripartism in England focuses on separate institutions as well as a separate curriculum. This is partly because of the marginal position of sixth form colleges in the FE reform process. These had been originally set up within school regulations, to provide traditional academic education based on 'A' levels, as part of a recognized comprehensive education system. It was often an old grammar school that was transformed into a sixth form college. The new post-sixteen funding arrangements abruptly moved them from the schools sector in 1993, giving them independence from LEAs with funding provided by the Further Education Funding Council (FEFC). They exist alongside the predominantly FE colleges, which have a very different history and ethos (Smithers and Robinson 1993). Research by Robinson and Burke (1994) suggests that many sixth form colleges are striving to preserve their elitist, academic ethos, based around provision of 'A' level to full-time 16–19 year old students. Many will not offer more than a token GNVQ curriculum in one or two occupational areas, though this is changing. The risk is that if high-status institutions like public schools and sixth form colleges do not take GNVQ seriously, the new middle vocational track will be squeezed every bit as effectively as were technical schools in an earlier age. Furthermore, a belief in a technical strand 'for other people's children' reinforces the status and sense of well-being for those who have succeeded on the academic route. From this point of view, a middle stratum that is weak in practice but strong in rhetoric meets the status needs of the academic elite. Thus, to succeed in the vacuum left by a failure to create technical schools, GNVQ has the task of breaking out of this vicious circle, and to avoid being 'diluted' by schools offering it without additional physical or human resources.

GNVQ AND THE 'MIDDLE GROUND'

One of many ideological conflicts relevant to GNVQ lies between classical humanism and what Skilbeck (1976) called reconstructionism. Within a reconstructionist ideology, the educational system is seen as a means of restructuring society normally for economic ends. This can be seen in the repeated calls for more or better vocational or technical education, in order to close the skills gap between Britain and her rivals, to make industry more competitive and to ensure future prosperity. Such beliefs are almost as strong as classical humanism within the ruling Conservative elite, and are advocated by the influential CBI, among many others. Such a reconstructionist argument is frequently restated in the official rationale for GNVQ, which stresses the need to raise the standards of education and training across the board. Hence the National Targets for Education and Training (NTETs) expressed government commitment to fifty per cent of any year group achieving NVQ Level three equivalence by the turn of the century, with these targets likely to be increased upwards in the immediate future.

Such universalist views of attainment run counter to the classical humanist view, that a norm-referenced hierarchical distribution of ability and therefore appropriate qualifications is part of the natural order of things. Paradoxically, the British government can, at the same time, proclaim NTETS as official policy and create new A* (starred) grades for 'A' level and GCSE because 'too many people are getting an A' grade. Moreover, constant talk of 'A' level as the gold standard has set GNVQs (and NVQs) a difficult cultural and educational task. To succeed, at least in the terms of those government directives that brought it into existence, GNVQ must establish a credible vocational middle track while simultaneously raising levels of education and qualification in ways that are acceptable to the mass of the English public, be they parents, young people, teachers, employers or politicians. Already there are rumblings that the maths and science levels in GNVQ are not high enough and that the modular base of GNVQ, compared with 'A' levels, renders it an 'easy option'.

There is also a growing gulf between GNVQ and NVQs (Hodkinson and Mattinson 1994). Unless students have topped up GNVQ with NVQ units, they may have few relevant workplace skills. This means that many young people leaving at eighteen or nineteen with GNVQ Advanced Level may need to take NVQ Level II once they start work. This shows that the official picture of three equivalent post-sixteen pathways, where the normal progression would be from Level III, including GNVQ Advanced, to Level IV or its equivalent, is oversimplified (Figure 1). Furthermore, young people with GNVQ Intermediate or Advanced may have turned down opportunities to train at NVQ Level II when they were sixteen-plus. They may, therefore, see a move into this level of training, following two or three extra years of full-time education, as a step backwards. Because the launch of GNVQ has been so closely linked with the value of qualifications in the labour market, it is likely that many of the young people flocking to take these new courses are doing so in the hope of gaining access to HE and getting a good job, or a combination of both. But education does not create jobs for students. Unless there are widespread changes to the ways in which labour markets, industry and job opportunities are organized, progression for many GNVQ students will be difficult, no matter now good the actual course provision may be (Finegold and Soskice 1991). Currently the legacy of recession and youth unemployment in Britain, including growing disparities in wealth and income, undermines qualification-led reform and the rhetoric of parity of esteem which goes with it. If there were hopes that the supposed skills revolution would counteracted the decline in manufacturing and the expansion of the service sector, then these have not been realized. Traditionally, industries such as engineering, construction and energy have had the highest concentrations of young people with formally recognized qualifications. With the decline of such traditional 'Fordist' industries the need for formal training has been increasingly determined by the demands of an expanding, mainly low-skilled service sector, and to a lesser extent by a minority recruited into high-tech 'post-Fordist' information-based industries, a division to which G/NVQs do not easily relate. Not surprisingly, recent aspects of post-compulsory education expansion reflect rather than challenge this trend, revealing stark contradictions between the rhetoric of up-skilling expressed in government reports and the reality of segmented 'casualized' labour markets. For Hutton (1995), the combination of New Right thinking, markets, and tripartite education policies has not only destroyed the post-war social and economic settlement but has also brought about a segmented 30–30–40 society. The first thirty per cent he describes as 'disadvantaged', the second thirty per cent are made up of the 'marginalized' and insecure; and the last category is that of the 'privileged' whose market power has increased since 1979. From this viewpoint, he argues, judgements about the appropriateness of youth and adult training provision have to be revisited in both economic and educational terms if they are not simply to replicate and reproduce such tripartite segmentation. Elsewhere, McCrae and others (1996) argue that such forms of inequality cannot be separated off from the ways in which post-compulsory institutions operate in the competitive market place. They point to the ways in which the dynamic of this market is inflected by class and ethnic relations – in the way class and ethnic composition of institutions is, for some 'choosers', a criterion for selection or rejection. The composition profile of a college can, for example, become part of the reputation and, subtly, the basis for the marketing strategy of FE institutions.

> We are perceived in the community as a black college...we don't attract people from the south of Mainwaring, Morland, moving towards Wentworth, the wealthy part of the LEA which is more white...we serve increasingly the north end of the LEA which is where the deprivation is...(a College Vice-Principal, quoted in McCrae, McGuire and Ball 1996).

In this context, where curricular, institutional and 'niche' market dynamics intersect with class and race, 'new' forms of structuring between institutions arise. Already, significant research on the transition from school to work stresses the stratification of such inequality (Furlong 1992, Banks et al. 1991, Bates and Riseborough 1993, Kerckhoff 1993). This contrasts sharply with policy assumptions based on individualism and free choice which accept the primacy of 'A' levels and offer G/NVQ as 'the alternative route'. Yet, despite increased student participation, the evidence is that the limitations on school leaver choice – between work, dole queue, Youth Training, 'A' level and full-time vocational education (now GNVQ) – remain much the same as a decade ago. Ostensibly, GNVQs are designed with the intention of enabling young people to progress either to higher education or into employment, allowing virement and freedom of movement between academic and vocational courses. Yet both transfer and progression are problematic within existing tripartite structures. So, what are the alternatives?

BEYOND TRIPARTISM

In the past five years substantial government reform has radically altered FE's voluntaristic tradition. In response to a combination of mounting social and economic pressures, recession, unemployment and lack of international competitiveness, a rapid series of reforms has been put in place. Following the influential White Paper: *Education and Training for the 21st Century* (1991), the sector has been re-engineered around the FE and HE Act (1992), involving NCVQ, FEFC and creation of the internal market. This arguably has had both beneficial and limiting effects. On the one hand it has increased student participation, and encouraged new models of curriculum delivery and greater institutional responsiveness. On the other, it has overstretched the financial resources of institutions, introduced false economies because of competitiveness and tripartism, and failed to significantly raise the education and skill level of the nation. A central problem has been the mode of *delivery* associated with putting quangos, qualifications and markets in place, in a funding-led model which has little to say about the process of teaching, learning and curriculum. Yet, as Flint (1996) has argued, the total picture is not quite so predetermined as it appears. There are signs, for example, that incorporation and PCET expansion has let the 'genie out of the bottle'. At college level there is evidence of an emerging unified, credit and modular-based system on lines advocated by the National Commission on Education, which has influenced new forms of school, FE, HE and community partnership. According to Flint (1996), the momentum of such change is not, however, likely to be best served by the amalgamation of NCVQ and SCAA into a single qualification authority (QNCA):

> Further education works well with schools generally, but its future is as part of a coherent post-compulsory system, not tied to and subsumed within a monolithic and schools-focused curriculum and assessment authority. Why not a National Tertiary Qualifications body, where the emphasis of 16–19 curriculum and qualifications would be at point of entry into higher levels of education and into work, rather than the culmination of an educational experience? The development of (G)NVQs at Levels IV and V would be overseen here, and the work of the lead bodies co-ordinated. (Flint TES 23.8.96).

Here, Flint draws attention to the importance of building on existing knowledge and experience of course design. As a college principal he adds weight to the argument that the latest resurrection of tripartism, with parallel 'A' Level, GNVQ and NVQ tracks, is a recipe for innovation without change. There has, of course, been much talk in the 1990s of bridging the academic/vocational divide by creating new pathways through modular-style course programmes. However, this, linked with an overarching national certificate or diploma overlaying unchanged 'A' Level, GNVQ and NVQ provision (Dearing 1996), will not go far enough, particularly in relation to a growing adult clientele. It not only fails to address the historic tensions referred to so far, but it also ignores weaknesses within existing academic and vocational traditions widely acknowledged as narrowly subject-based, and also age-, gender- and occupationally specific. The feature of over-specialization, most noticeable in 'A' Level and NVQs, sets Britain, and particularly England and Wales, apart from most other nations, and provides further indication of the tension between nation state planning and the requirements issuing from globalization. It also ignores Hutton's (1995) analysis of a '30–30–40 workforce', where many are unemployed while others have to survive on insecure short-term contracts. Traditional specialisms have been based on assumptions of full employment and careers for life, rather than the need for lifelong learning. In a 21st century that promises a further acceleration in the explosion of knowledge, young people will not be well served by a post-compulsory education sphere defined largely on the basis of past experience of employers' needs.

In these circumstances, challenging tripartism is not just a technical or a curricular matter. It would be naïve, for example, to regard government policy on Youth Training, City Technology Colleges, G/NVQ and Modern Apprenticeship as isolated policy incidents disconnected from broader New Right political agendas. The current policy discourse which surrounds vocationalism and the plethora of other recent training initiatives in the 1980s is positioned within several favoured projects central to the previous Conservative Government's overall social and economic strategy, one of which now includes New Labour's Welfare to Work programme. These projects include fiscally driven social, economic and welfare policies for restructuring the workplace, for controlling the inner cities, for Trade Union and industrial relations reform and for replacing planned education, housing and welfare with market-oriented provision. Increasingly, marketization, competition and corporate status for schools and colleges are having limiting educational effects: first in ensuring adherence to an ever-decreasing funding base and, second, in bringing forward uncomfortable decisions about how institutions should compete rather than co-operate in the market place.

Such factors not only reinforce and reproduce principles of inclusion and exclusion associated with social class, gender and race, but they also underpin a political system which encourages passivity rather than active participation and learning in the public domain. Taken seriously, Young's (1993) and Brown and Scase's (1994) view that new technology and a combination of academic and vocational options prove the potential to enable young people to become multi-skilled is important. This needs to be tempered with the realization that it is knowledge combined with democracy which provides the substantive basis for a learning society (Avis and others 1996).

In challenging tripartism, therefore, it is necessary to address a broader vision of citizenship and learning, in fact, a different vision of post-compulsory education which will sustain the personal development of all. New concepts of specialism will need to be found in which a broader integration of theoretical and practical knowledge is provided for and where traditional knowledge categories and boundaries are transcended. This will not be provided for by bridges or by bolting on key or core skills at 16–19 or beyond. Young's (1992, 1993) work on organic specialization is important here, in drawing attention to *relational* aspects of knowledge, experience and skill in the curriculum. At the same time it is crucial to revise Crowther's original notion of 'the practical' as a way of enhancing the process of academic and work-based learning, a message that has been lost along the way. To avoid reinventing the wheel it is important to remind ourselves of the historical route we have travelled, and to ask awkward questions concerning what Crowther refers to as 'the rehabilitation of the practical'. My intention in raising such questions here is to stimulate debate rather than to provide in the short space available a thoroughgoing analysis of the aims of polytechnical education.

1. Does Vocational Education Have to be Non-Academic?

We know that many forms of education directly linked to employment are not seen as 'vocational' education. These include the high-status courses, such as degrees in medicine and law. Their place in higher education is never challenged. But what of those which do not command such status? Can we not devise courses in catering, engineering, hairdressing or business and administration that also contain a coherent mix of critical theory and practical application? Within 16–19 education in Britain, there is a strange polarization in current vocational provision. For those in work, NVQs emphasize practice to the extent that theory can be entirely missing. On the other hand, GNVQs, designed for full-time education, have no requirement for practical experience in the workplace – real or simulated: and both are fundamentally uncritical.

2. Why Does Vocational Education Have to be Closely Tied to Assumptions about Employers' Interests?

There are two related issues here. The first relates to the desires of some young people for an education that prepares them for work and training. If this is acceptable for those studying science in order to go on and read medicine to become doctors, why should it not also apply to those who wish to have an education that can lead them to a career in catering or motor vehicle maintenance? Perhaps we need to consider the links between education and employment from the young person's perspective, rather than assuming this is always the same as that of employers. We also need to examine more carefully the balance between specialisms which are seen by some as career-specific, and the benefits of a broader-based general education.

The second issue relates to a central theme of this paper. It has been argued that education should not be determined by an economic imperative based on outmoded divisions. Therefore, if what are now called vocational studies are to be included across the post-compulsory curriculum, should they also be subjected to scrutiny for the intrinsic interest they can command, and for their contribution to citizenship, democracy and a sound general education? This is the kind of question that Dearing, among others, has brought to the fore, but it still needs consideration.

3. What is the Place of the Practical in General Education?

Once the vocational curriculum is separated from the 'causal' link with employer needs, we require other reasons for its inclusion. One of these must relate to the need for practical education to balance more restrictedly academic approaches. This raises the currently neglected question about what practical education is, and what and who it is for. Here, four different types of answer present themselves, and hence four different reasons for the inclusion of the practical, although the list is not definitive:

- The first concerns the benefits of learning from practical experience. If the key aims of learner autonomy and citizenship are to have more than rhetorical value, all learners must acquire the means of generating their own theoretical understanding. The uncritical rehearsal of others' theorizing is not sufficient. Knowledge and understanding must square with learners' personal practical experiences if they are to have proper meaning and value and, for this, learners will need at their disposal the skills necessary for their continual critical examination of practical experience.

- The second stresses the practical application of theory or knowledge. This can take place in almost any subject, and might include putting on a play, conducting a scientific experiment or running a simulated business. The important point is that knowing and understanding are not enough – that education must go further.

- The third type of practical application concerns physical dexterity and the notion that education should not neglect physical skills. Once more, these skills could be developed in a wide variety of contexts, not all currently included in 'vocational' education. Hairdressing, cooking, mechanical engineering, laboratory experiments and making electronic circuits are just a few examples.

- The fourth type is of a different order. Practical, in this sense, implies the ability to be proactive in a practical way, rather than expecting someone else to either give a lead or do things for you. Often, though not always, this type of 'practicality' is a team and community effort. Examples would be when students organize their own events, become involved in local community events, run a college newsletter or produce their own concert. The central question then becomes: can we ever justify a general education that does not celebrate and develop all these forms of the practical, for all young people?

4. What should be the Role of Learning in the Workplace?

Attention has already been drawn to the current paradox, whereby vocational courses in full-time education may have no requirement for work-based experience, while work-based training programmes have no requirement for off-the-job experience. Yet we know that most young people identify with work experience of various types, not least because they are treated as adults in adult surroundings, in sharp contrast to what they see as the infantilization of full-time schooling. As school-leaving ages continue to rise, with a growing number staying in full-time further education until they are twenty or older, this issue is of growing importance. Furthermore, is it not at least plausible that work environments could release novel learning opportunities which, for many young people, could be profitably blended with other experiences in their post-sixteen education? This relates to the previous question. Where relevant, the understanding of applied practical skills is likely to be greatly enhanced in a working environment linked with post-compulsory education and training. It is time to be less squeamish about such matters if policy-makers are to take the education–industry relationship seriously.

If a current problem for educationists, policy-makers and politicians is one of how to respond to such questions, the reality is that the same questions have been on the table, unaddressed, since Crowther (1959). In the post-Dearing and post-election climate the situation is more complicated as current principles of marketization and managerialism, as well as the previous ones of democracy and professionalization, are all under siege. Some policy rapprochement between the two approaches looks on the cards, but will it be enough? In contrast with more unified approaches being developed in Sweden and Scotland, there remains a lack of policy consensus or political will in England to move in this direction. According to Spours and Young (1996) there is a danger in forcing through a response to Dearing based on an Advanced Diploma, which has neither the backing of Higher Education and employers and, importantly, where the principles of integration linking academic, vocational and work-based knowledge remain unclarified. According to Spours and Young (1997), research on professional opinion among teachers and lecturers favours strengthening the framework offered by Dearing rather than trying to move directly to a Baccalaureate-type Diploma.

> If qualifications reform is undertaken in an incremental, planned and well-managed way with adequate resourcing at each stage, a consensus for change can be established in a system far more fragmented and complex than north of the Border . . . if lessons can be learned from TVEI, and it is recognized that much of the capacity for innovation in England is local, not national, it is not unrealistic to envisage a unified system within ten years.

The message here is that we are at a 'half-way house' in a transition that is likely to proceed slowly and incrementally. In the meantime, the lesson from TVEI (Gleeson and McLean 1994) of teachers implementing real change in spite of rather than because of any direct lead from government looks set to continue. Perhaps if policy-makers expressed less frustration with educationists and social scientists for failing to provide them with answers to their problems, they might just reflect on this lesson. 'Fat chance', one might say. Put another way, there is a need to understand the way *values* inform new policy thinking, whose values these should be, and how they should be represented? As Avis and others (1996) have sought to argue, in spite of the apparent importance attached by the New Right to education and training in revitalizing the British economy, the reality has been an 'economizing of education' (Kenway 1994), dominated by downsizing and fiscal objectives, which have led to a serious fracturing of Britain's public sector institutions without adequate replacement. Instead of becoming the socially progressive post-Fordist society advocated by some commentators, Britain has gone down a selective and market-driven route, in which the rights and opportunities of citizens and workers have been increasingly diminished. The danger is that piecemeal market funding and qualification-led reform will reinforce this process by driving the lifelong learning agenda into a franchised cul-de-sac, creating a 'Marie Celeste' model of learning in which real teachers and students rarely meet but are nevertheless 'on roll' (Frankel and Reeves 1996). This model of the *virtual student* may satisfy the accounting procedures of funding agencies, but in this form it represents little more than an educational version of 'care in the community', serving mainly the interests of a low-skill service economy.

It may well be that full employment is a thing of the past: but that does not necessarily mean full-time work is at an end or that FE cannot make a contribution to the economy and jobs. Rather, it requires new thinking about the nature of work, including its construction, distribution and relationship with education and society. The conviction that no such alternative strategy is possible has been sustained by a populist cultivation of nationhood and vocationalism, backed by a corresponding state craft which has ensured that New Right and now New Labour education policy has remained unchallenged by internal dissent, or external critique – at least, until recently. Yet, as the limitations of nation-state vocationalism as a basis for enlightened reform become more obvious, there remains little to build on in terms of alternative values and priorities. If, in Hutton's terms (1996) 'a great opportunity may yet go begging' – presumably a message to New Labour – it is worth remembering that lifetime learning is not just about markets and economic competitiveness: it is also crucial to a developing national culture and quality of life. The two, however, need not be separate. Driving unemployed youth and adults into training as an 'acceptable alternative' to unavailable work – in the form of welfare into work – is, however, unlikely to support this end. Neither is the reduction of the '21-hour rule' to sixteen, as the number of hours per week of formal teaching which a student can receive from a college before losing entitlement, likely to inspire educational access to the most needy, including those with special educational needs.

At present the combination of centralized fiscal restraint and a tendency for the DFEE, FEFC and other bodies to hide behind the crumbling market which they helped to create, is limiting FE's room for manoeuvre. What is called for now are funding and support mechanisms which place learning as much as funding at the centre of post-compulsory education policy and practice. This will require greater recognition on the part of New Labour of the strategic national importance of FE in delivering quality learning, at local level. A strong FE system will, at college level, be greatly enhanced by:

- placing learning, knowledge and skill at the centre of its operations;
- developing a unified curriculum which accommodates progression across the 14–19 and adult age range, involving academic, vocational and work-based learning for all;
- ensuring that managers, lecturers and governors work co-operatively in defining the FE curriculum;
- making decisions based on independent evidence where labour market and community needs are held in balance;
- being accountable to a National Further Education Council, which subsumes FEFC funding arrangements alongside a broader professional, pedagogic and research remit.

What I have sought to argue is that it is in the public interest to encourage greater breadth of further education and training than the current limitations of market, funding and National Vocational Qualifications permit. Wholesale changes now taking place in the methodology of funding and provision for post-compulsory education reflect outcome-rather than process-based considerations, when clearly the two must connect. Moreover, attempts by the Department for Education and Employment (DfEE), FEFC and the National Council for Vocational Qualifications (NCVQ) [now QNCA] to colonize youth and adult provision with a tripartite formula is not best placed to secure the diverse learning needs of PCET students, or the conditions of a learning society for the 21st century (Hyland 1994). Such an approach is altogether too narrow, restrictive and out of step with growing provision in colleges which falls largely outside the traditional frame of GCSEs, 'A' Levels, NVQs and GNVQs. The reality is that a majority of young people and adults work and study via a combination of routes, modes and approaches which a tripartite curriculum, training and accreditation approach barely accommodates (Kennedy Report 1997). In Flint's (1996) terms, 'the genie is now out of the bottle'. However, claims about the importance of FE in the process of national economic regeneration will remain simply slogans unless there is a serious recognition that the requirements of youth and adult learning consist of much more than the limited conditions of tripartism allow. It is to this neglected aspect of the post-Dearing policy debate that this chapter is addressed.

ACKNOWLEDGEMENTS

I am grateful to fellow members of the Further Education Researchers' and Writers' Group, James Avis, Martin Bloomer, Geoff Esland and Phil Hodkinson, for allowing me to draw and develop ideas from our recent book, *Knowledge and Nationhood: Education, Politics and Work*. I am particularly indebted to Phil Hodkinson for letting me develop ideas on GNVQ which we have worked on jointly, and to Geoff Stanton, Senior Research Fellow (Greenwich University), for detailed comments on an earlier version of this chapter which first appeared in *A Basis for Development: Breaking from Past Divisions* (Further Education Development Agency, 1998).

9 Education and IT Policy: Virtual Reality?

Phil Wild and Peter King

The annual British Educational Technology and Training (BETT) exhibition is a showcase of the best in British IT, revealing the power and range of possibilities available (at a price) to enhance the process and practice of education. It is a place to indulge in the best of educational visions and dream of the attainable in the IT and education heaven. Yet walking around it in the company of hard-pressed teachers is to be made acutely aware that, too often, their vision is blurred and they are subject to an only too rude awakening from the insistent shaking of reality. One visitor to the exhibition in 1997 expressed this when he wrote that BETT was 'a great place for dreams – and for nightmares. For some schools – especially in the least affluent areas – it's an annual reminder that they are falling hopelessly behind in the race to equip the classrooms of tomorrow.' (Evans 1997, p. 2). How can it be that the UK can be so strong in the pioneering of some key aspects of IT and yet, in the late 1990s, many observers of the educational scene can feel like this?

This same observer goes on to claim that 'BETT will attract delegates from around the world eager to capitalize on our pre-eminence in creating educational software and implementing IT in the curriculum. What they won't see, as they glance admiringly at the 350 exhibitors' stands, is the gaping chasm that separates the best-equipped schools from the vast majority of others where staff are underresourced, undertrained' (Evans 1997).

The growth and changes in information technologies have been dramatic during the last twenty years. The effect on education has been much less dramatic. The educational IT policy has been very largely state-directed during most of this time (Boyd-Barrett 1990) and the Conservative government which was in power during those years appears to have operated from a simplistic and superficial vision characterized by an acceptance of the appearance of shop-windows like BETT rather than the reality of the schools, as is exemplified in this comment from the then Minister for Science and Technology when he visited the same BETT as Evans: 'When I walk around the BETT show I'm heartened by how much IT is being used in schools.' To confuse in this way what is visible at BETT with what is happening in the majority of schools is to mistake a vision for the reality. It is the fact of such a limited understanding at the level of government which has been greatly to blame for the constraints on the use of IT in schools and the failure to produce a genuinely effective national strategy in IT in education.

So while it may be true that government has attempted to direct IT in education, it is equally clear that such direction has yet to produce a properly integrated national strategy for the provision of IT and the influence and dissemination to all schools of the use of IT as a genuine teaching and learning experience for teachers and pupils alike. There has been much political rhetoric and pious intention but policies have been unremittingly *ad hoc*, limited by short-term investment and restricted in their uptake by too little attention to teacher training and teachers' needs.

The Labour government elected in 1997 renewed in office its earlier party pledge to make education a priority in its policy making and within that to rapidly develop IT at all levels through supporting a National Grid for Learning. The question remains as to how this can be achieved when it chooses to work within the same economic framework and embrace the same public spending targets as its predecessor government? The question is raised as to what is needed to provide a properly integrated national strategy for educational IT and whether there is evidence of the necessary planning, practical application and political will to suggest that the current government can succeed by 2002 where its predecessors failed over the last twenty years?

Evaluations of these previous government strategies to promote the wider use of computers have been scathing ever since the early 1990s. Casting a brief look back at some of those policies may help identify the pitfalls to be avoided in the immediate future and reveal how the virtuous rhetoric might be turned into an achievable reality.

Kirkup complains that 'Britain's IT policy was centrally generated, it did not grow out of demands or the needs of pupils or teachers' (Kirkup et al. 1978, p. 27). Such ill-founded policy had given birth at the beginning of the 1980s to the first attempt to support IT development on a national front through the Micro-Electronics Education Programme (MEP) and the Computers in Schools initiative from the Department of Trade and Industry (DTI). The MEP ran from 1981 to 1986 and was established to ensure that the microelectronics advances were exploited within schools. It ran in parallel with the DTI scheme during 1981 to 1984 and gained from the latter's earmarking of funds to be passed directly into the hands of individual schools for the provision of hardware.

It is true to say that these government-backed initiatives did generate some activity which impinged a little on the classroom, but from the perspective of an evaluative study made in 1987 it was clear that severe criticisms of their effectiveness could be made. Ennals declares that

> The MEP was a short-term ephemeral initiative, part of a growing tradition in British government technology policy. A problem was identified, a political posture was struck, a programme was launched. A public relations victory was scored, a limited scale and duration budget was committed. Underneath little may have changed (Ennals 1987 p. 194).

Boyd-Barrett (1990) notes that 'a condition of DTI subsidy was that at least two teachers in each receiver school should acquire relevant training.' Such a requirement, which at face value looks reasonable, placed an obligation on the mode of working of MEP before it even got off the ground, and there is much reported concern that the DTI involvement was purely to protect the home computer markets (Boyd-Barrett 1990), which in itself could have been a cause of slow development in UK schools owing to the small market open to educational software publishers. In any case, the INSET provision related to the DTI scheme was described as 'totally inadequate' in an evaluation (CARE 1988). The pace and direction were therefore being controlled by government without due regard to the real educational needs of pupils and teachers; the technology was dominant over the learning needs. After all this, an analysis of available statistics on the use of computers by teachers carried out in 1992 by McCormick concluded that 'the general picture is that the curriculum has not been affected radically, with the computer being accommodated into a subject, whether it be a traditional one or the new one of computer studies/information technology'(McCormick 1992, p. 34). It was clear that many teachers, even if they did use the computer, felt that it was most appropriate for reinforcing current classwork rather than initiating new types of learning. Computers appeared to be motivating, but teachers were not always aware when gainful work was in progress when computers were in use. In addition, the short out-of-school courses which were the staple diet of MEP were not meeting the actual training needs of teachers, because they did not provide sufficient time for pedagogical issues to be considered or classroom experimentation to be followed up; the emphasis was too much on the hardware.

The debate over education which began in the late 1970s led eventually to the 1988 Education Reform Act which embraced state direction of education to an unprecedented degree. However, the opportunity to affect every teacher's attitude to and utilization of IT by making IT an integral learning activity for each subject was overlooked when the National Curriculum which emerged from the ERA legislation led to IT being separated into another National Curriculum subject of its own. After that teachers obsessively withdrew into their own subject guides and now had the excuse that IT was someone else's responsibility. The pious principles and hopes for the integration of IT were set back, and the many documents which tried to redress the balance failed to have much general impact. The National Council for Educational Technology (NCET) fought hard to promote wider use. In 1993 they published the results of seminars to focus thinking specifically on the use of IT within NC subjects and tried to break the technology link. They reported that 'The National Curriculum does not yet fully reflect the skills, knowledge and understanding which are made possible through new technologies and which are likely to be a requirement for learning in the future' (NCET 1993, p 25). Such comments were a strong indictment of the government of the day and reflected a judgement that the NC had inbuilt IT stagnation. The Dearing Review of 1993 partially retrieved the situation through categorizing IT as a basic skill alongside numeracy and literacy. However, even this reflects a narrow view of IT as a vocational skill rather than as a learning tool integrated in the school curriculum, and as such it was a step backward from the previous DES document in 1987, 'New Technology for Better Schools', which had clearly promulgated the view that computers in education were important to improve the delivery and quality of education. There was an attempt to broaden the position through the statement attached to each NC subject (although physical education was excluded from this) which required that IT should be used where relevant. More recently, at their 1996 conference, the School Curriculum and Assessment Authority (SCAA) has tried to identify a number of key issues which they consider should move IT forwards within education to bring it into line with the great changes evident in industry and commerce. The key issues identified and reported by Niel McLean (1997) are:

- How do we ensure that the skills of information handling and critical thinking are represented in the curriculum?
- How do we ensure that IT resources are used to support priority areas such as literacy and numeracy?
- What is the balance between generic skills and specific knowledge?

• How do we [SCAA] support the production of software that addresses schools' particular needs?

Individually these are discrete points and are implied in the SCAA (1997) publications which are being widely distributed to try to influence the directions of IT developments, but they should rather be explicitly expressed as a group of questions the answers to which clearly demand a unified national strategy.

How is such a strategy to emerge? It seems that all the main political parties are keen to show that they understand the importance of information technologies for schools and learners, but there is little evidence that they really understand the underlying issues of why IT is not seen by many teachers as the 'answer' for improving education in the classroom. The idea of a computer for every child does not address the issues of space in overcrowded classrooms or the inability for everyone to print out at the end of the lesson to the one printer in the corner of the next-door room. In the 1997 election campaign, all the main political parties were making ample references to 'the information age' and claiming 'IT is integral to the learning process'. However, the emphasis on the 'old values' of whole-class teaching made by the Conservatives and that on 'traditional' styles of teaching which was cited by Labour were in stark contrast to the independent (but managed) learning environment provided in a true IT culture.

Recently there has been a change in emphasis towards the use of IT for learning. Robert Wagner, author of successful school-focused software, sees that

> Technology is changing student activities in the classroom itself, moving from the situation where the teacher stands at the front of the room 'spraying knowledge' at their students.... To a situation where the students are much more active participants in the topics of learning. The processes of gathering and assembling information, and learning how to share the results with others (quoted in Davitt 1997).

The use of CD-ROMs and the Internet moves the emphasis to the individual 'finding out', which is the basis of individual or small-group investigations or projects, but the emphasis on terminal examinations in GCSE syllabuses removes the opportunity for such modes of learning being assessed in the 14–16 age range. George Cole, reporting in the *Times Educational Supplement* recently, focused on this particular problem, with well-known workers in the field of IT in education such as

Stephen Heppel, Martin Kilkie and Heather Du Quesnay all supporting his case for 'a national crusade, a programme of renewal for IT in schools' and agreeing that 'we need the political leadership, will and imagination to keep IT moving forward' (Cole 1997).

There has long been a broad consensus that it is the skills and know-ledge of teachers which permits change to succeed. This is clearly the case in implementing IT, where the technology is new to the majority of teachers. The support that teachers receive to take on these new skills has decreased just at the time when the politics has been more demand-ing. Earmarked Grants for Educational Support and Training (GEST) were removed in 1993 just at the same time as the IT support infrastruc-ture of LEAs were crumbling and when many IT advisors and the bands of advisory teachers had been pensioned off. The expertise once avail-able has declined, reducing the local infrastructure of support and making it even more difficult for national agencies such as NCET to have local influence, therefore limiting any possible resurgence of a national infrastructure.

Current research being carried out in the Department of Education at Loughborough University, which is investigating the IT needs of teachers, clearly illustrates the skills and knowledge famine amongst teachers. Many teachers have seen the media hype on the potential of the Internet as an information source. As part of a project to examine how the University could support the use of the Internet within the local community, groups of teachers from schools were given the opportunity to learn how to use the Internet and at the same time develop their own ideas, with guidance, of how it might affect their own teaching. The research was looking at these subsequent ideas. However, the outcomes were limited by the fact that many teachers first had to be taught such simple skills as how to use a mouse and scroll bars on screen to move down text, and how to 'point and click' on hyperlinks to navigate through searches. Obviously many pupils are already beyond this stage, so this lack of skills and the associated decrease in confidence make teachers even more wary of using such facilities with pupils.

Similar deficiencies in teacher IT skills were found when researchers were investigating the use of IT in science. In this subject, for instance, there is ample opportunity to mimic industrial monitoring and record-ing processes by using data logging. Those teachers who have used such IT methodology report their pupils as working to higher NC levels as a result of the quality of data achievable with IT and the analytical power of IT, and this brings its own academic gains (Rogers and Wild 1996). The latest reports suggest that the vast majority of science teachers do not take advantage of this educational power, and 'secondary science teachers are the least likely to use information technology in their teaching' (McFarlane 1997). This is a particularly serious setback to the concept that schools provide pupils with relevant skills for industry.

A further example reveals the way in which, notwithstanding NC requirements, many teachers are either not in a position to further IT skills in their pupils or are even unwilling to acknowledge this as a serious deficit in their teaching. A 1996/7 small-scale survey within the Loughborough University Initial Teacher Training Programme looked at the IT experiences gained by PGCE trainees in English during their school placements. It was found that only two out of twelve trainees had been able to use IT skills with their classes during a twelve-week teaching practice. The group of schools involved served the 11–14, 14–18, or 11–18 age range. This was the case even though the training programme required partner schools to make such an IT experience available to every trainee. When this low level of provision was investigated, the English mentors supervising these trainees accounted for the lack of provision in one of two ways: (a) they cited difficulties in making resources available (for example, the obstacles to a regular booking of the computer room), or (b) admitted that their own lack of confidence or commitment to IT was the root cause. When it was suggested to the mentors that this situation not only undermined the professional development of the trainees but also implied their own departments were not delivering a mandatory part of the English National Curriculum, there was widespread acceptance of culpability. They went on to admit that Ofsted inspection reports on their own schools had drawn attention to the deficiency in IT delivery within English but it appeared that because this deficiency was perceived to be a widespread condition across the country it was not necessary for them to prioritize it among their own problems! Spreading the fault appears to lighten the responsibility to such an extent that no individual feels the need to change, or so it would seem.

This is a clear example of how even mandatory National Curriculum criteria will not be met while the teaching profession looks around and perceives a wholesale ignoring of the need for provision of IT resources and professional training. Teachers cannot be persuaded to use IT in their work if there is no systematic provision of such resources and training. Furthermore, new teachers during the university element of their courses are being trained to appreciate and utilize IT within their training, but this is being undermined during school-based teaching practice experiences where there is a cynical dismissal of IT by mentors as not an important priority when faced by the reality of the harassed teacher's everyday classroom.

This same theme was taken up by Margaret Bell, Chief Executive of NCET, when she referred to 'the missing two thirds' of teachers not using IT. NCET is the government quango charged with advising on the development of IT policy and supporting its implementation, but it has an organizational role beyond its means. Bell confirms and concedes that there have 'been many initiatives to train teachers and encourage them to use IT but, it seems, none have been able to persuade teachers to use IT in their work' (Bell 1996). She obviously had vision for what IT can and should be doing to enhance education. Many NCET publications are used by many teacher educators to promote subject-specific and wider policy issues of using IT. Much evidence has been gathered together of the important effects of using IT, such as motivating slow learners, developing graphical interpretation skills and evaluating the true power of newer technologies such as the Internet and multimedia CD-ROM in school libraries. Many stories of success have been used as evidence that IT improves education, but hard evidence is difficult to gather in the short-scale and low-funded projects which seem to be the basic diet of NCET. Bell acknowledges that there is a need for an overarching organization to embrace all teachers and teaching, a view supported by Heather Du Quesney, Chair of NCET. However, her view that the LEAs should play a bigger role in a developing IT infrastructure appeared to immediately diminish her credibility with her political masters. But government policy with regard to LEAs had led to a slow starvation of their power and funding so that they have retained very little, if any, IT infrastructure. Soon after saying this Bell resigned, arguing that 'There are far too few learners experiencing the benefits of technology. In order to make real progress in this, it is necessary to challenge current systems and structures; this can cause obvious tensions when this is initiated by an organization which is government-funded' (quoted in John 1997). It seems that questioning DFEE strategy in relation to IT developments can become incompatible with remaining in your job.

Bell's resignation must be seen as an admission of the impossibility of persuading the (then) government to properly support NCET in becoming an overarching organization to reach all teachers and classrooms. Du Quesney continued to serve as Chair of NCET and appeared to believe that some coherent strategy was just around the corner, saying that 'I don't believe in large bureaucracies trying to control what goes on in school' – conveniently ignoring the fact that in the circumstances a lack of any overall bureaucracy remains itself a form of policy by omission. She continued to talk about partnership to bring about the developments sought in schools by NCET but forgot that the old partners who might support teachers were no longer available, and the few that were could have little impact on the scale required. Other attempts to seek 'partners', such as the Link-IT scheme involving Higher Education (HE) institutions, are doomed to fail in an environment of 'efficiency' cuts, as such institutions cannot work without full-cost returns. The age of goodwill has been removed by government financial restraint (otherwise known as tax cuts). Agencies such as the Teacher Training Agency (TTA) and SCAA (now known as the Qualifications and Curriculum Authority) were talked of as new partners, but they cannot themselves implement policy and support teachers in the role of professional partner when much of their own policies appear to the teachers and to their trainers to be instituted without genuine consultation. Their preferred action appears to be to work up schemes of 'sticks' with which to beat the schools and HE into new paths (e.g. by defining the outcomes of ITT in terms which will remain unattainable within the funding reductions to HE). Any 'carrots' are hard to find when there is no increase in funding for the addition to the menu required by an extra serving of IT.

By the end of the Conservative Government's period of office it was obvious that there was no question of a national IT strategy. Obviously this was because there was no internal consistency between what was needed to make support possible and what remained available at the time to support the need. This had been concisely outlined by Kenny (1996) when he said that 'the success of the Grants for Education Support (GEST), which targeted money on IT, was followed inexplicably by reduced funding'. In addition he suggests that IT suffers for a number of important reasons, the main ones being: schools have many demands on delegated money, so reducing the priority of training and subscribing to IT support packages now charged by the LEA; there is only a weak direct link between NC subjects and the use of IT; schools are unable through lack of knowledge to support ITT students now put there for longer; and, most important of all, there is now only a limited and frail support network. He concludes that 'one crucial point that comes out of the NCET's work is that without a strong national support network it will be difficult to implement any national strategy for information technology. What national strategy? Perhaps that is where it should all start – with a national strategy.' Perhaps we should add 'What national support?'

It should be obvious that any forceful strategic drive which is to give a positive steer to the direction of practice in all schools must meet some fundamental needs of teachers and schools and clearly identify how professional skills and understanding of the learning environment can be interfaced with the technology. If anything, history has surely taught us that the technology alone cannot bring about change; teachers must be carried forward with it. History has also taught us that teachers will not respond to professional development if the resources are not in place to implement change, so parallel and complementary strategies are essential. This will require a push from the centre to produce a critical mass of active teachers in every subject. For example, Singapore has policies which put a large number of computers into all schools and send all teachers on training courses to provide the critical mass needed for the programme to be self-supportive. This provides a dilemma for our politicians who made such an issue out of developing IT in schools. It is now quite obvious that more pilot projects with yet more small-scale evaluations will continue to be ineffectual. Enough is now known to develop an overarching policy of access and training which will enable teachers and pupils to work with IT. Once the policy is established, the strategy for implementation can be developed, working with schools, LEAs, HE, industry and commerce, possibly through and with the NCET, clearly identifying the role of each. This would be perceived by politicians as opening the door to writing a blank cheque, which is obviously untenable. However, there are examples closer to home where national strategies are being developed.

Nigel Pain of the Scottish Council for Educational Technology is promising that Scotland's schools will be fully wired by the end of 1997, including the most remote of communities. This policy is being developed in parallel with a planned training programme over a three-year period specifically focused on the communication aspects of the new technologies. A basic system will be installed and operable at no cost to schools. Such a move will provide more than the critical mass of schools needed for teachers to see the benefits both for managing schools and sharing ideas with other teachers, as well as being able to share teaching materials throughout Scotland. The one hundred per cent coverage will provide greater social cohesion and overcome the potential problem of the technology creating an acceleration of disadvantage, with the information-rich and information-poor perpetuating a divided society.

So it becomes clear that a genuine national strategy would be a government-directed programme for advancing on three fronts in IT: (i) creating a skills-based teaching force; (ii) developing a coherent and integrated curriculum platform; (iii) providing a coherent and compatible infrastructure. Each of these fronts would be supported by specific action.

The teachers would be encouraged to gain the necessary skills through a national training and development programme for teachers, possibly by giving NCET a more directive role. This raises issues of professional autonomy and central bureaucracy, but it is clear that merely pointing teachers and schools towards good practice, which is NCET's current role, allows excuses for non-adoption to flourish. We may hope that the powers of the TTA can be combined with the professional knowledge of IT educationalists to make the outcome realizable. However, this will need to be extended to teachers already in post, perhaps through 'contracts of implementation' linking with training and resource provision. Furthermore, tax incentives could be used to encourage teachers to purchase their own personal computers. There is certainly some evidence from in-service training in the mid-1980s that providing teachers with the resources does encourage implementation of ideas derived from courses (Wild 1989).

To develop a coherent and integrated curriculum base it will be necessary to make it mandatory for all subjects to be audited for IT delivery via Ofsted inspections, but with follow-up developmental advice being regarded as of equal importance to any summative report. A consultation network for staff and curriculum development would be made available. Within the more mandatory framework for the training of teachers, this advice network would recreate the infrastructure based on LEAs, HEIs and more local support clusters of schools working on joint IT development and sharing dissemination of NCET-identified good practice. Such activities might be focused through each school being required to formulate a three-year action plan for the implementation of an acceptable level of IT delivery. Earmarked funding, including GEST-type initiatives, could be resurrected to support developmental policies in individual and consortia of schools. QCA should promote changes in the examination system to encourage pupils to show IT skills, perhaps by recognizing and rewarding the relevant use of IT in the marking structure of coursework. At the moment, to use or avoid IT does not actually impinge on performance tables.

To provide a compatible and coherent infrastructure will require, at the very least, a government commitment to realistic resourcing policies, perhaps by promised matching government funding to private finance initiatives and commercial sponsorship schemes, for a regular hardware upgrade. Such upgrades are absolutely vital: at the present time, figures for PCs in schools hide the true state of this need. The latest figures from the DFEE (November 1997) show that primary schools in the UK have an average of thirteen computers each and secondary schools have an average of 96. In primary schools computers contribute to 43 per cent of lesson time in any week and to 23 per cent in secondary lessons. At first glance this seems to be an impressive set of figures. The UK is in third place in any international comparison of the numbers of PCs in use in schools. Only the USA and Singapore have proportionately more in use. However, both Germany and Malaysia are about to overtake the UK. In this country 1996 saw a four per cent drop in the purchase of equipment in primary schools and overall UK expenditure on educational IT equipment has remained at around one per cent of total education expenditure for several years, in contrast to the five per cent spent by the USA. Furthermore, these raw figures hide the actual rate of replacement and upgrading of hardware and software. Half of the PCs in schools are more than five years old and many have reached a terminal stage of unreliability. Most schools are simply unable to keep up with the necessary upgrading (since 1993 the total budget surplus of all UK schools has decreased from £600 million to less than £100 million) even if they could overcome the chaos of choices resulting from a lack of any clear national agreement over appropriate provision. The Stevenson Report (Stevenson 1997), an independent inquiry into Information and Communications Technology (ICT) in UK schools, states boldly that 'the state of ICT is primitive and not improving.'

An essential for any strategy that seeks a compatible and coherent infrastructure is the connection of schools to the Internet. The most effective means to this would be to enable British Telecom and the various cable companies to bring every school on-line in a low-cost (or preferably no cost) JANET-type users' network within a short time scale of perhaps three years. The Joint Academic Network (JANET) in HE provides a free access at the point of delivery and this has certainly created that critical mass generally accepted as the prerequisite for wide and effective use of the communications facilitated by IT. However, no single company (certainly not BT alone) should be given this monopoly for schools, but rather regulated consortia could be supervised in such a way as to balance commercial gain against educational advantage.

The Prime Minister is on record as claiming that 'Education is the best economic policy there is, and it is in the marriage of education and technology that the future lies.' Under his government it might be thought possible to believe with confidence that such a national strategy would be implemented. Indeed, policy proposals from the present Labour government do come much closer than any from the previous administration to putting such a strategy into place. But can this government actually deliver when it has tied itself to existing public spending limits? Already the Labour government's desire to see the creation of a national information grid linking all schools and colleges in order to facilitate the widespread sharing of ideas and resources has been severely compromised by its complementary decision to act only as a licensing agency and requiring such a grid to be self-funding. Their suggestion that GEST (Grants for Education Support and Training) be used once again for targeted funding of training may be only one small step towards fulfilling one element of that national strategy, but far more confident strides need to be made if the long march to justifying Mr Blair's claim is to be accomplished.

In October 1997 the new government published a Green Paper, *Connecting the Learning Society*, which is its proposal for a national IT strategy. The White Paper, *Excellence in Schools*, also commits the government to the creation of a National Grid for Learning. Subsequently it appears that this is envisaged as being run by a consortium of IT companies and designed to link all schools to the Internet by 2002. At the same time, funds from the National Lottery are to be used to provide a nationwide programme to train every teacher in the use of IT. At the present time only one-third of secondary schools and few primaries are connected to the Internet; and no more than a small minority of serving teachers have received any formal training in IT. Therefore, this is an aim to be supported as an essential part of any national strategy.

There remain two dangerous traps into which a plan such as that outlined by this government could yet fall. The first is external to schools and concerns the means of funding the proposals. The second is internal to the schools themselves and reflects the attitude of the teaching profession.

The question of external funding hinges on the source, control and exact purpose of such funding. As presently conceived, the government appears not to be committing new public spending. Additional revenue will come from the existing schools equipment budget, the National Lottery and from businesses in the IT and telecommunications industry. In itself this does not justify criticism of the policy but, nevertheless, reliance upon business consortia to provide essential hardware and software does open the path to the possibility of purchasing decisions being dominated by marketing aims rather than best educational practices, and it can mean leaving important elements of the national strategy to the push and pull of business economics and investment. The disinterested observer might well conclude that a government not prepared to put its own money where its mouth is will be a government that does not believe as strongly in what it does as in what it says to get votes.

Even if this external trap is to be avoided, any success for the government's proposals remains dependent on persuading the teaching profession to support what it intends; this internal constraint must be loosened. Ofsted reports on the standards of IT teaching have shown how patchy are the results. Alan Teece, general manager of ICL Education Systems, believes the biggest task remaining is to persuade teachers of the importance of IT as a learning tool. He says, 'We must address the skills required – and overcome the fear and reticence of using the equipment. . . . That is something we have not quite cracked yet.' This may be partly overcome by ensuring IT is part of the compulsory core for all teachers in initial teacher training by including IT in the national curriculum for such training. The first step in accomplishing this will be taken in 1998 by the publication of a curriculum by the Teacher Training Agency, to which Mr Teece is himself an advisor. For teachers already in post, a training programme is promised, but full details have not emerged at the time of writing.

It remains very hard to see how a genuinely effective national strategy for IT can be made a reality even in the form proposed by this Labour administration, if there is no commitment to raising existing public financial support for IT in education. Over the last fifteen to twenty years we have seen an ever-increasing gap between the rich and poor in UK society which has been exacerbated by a dominant economic, social and political ideology that places importance on individual rather than group values. This social division is in danger of being shadowed by an equally serious educational division between schools richly resourced in IT terms and those poorly resourced in this area. So long as the development of an IT infrastructure is left to piecemeal local innovations and not to the creation of a national strategy, this division will get steadily worse. Such a situation would be more than an educational tragedy because it is precisely through widespread provision of IT in schools that we can prevent the accelerating disadvantages of a two-tier IT skilled workforce and society. Some other countries, like Singapore, are already putting into place sophisticated and ambitious IT strategies in their schools. Such countries have already progressed beyond the debates about what might be done and are acting decisively to resource infrastructure and the training of teachers in a way which leaves the UK's ad hoc developments far behind. As Margaret Bell wrote in the TES 'Expanding teachers': 'IT use needs a clear statement of expectation, a change of attitude and access to the technology' (Bell 1996). In order to provide this, government must take the lead in implementing a national strategy for IT in partnership with the profession. Time and political ideology are running out.

10 Education Policy: The Next Ten Years
Stuart Sexton

Let us look into the future – say, the next ten years – keeping in mind that this can only be done with reference to the present and with cognizance of the past. We can never start again on policy making for education from a clean sheet (nor, for that matter, can we for any other area of government intervention). We have to start from the current situation, warts and all, and, if we are wise, we have to take into account past policies: those that failed and those that succeeded.

Given that all of this is within the context of contemporary party politics, in trying to forecast the future turn of policy we also need to take into account the past record of political parties, their current attitudes and their statements on future policy, and then exercise a justified measure of scepticism as to what they would do rather than what they say they would do.

In this chapter I propose to chart the likely course of education policy over the next ten years; to recommend what ought to happen, and to see if and when and how closely my ideal policy will be reached.

It is a popular myth, especially in regard to education policy, to suggest that there is a remarkable degree of consensus between the principal three political parties, such that policy making would be much the same whichever party had formed the present government and, more importantly, whichever party forms the next one. It is a myth that the media has encouraged because they were bored with the same party in government for seventeen years, and a myth that the Labour Party subtly promoted because they needed to cultivate erstwhile Tory voters in order to win the election – and such voters do not, in practice, want a change in policy.

It *will* make a great deal of difference to education policy over the next five years now that Labour has won, and again which party wins in five years' time. I do not approach my task of presenting a glimpse into the future from an unbiased position; I am not an impartial observer. Let me therefore put the cart before the horse and tell you first what ought to happen – what the ideal policy should be – and then say how far actual policy is likely to fall short of that ideal.

I first began considering what ought to be done with State-funded schooling back in the 1960s when I was a local councillor serving on an Education Committee. (I shall turn to the matter of higher education later in this chapter). Much analysis and discussion, in the course of visiting schools and talking to teachers, polished and refined those early thoughts during the 1970s and put together the first policy steps which became the then Conservative Opposition Policy. I then assisted as Special Advisor to the Government from 1979 to 1986 to put those policies into effect. We did not achieve all we set out to do, we made mistakes, and since 1986, policy took several swings in the wrong direction.

The ideal policy which emerged from that extensive consultation is that all schools should be independent, by which is meant independent of political control, both local and national government. They should be owned and run by an independent body, probably a charitable trust, but not necessarily so. They must operate within a competitive market; such an environment is essential if the schools are to respond to the wishes of the parents and the needs of the children. Then they respond to pressures from the world of academia, the world of business and society as a whole; then they aspire to and achieve high all-round standards, and then they are able to achieve maximum effectiveness and efficiency from the resources available to them. In short, as with any good service, it needs to be consumer-led, not producer-dominated.

Ideally we should all have enough of our own money in our own pockets to pay directly to the school of our choice; such completes the direct link between producer and consumer. It excludes others, such as politicians, with no parental responsibility for our own children, from influencing our choice of school and style of education; and it is necessary for a competitive market.

Some seven per cent of children are paid for directly by their parents, into the present independent sector of schools, and such is therefore as perfect a schools' market as you are likely to get, at least at present. But those parents are paying twice, once through fees and once through taxes. If parents were to be given the choice of paying school fees or paying the schools' element of taxes, it is highly likely that fifty per cent or more would choose to pay fees to independent schools, and could afford to do so. The independent schools' market would expand considerably to meet this new demand. That, however, still leaves a large percentage of parents who wish to pay school fees but could never afford to do so.

If, therefore, all children are to receive a high standard of education – and most people accept that such is socially, morally, politically and economically necessary – there does have to be some measure of cross-subsidy from those that can afford it to those that cannot. If we pursue this argument to its logical conclusion, we finish up with some form of voucher, whether we call it a voucher or not.

We could tax everyone on an income scale, as we do now, and then give every parent, regardless of income, a cheque or voucher to pay for schooling at any school; or we could exempt parents from that element of taxation if they are paying fees and give vouchers to the rest; and/or we could tax everyone far less, so that most could afford the fees anyway; or we could issue everyone with vouchers but make those vouchers taxable so that, in effect, they are income-related; or there are very many more variations which are determined not by education policy but by considerations of taxation and redistribution policies. The essence of all of them is that every parent of every child should have a combination of cash and an education cheque in their own hands in order to go out and buy what they regard is the best education for their child, not for anybody else's child, within a competitive market of schools.

In the above ideal, government has no need to set certain standards; the market will do that, and do it better. There is no need to exhort greater effectiveness and efficiency, greater managerial skills, high-quality teaching; the competition will ensure that. No need to set a National Curriculum, or control examinations or testing, or in any other way control content; the market of parents, children, employers and universities will do that better, more flexibly and more effectively. Government (or rather Parliament) will have no greater part than collecting the taxes and paying out the vouchers. In so doing, Parliament will decide the value of the voucher and of any increased value year on year, thus leaving the parents to top-up or not as the case may be. The only exception to such a non-interventionist stance by Government and Parliament is likely to be the provision of an Inspectorate or Ofsted as we have today. Most parents are likely to want to exercise their judgement in this free market of schools with the advice or guidance or assurance of an independent Inspectorate as a guarantee of minimum standards. Most governments and Parliaments are likely to want to have taxpayers' money, through the voucher, paid out only to bona fide schools and not to charlatans – and not even charlatans that a parent has chosen.

Even under a voucher scheme, it is taxpayers' money being spent, tax payers as a whole, as represented by Parliament, will not be willing to see 'their money' spent on what they regard as poor-quality education, or worse still on subversive education. Therefore some form of inspection and registration is always going to be necessary, and I would say rightly so.

A free competitive market of schools would greatly reduce the number of poor-quality schools (although it would not eliminate them altogether) but the taxpayer should not have to support them.

This ideal for future education policy seems to me to be so logical, so appositely meeting the needs and wishes of the customers, parents and their children, that once some of the benefits become apparent to those parents, the public at large would insist upon further measures until an ideal free market with vouchers was achieved, regardless of what individual politicians, or even political parties, might say. What will differ, according to changes of political control, is the speed, the number of years, needed to achieve this ideal.

The first steps on this road to the utopian uplands have been taken. Removal of party political control of school governors was an early step, although in some parts of the country such control still exists in practice. The self-managing LMS – school, with financial controls at school level and annual school budgets – all of that was a big step towards the ideal policy. Better still was the further step of Grant Maintained schools, an even greater measure of independent control and financial management by the school. It seems to me that the benefits of those recent reforms are now so obvious that even those who were once sceptical of their introduction now accept and even welcome them.

The Labour Party vigorously opposed Local Management of Schools, but later on conceded its benefits to the extent of forgetting that they ever opposed it in the first place. Now in government, however, Labour intend to reassert bureaucratic control over LMS schools and effectively scrap the Grant Maintained schools by putting LEA control, through the governors, back in place, as well as taking away some of their budget.

Policies of self-management and financial control would have continued under a Conservative Government. The Conservatives would have reduced the percentage of the budget held back by the local authorities for LMS schools until in practice they all became Grant Maintained. The new Labour Government, on the other hand, will reverse the whole process over the next five years, though possibly not quite back to square one. I hope a measure of independence is still left to schools. If at the end of those five years Labour were to win again then I fear that we would enter another era of bureaucratic and political control over the schools, and political control of an even more dictatorial nature. If, however, the Conservatives regain office in five years' time, I think they would go rapidly to an all-Grant Maintained Schools policy, or even straight through to vouchers.

By this point you may be saying that I dwell too much upon the reform of management and finance and not enough upon the curriculum, examinations, teaching standards and methods, and so on. This is not because all these questions of quality and content of education are not important (they most certainly are), but because if we work inexorably towards that free competitive market with vouchers described earlier, then all the rest falls into place in response to that market, without government direction or control.

Because, however, we have not yet reached the utopia that I describe (and which I believe will inevitably come), the recent Conservative Government attempted to gainsay what that market would demand, to substitute their judgement on standards and content in the absence of a clear market lead. The danger of doing that, of course, is the risk of substituting your own judgement for that of the majority of consumers as a whole, and the danger for the Labour Government is the same: substituting their values for those of the Conservatives and for those of the consumers.

Should we therefore pursue the measures needed over the next few years to arrive at a system of independently run and independently owned schools? This requires the means to pay the fees, and thus effectively a system controlled by the market. If we do so, we accept, in the interim period, less than ideal standards and content. Alternatively, should we attempt to prejudge or pre-empt what that ideal market would dictate through regulatory control?

My own inclination is to accept laissez-faire, even now, in the belief that the present imperfect market is still better than the best of well-intentioned ministerial intervention. Hence, I *opposed* the introduction of a National Curriculum; hence, I stood down as Special Advisor because Kenneth Baker and I differed over such a measure of centralized control.

In practice there is a sensible compromise between these two extreme positions. On the one hand, regulate the whole curriculum and all standards; on the other, regulate nothing. The compromise is to regulate as much as even the most sceptical observer like me can accept as representing the general will of the consumers, or if you wish, of society as a whole.

It does seem that there is little dissent that children should be able to read, write and speak fluently and effectively, and whilst definition of what is fluent and effective is difficult, there is a general view of what is the acceptable minimum standard. A colleague of mine once said that two-thirds of the population were illiterate because they only read *The*

Mirror or *The Sun*! There is also a reasonable agreement that children should reach a certain level of numeracy, should have an understanding of science and technology, should know and understand the history and culture of the United Kingdom, of which they are a part, and so on.

The 1988 National Curriculum was far too prescriptive. Ministers at the time ignored protests that it went far too far in specifying what should be taught and how much time should be spent on each subject. Indeed, we used to say that far from prescribing ninety per cent of the timetable as claimed, it attempted to prescribe about two hundred per cent of the time.

In recent years those early mistakes have been remedied to some degree, thanks in practice to market pressure. The National Curriculum is being reduced to manageable proportions. That process may now be reversed under Labour. Under the Labour Government there is a grave risk of 'politically correct', cultural, ethnic and social theories being rammed into the National Curriculum. There is risk of further turmoil ahead, only to be resolved, as the Conservative turmoil was resolved, by the Government backtracking to the essential elements of the curriculum.

'Standards' is a related issue. In the 1970s, under the then Labour Government, 'standards' meant standards of provision – that is, the amount of money spent, the input. One success of the then Conservative Opposition, later to become the Conservative Government, was to change the criteria to that of output: what did the pupil achieve, what standards of skill and knowledge were gained after all that compulsory schooling? It is indeed fascinating to someone like me who has lived through these changes to see 'new' Labour now concerned over the quality of education – something which escaped them twenty years ago.

Although it is now generally accepted that 'standards' ought to mean standards of achievement, of output, there remains a residual belief amongst some that the greater the input necessarily the greater the output. Such a statement is patently untrue. To use a phrase so frequently written into speech after speech, it is not how much you spend: much more important is how effectively you spend it. Britain pumped money into its schools in the 1970s to little effect: standards of output were poor. Of course, there has to be sufficient money and, of course, rather like the Health Service, there is a bottomless pit of desirable spending into which money could always be poured. No matter how important you regard education or health, there will always be a finite sum available to spend on it.

In the last decade the expenditure on education has vastly increased: it is now far more per pupil in real terms (allowing for inflation) than ever it was. Although recent reforms have greatly improved the efficiency and effectiveness of the provision of that money, it seems to me that there is still plenty of room for effective financial control to achieve yet better value for money; so much so that such improved effectiveness needs to be implemented first before we even contemplate asking the tax payer to pay even more.

Here, then, lies a further difference between the political parties. The Conservatives would have continued to pursue measures to ensure that present budgets are more effectively spent – and there is still plenty of scope for that, in effect letting all schools become Grant Maintained, plus taking the necessary measures to ensure that such schools have the best available management. The Conservatives would probably have maintained the current level of spending on education, in real terms, but would not have increased it, nor is there any need to increase it. The Liberals clearly stated that they would tax more in order to spend more on education, without any promise of more effective and efficient spending. Labour says it will keep to Conservative spending plans but is under pressure from 'old' Labour to spend more. The previous Labour Government spent proportionately far less on education than did the subsequent Conservative Government. Would Labour do that again? Probably not. They are likely to follow the Liberals and to increase spending (and thus taxation) but without Grant Maintained Schools and other measures to improve efficiency.

So, under the present change of government, the term 'standards' is likely to regress to one of input rather than output. That said, the present climate of examination results and league tables is here to stay by parental demand, such that no government will be able totally to ignore standards of output and standards of achievement.

I am not so optimistic as to believe that the present Labour Government will do the right thing and pull out of government control in examinations altogether; they should do, but I doubt that they will. It was Kenneth Baker's 'great Education Reform Act' that first gave Government control of the public examinations system. Ideally that should be reversed and the examination boards should become independent once more, based firmly on the universities.

The same observations can be made of all the testing now made throughout a child's school career. In my view it is far too complex and far too bureaucratic, and I remain to be convinced that such political intervention is a satisfactory substitute for the control of standards by the market.

Not only will Labour retain control over public examinations, the various school tests, and all the rest of the paraphernalia, but it will increase it. Furthermore, rather like *Alice in Wonderland*, it will make everyone a winner, as in the Caucus race. Such control, of course, would eventually defeat the whole process (no one would respect it any more), so I suppose we could gain in the long run from such a disastrous interlude by regaining independent examinations.

Teacher training is the one area of schools education which the last Conservative Government should have tackled long ago. Some may remember that Shirley Williams, when Secretary of State for Education, closed many colleges of education and forced others to amalgamate. It was said we had too many places for teacher training. However, her criteria were more financial and political rather than measures of quality. Certain half-hearted efforts were made under Keith Joseph to tackle the problem of poor education courses. We all said that there was too much theory, and dubious theory at that, and not enough practical experience in teaching how to teach – but we did little about it.

I once asked the Headmaster of a well-known independent school from which teacher training colleges he drew his new teachers, and he replied 'None of them if I can help it.' He sought a good subject degree, preferably from Oxbridge, and then they, the school, taught the new graduate how to teach. Back in the 1970s Rhodes Boyson was saying that the proper way to train teachers was through a form of apprenticeship: take a graduate with a good subject degree and employ him or her on an apprentice basis under the guidance of an experienced, competent senior teacher.

If, as I expect, we finish up in ten years' time with a system of all independent schools and a means to pay the fees, then I would expect those schools to exercise their judgement, far more than they do today, as to the competence of the teachers they employ; to introduce apprentice-type training schemes; and thus to require the education departments to compete much more than they do now for their bit of the market in teacher training.

In the meantime, without that 'perfect' market, I can see the Labour Government using the tight curriculum proposals for teacher-training institutions recently proposed by the Conservatives in order to introduce their own concept of what a teacher should teach, and how – a concept likely to be at strong variance with what and how I think a teacher should teach.

Under the Conservatives, education departments would have faced increasing competition and therefore would have had to get their act together. Under Labour, their act will be got together for them, but not perhaps as they would wish.

As far as university education is concerned, there are parallel arguments to those advanced above for the schools. The universities have lain down like doormats and have let successive governments walk all over them. They have sought the cosy world of assured income from the taxpayer in exchange for loss of independence. Now that the student population has expanded (in accordance with the previous Government's policy) to one-third of the peer group, and is still growing – it is vastly greater today than it was twenty or more years ago – both the nature and the funding of that undergraduate education has to change, and that is true under any government. The taxpayer will just refuse to pay the greatly increased sum implied by such continued expansion. Not even an extreme socialist government, if there ever were one, would not dare to do so – or not for long, for they would be out of office.

It follows that a system of funding parallel to self-managing independent schools and the use of the voucher is inevitable for the universities, and the difference between the political parties is the speed with which such would be introduced. A Conservative government is likely to have conceded the need for such rather earlier than a Labour one. But the longer the present situation persists, the greater the damage done to our universities.

I suspect it will not be long before all British universities charge full-cost fees, and each university will make their own judgement as to what the full cost is for each particular course at that university. The government, in other words the taxpayer, will pay much of that fee, but probably not all of it, and it will do so with the equivalent of a voucher, even if without the piece of paper called a voucher. A student will therefore choose a course and choose a university, apply and hope to pass the entry requirements, and if successful commence that course, paying the fee directly to the university, partly out of taxpayers' money and making up any difference out of his own pocket. That pocket would of course be his own money (or his parents' or an employer's money) or a loan to pay back after graduation.

Current maintenance grants I expect to be phased out altogether. A student will pay for his own accommodation and living expenses and do so out of his own resources, most likely out of a loan. All of this is likely to come about within the next five years because the current university position cannot last longer than that. The Labour government is likely to be brought kicking and screaming to this same conclusion.

The content and standards of education in our universities are properly the concern of the market, that interplay between the providers and the consumers. It is not something for governments to be concerned with. Since I expect universities to return to the free market within five years, because of financial necessity, I expect that the free market will then dictate the content and standards of education once more. Neither I, nor any government, need propose what those will be. Nevertheless, I am entitled to attempt to forecast what they will turn out to be.

In no way can one-third of the population reach the high academic standards in specific subjects as is implied by an honours degree, and as was once achieved when only five per cent or so of the peer group took honours degrees. That applies however good our schools become in the future. Nor, for that matter, should we expect one-third of the peer group to be able to do so, or to want to do so. Many will be highly skilled but not necessarily in the academic learning implied by a good honours degree.

My expectation, therefore, is that the student population will go on rising but that for most of them their first degree will be a general degree which they will take only two years to achieve. Some will then go on to an honours degree (or whatever it may then be called) in a specific subject. Most will go on into employment, satisfied that the general degree is sufficient formal training before such employment, and that any further specific training needs to be done on the job. Those that do go on to the honours degree are likely to go to the top academic jobs after that, or to research. Some undergraduates, the brightest, may still – as now – go straight to an honours degree, without the need for the general degree. The above is, I think, the likely pattern of higher education in the free market shortly to be upon us.

Where, then, does all this lead us as to the future course of education policy? I hope I have given enough evidence to show that there is by no means a consensus – and thus, the future course of policy in the short term will change with the new Labour government; in the longer term, it depends upon who wins the next election. Upon such political differences will depend both the pace of change and the direction of change. The direction of change in the long term is largely dictated by that complex interplay of users and providers, observers and commentators – in a word, 'the market'. In a democratic system the government has eventually, even if not initially, to follow that market.

If the Conservatives had won the election in 1997 there would have been further measures towards greater self-management and financial control for all schools; no more money in real terms, but continued pressure for more effective use of resources; a relaxing in the prescriptive nature of the curriculum and testing; and further toes in the water towards an eventual voucher system. Nursery classes were a start. Proposals to improve teacher training would have been followed up with some vigour and no little controversy, and more alternative avenues towards qualified teacher status opened up. As for the universities, the days of block funding would be numbered and funding far more related to the per-student basis – but with government no longer paying the full real cost of each course. The Principals and Vice Chancellors would introduce, no matter how reluctantly, full-cost fees.

With Labour winning in 1997, I expect them to put a hold on further devolution of management to schools and to attempt to reverse that already given. They will scrap GMS in practice if not in name, forcing such schools to take a renewed measure of political control and less than one hundred per cent control of their budget. In spite of the rhetoric of 'New Labour' I expect this Labour Government to revert to type, and to reassert centralized control from the Department for Education even more so than Kenneth Baker attempted. Such control is likely to extend to teacher training, but probably not in the way that the colleges and departments of education would wish. Labour will scrap the Assisted Places Scheme and try once more to squeeze the concept of academic selection.

The universities are likely to try to hold to the present position, with financial constraints forcing them off it – perhaps after two years, after which they would have to follow something like the reform described above under a Conservative Government.

How much positive damage this Labour Government will do to earlier reforms is difficult to say. If, however, there were another Labour Government in five years' time, then I think we would see a destruction of many of the Conservative reforms and, as far as I am concerned, I would regard that as going back to square one, as in 1965.

On the other hand, if this Labour Government is replaced in five years with a Conservative Government, as I believe to be most likely – Labour will have made itself highly unpopular by then – I would expect that Conservative Government to consider that it had the mandate to pursue the ideal reforms in both schools and universities, and thus to complete the process within the lifetime of that Parliament, around the year 2007.

Paradoxically, I may well see my utopia earlier if Conservative follows Labour, rather than if the Conservatives had won in 1997. We will still reach those delightful uplands, but earlier still!

Bibliography

Adam Smith Institute (1984) *Omega Report: Education Policy*. London: The Adam Smith Institute.

Ahier, J., Cosin, B. and Hales, M. (eds) (1996) *Diversity and Change: Education Policy and Selection*. London and New York: Routledge in association with the Open University.

Ainley, P. (1994) *Degrees of Difference*. London: Lawrence and Wishart.

Ainley, P. and Green, A. (1996) 'Education without Employment: Not Meeting the National Education and Training Targets,' *Journal of Vocational Education and Training*, 48:2.

Ainscow, M. (ed) (1991) *Effective Schools for All*. London: David Fulton.

Aitkin, M. and Longford, N. (1986) 'Statistical modelling issues in school effectiveness studies.' *Journal of the Royal Statistical Society*, Series A: 149:1.

Anderson, B. (1983) *Imagined Communities: Reflections on the Origin and Spread of Nationalism*. London: Verso.

Anderson, B. (1991) *Imagined Communities: Reflections on the Origin and Spread of Nationalism*. Revised edition. London: Verso.

Apple, M. (1997) 'The Politics of Education in a Conservative Age.' The Charles Degarmo Lecture, American Educational Research Association, Chicago, March.

Arnot, M., David, M. E. and Weiner, G. (1996) *Educational Reforms and Gender Equality in Schools* (Research Discussion Series Number 10). Manchester: Equal Opportunities Commission.

Audit Commission (1996) *Trading Places: The supply and allocation of school places*. London: Audit Commission.

Auld Report (1976) *The William Tyndale Junior and Infants Schools*. London: Inner London Education Authority.

Avis, J., Bloomer, M., Esland, G., Gleeson, D. and Hodkinson, P. (1996) *Knowledge and Nationhood: Education, Politics and Work*. Cassell: London.

Back, L. (1996) *New Ethnicities and Urban Culture: Racisms and Multiculture in Young Lives*. London: UCL Press.

Ball, S. J. (1990) *Politics and Policy-making in Education*. London: Routledge and Kegan Paul.

Ball, S. J. (1994) *Educational Reform: A Critical and Post-Structural Approach*. Milton Keynes: Open University Press.

Banks, M., Bates, I., Breakwell, G., Bynner, J., Elmer, N., Jamieson, L. and Roberts, K. (1992) *Careers and Identities: Adolescent attitudes to employment, training and education, their home life, leisure and politics*. Milton Keynes: Open University Press.

Barber, M. (1997) Educational leadership and the global paradox, in Mortimore, P. and Little, V. (eds) *Living Education*. London: Paul Chapman Publishers.

Barber, M. (1997) *The Curriculum, The Minister, His Boss and Her Hairdresser: The Rise and Fall of Kenneth Baker's Plan*. London: British Curriculum Foundation.

Barker, M. (1981) *The New Racism: Conservatives and the Ideology of the Tribe*. London: Junction Books.

Bates, I. and Riseborough, G. (eds) (1993) *Youth and Inequality*. Buckingham: Open University Press.

Batteson, C. (1997) 'A Review of Politics of Education in the "Moment of 1976"', in *British Journal of Educational Studies*, 45:4.

Beaumont, G. (1995) *Review of 100 NVQs and SVQs* (A report to the Department for Education and Employment). Sheffield: DfEE.

Bell, M. (1997) 'The missing majority', in *The Times Educational Supplement Computer Update*, 18 October.

Benn, C. and Chitty, C. (1996) *Thirty Years On: Is Comprehensive Education Alive and Well, or Struggling to Survive?* London: David Fulton.

Bernstein, B (1997) *Class, Codes and Control: Towards a Theory of Educational Transmission*. London: Routledge.

Bernstein, B. (1990) *The Structuring of Pedagogic Discourse: Class Codes and Control*. London: Routledge.

Bernstein, B. (1996) *Pedagogy, Symbolic Control and Identity*. London: Taylor and Francis.

Bernstein, B. and Brannen, J. (eds) (1996) *Children, Research and Policy: Essays for Barbara Tizard*. London: Taylor and Francis.

Bhabha, H. K. (ed) (1990) *The Nation and Narration*. London: Routledge.

Bilefsky, D. (1998) 'Welcome to the (l)earning zone', *New Statesman*, 20 January.

Black, P. (1998) *Testing: Friend or Foe?* London: The Falmer Press.

Black, P. and Wiliam, D. (1998) 'Assessment and classroom learning', in *Assessment in Education* (in press).

Blair, Tony (1994) Interview with Hargreaves and Macintyre, in *The Independent*, 23 December.

Blair, Tony (1995) Speech to the Labour Party Annual Conference, October.

Blair, Tony (1996) *New Britain: My Vision of a Young Country*. London: Fourth Estate.

Blair, Tony (1996) Speech to the Labour Party Annual Conference, October.

Blunkett, David (1994) 'Tables are here to stay', in *The Times*, 21 November.

Blunkett, David (1997) Labour Party: Response to Education & Equality: Twelve questions for political parties. *The Runnymede Bulletin*, February.

Bocock, R. and Thompson, K. (eds) (1992) *Social and Cultural Forms of Modernity*. Cambridge: Polity Press.

Bosanquet, N. (1983) *After the New Right*. London: Heinemann.

Bosker, R. and Scheerens, J. (1997) *The Foundations of School Effectiveness*. Oxford: Pergamon Press.

Bourdieu, P. (1984) *Distinction: A Social Critique of the Judgement of Taste*. London: Routledge and Kegan Paul.

Bowe, R., Ball, S. J. and Gold, A. (1992) *Reforming Education and Changing Schools*. London: Routledge.

Boyd-Barrett, O. (1990) 'Schools' Computing Policy as State-directed Innovation', *Educational Studies*, 16:2.

Broadfoot, P. (1996) *Education, Assessment and Society*. Buckingham: Open University Press.

Broadfoot, P. (ed) (1984) *Selection Certification and Control*. Lewes: The Falmer Press.

Brown, P. and Lauder, H. (1992) 'Education, economy, and society: An introduction to a new agenda', in Brown, P. and Lauder, H. (eds) *Education for Economic Survival: From Fordism to Post-Fordism?* London: Routledge.

Brown, P. and Scase, R. (1994) *Higher Education and Corporate Realities: Class, Culture and the Decline of Graduate Careers*, London: UCL Press.

Brown, S., Duffield, J. and Riddell, S. (1996) 'Possibilities and problems of small-scale studies to unpack the findings of large-scale studies of school effectiveness', in Gray, J., Reynolds, D., Fitz-Gibbon, C. and Jesson. D. (eds) (v.i.).

Bruner, J. (1996) *The Culture of Education*. Cambridge, Massachusetts: Harvard University Press.

Bush, T., Coleman, M. and Glover, D. (1993) *Managing Autonomous Schools*. London: Paul Chapman Publishers.

Caldwell, B. J. and Spinks, J. M. (1988) *The Self-Managing School*. London: The Falmer Press.

Campbell, J. and Neill, S. (1994) *Curriculum Reform at Key Stage One*. Harlow: Longman.

Capey, J. (1995) *GNVQ Assessment Review*. London: NCVQ

CARE (1988) *DTI Micros in Schools Support 1981–1984: an independent evaluation*. Norwich: Centre for Applied Research in Education.

Cauldwell, J. and Reid, I. (1996) 'Grant-maintained headteachers' reflections on opting-out', *Educational Studies*, 22:2.

Chapman, P. D. (1988) *Schools as Sorters*. New York: New York University Press.

Chubb, J. and Moe, T. (1990) *Politics Markets and America's Schools*. Washington DC: Brookings Institute.

Coffey, D. (1992) *Schools and Work: Developments in Vocational Education*. London: Cassell.

Coldron, J. and Boulton, P. (1991) 'Happiness as a criterion of parents' choice of school.' *Journal of Education Policy*, 6:2.

Cole, G. (1997) 'Dangers of staying on a plateau of complacency', in *The Times Educational Supplement Computer Update*, 14 March.

Coleman, J. S. (1969) 'What is meant by an "equal educational opportunity"?' *Oxford Review of Education*, 1:1.

Commission for Racial Equality (1992) *Set to Fail? Setting and Banding in Secondary Schools*. London: Commission for Racial Equality.

Connolly, P. (1994) 'All lads together?: Racism, masculinity and multicultural/anti-racist strategies in a primary school', *International Studies in Sociology of Education*, 4:2.

Coopers & Lybrand (1988) *Local Management of Schools*. London: HMSO.

Creemers, B. P. M. (1994) *The Effective Classroom*. London: Cassell.

Creemers, B. P. M. and Osinga, N. (eds) (1996) *ICSEI Country Reports*, 7:2. Leeuwarden: GCO.

Creemers, B. P. M. and Reynolds, D. (1996) 'Issues and Implications of International Effectiveness Research', in *International Journal of Education Research*, 25:3.

Creemers, B. P. M. and Scheerens, J. (eds) (1989) *Developments in school effectiveness research*.

Crowson, R. L., Boyd, W. L. and Mawhinney, H. B. (eds) (1996) *The Politics of Education and the New Institutionalism: Reinventing the American School* (The 1995 Yearbook of the Politics of Education Association, Washington, D.C.). London: The Falmer Press.

Crowther Report (1959) *15–18: Report of the Minister of Education's Central Advisory Committee*. London: HMSO.

Dale, R., Ferguson, R. and Robinson, A. (eds) (1988) *Frameworks for Teaching*. London: Hodder and Stoughton.

Daly, P. (1991) 'How large are secondary school effects in Northern Ireland?' *School Effectiveness and School Improvement*, 2:4.

Damario, A. R. (1994) *Descartes' Error: Emotion, Reason and the Human Brain*. New York: Crosset-Putnam.

Daugherty, R. (1995) *National Curriculum Assessment: A Review of Policy 1987– 1994*. London: RoutledgeFalmer.

David, M. E. (1993) *Parents, Gender and Education Reform*. Cambridge: Polity Press.

David, M. E., Edwards, R., Hughes, M. and Ribbens, J. (1993) *Mothers and Education Inside Out? Exploring Family Education Policy and Experience*. London: Macmillan.

David, M. E., Davies, J., Edwards R, Reay D. and Standing, K. (1997) 'Mothering Choice within constraints', in *Gender and Education*, 9:4.

David, M. E., Davies, J., Edwards, R., Reay, D. and Standing, K. (1996) 'Mothering and Education: Reflexivity and Feminist Methodology', in Walsh, V. and Morley, L. (eds) (v.i.).

David, M. E., West, A. and Ribbens, J. (1994) *Mother's Intuition? Choosing Secondary Schools*. London: The Falmer Press.

Davitt, J. (1997) 'The ultimate good shepherd', in *The Times Educational Supplement Computer Update*, 3 January.

Dearing, Sir Ron (1996) *Review of qualifications for 16–19 Year Olds*. London: SCAA Publications.

Deem, R., Brehony, K. J. and Heath, S. (1995) *Active Citizenship and the Governing of Schools*. Buckingham: Open University Press.

Demaine, J. (1980) 'Sociology of education, politics and the left in Britain', *British Journal of Sociology of Education*, 1:1.

Demaine, J. (1981) *Contemporary Theories in the Sociology of Education*. London: Macmillan.

Demaine, J. (1988) 'Teachers' Work, Curriculum and the New Right', *British Journal of Sociology of Education*, 9:3.

Demaine, J. (1989) 'Privatisation by Stealth: New Right Education Policy.' *ACE Bulletin* No. 28. London: Advisory Centre for Education.

Demaine, J. (1990) 'The Reform of Secondary Education', in Hindess, B. (ed) (1990) (v.i.).

Demaine, J. (1992) 'The Labour Party and Education Policy', *British Journal of Educational Studies*, 40:3.

Demaine, J. (1995) 'English Radicalism and the Reform of Teacher Education', *Journal of Education for Teaching*, 21:2.

Demaine, J. and Entwistle, H. (eds) (1996) *Beyond Communitarianism: Citizenship, Politics and Education*. London and New York: Macmillan and St Martin's Press.

Department of Education and Science (1983) *School Standards and Spending: Statistical Analysis*. London: DES.

Department of Education and Science (1984) *School Standards and Spending: Statistical Analysis. A Further Appreciation*. London: DES.

Department of Education and Science(1987) *New Technology for Better Schools*. London: HMSO.

Department of Education and Science (1988) *Information Technology from 5 to 16*. London: HMSO.

DES (1988) *Report of the Task Group on Assessment and Teaching*. London: Department of Education and Science and Welsh Office.

Department for Education (1992) *Choice and Diversity*. London: HMSO.

Department for Education and Employment (1996) *Self-Governing Schools*. London: HMSO.

Department for Education and Employment (1997) *Connecting the Learning Society*. London: HMSO.

Department for Education and Employment (1997) *Excellence in Schools*. Cmnd. 3681. London: HMSO.

Department for Education and Employment (1997) *Teaching: Higher Status, Higher Standards. General Teaching Council: A Consultation Document*. London: HMSO.

Dewey, J. (1901) 'The situation as regards the course of study', *Journal of the Proceedings and Addresses of the Fortieth Annual Meeting of the National Education Association*.

Donaldson, M. (1978) *Children's Minds*. London: Fontana.

Douglas, J. W. B. (1964) *The Home and the School*. London: MacGibbon and Kee.

Drew, D., Fosam, B. and Gillborn, D. (1995) '"Race", IQ and the Underclass: Don't believe the hype', *Radical Statistics*, 60.

Echols, F. and Willms, D. (1995) 'Reasons for school choice in Scotland', *Journal of Education Policy*, 10:2.

Edwards, R. (1994) *Mature Women Students: Separating or Connecting Family and Education*. London: Taylor and Francis.

Edwards, T. and Whitty, G. (1997) 'Marketing quality: traditional and modern versions of educational excellence', in Glatter, R., Woods, P. and Bagley, C. (eds) (v.i.).

Edwards, V. and Redfern, A. (1988) *At Home in School: Parent participation in primary education*. Milton Keynes: Open University Press.

Eggleston, J. Dunn, D. and Anjali, M. (1986) *Education for Some: The Educational and Vocational Experiences of 15–18 year old Members of Minority Ethnic Groups*. Stoke-on-Trent: Trentham Books.

Elliott, J. (1997) 'School effectiveness research and its critics: Alternative visions of schooling'. *Cambridge Journal of Education*, 26:2.

English, D. (1987) 'Maggie: "What we still have to do": An Interview with Margaret Thatcher', *Daily Mail*, 13 May.

Ennals, R. (1987) 'Difficulties in managing innovation', *British Journal of Educational Technology*, 18:3.

Epstein, D. and Kenway, J. (1996) 'Feminist Perspectives on the Marketisation of Education', in *Discourse: Studies in the Cultural Politics of Education*. (Special issue) December.

Esland, G. (ed) (1991) *Education, Training and Employment, Volume 1: Educated Labour – the Changing Basis of Industrial Demand*. Wokingham: Addison-Wesley.

Evans, A. (1997) 'Dreaming of a computer for every child', *The Times Educational Supplement*, 3 January.

Figueroa, P. (1991) *Education and the Social Construction of 'Race'*. London: Routledge.

Finegold, D. and Soskice, D. (1991) 'The Failure of Training in Britain: analysis and prescription', in Esland, G. (ed) (v.s.).

Fitz, J., Halpin, D. and Power, S. (1993) *Grant Maintained Schools: Education in the Marketplace*. London: Kogan Page.

Fitz, J., Halpin, D. and Power, S. (1997) 'Between a rock and a hard place: diversity, institutional identity and grant-maintained schools', *Oxford Review of Education*, 23:1.

Fitz-Gibbon, C. T. (1985) 'A-level results in comprehensive schools: The COMBSE project, year 1.' *Oxford Review of Education*, 1:1.

Fitz-Gibbon, C. T. (1992) 'School effects at "A" level – genesis of an information system', in Reynolds, D. and Cuttance, P. (eds) (v.i.).

Fitz-Gibbon, C. T. (1996) *Monitoring Education : Indicators, Quality and Effectiveness*. London and New York: Cassell.

Fitz-Gibbon, C. T., Tymms, P. B. and Hazlewood, R. D. (1989) 'Performance indicators and information systems', Reynolds, D., Creemers, B. P. M. and Peters, T. (eds) (v.i.).

Flint, C. (1996) 'Knights of a not-so-round table', *The Times Educational Supplement*, 23 August.

Floud, J. and Halsey, A. (1957) 'Social Class and Selection for Secondary Schools'. *British Journal of Sociology*, 8:33.

Floud, J., Halsey, A. and Martin, M. (1957) *Social Class and Educational Opportunity*. London: Heinemann.

Flude, M. and Hammer, M. (eds) (1990) *The Education Reform Act 1988: Its Origins and Implications*. Basingstoke: The Falmer Press.

Frankel, A. and Reeves, F. (1996) *The Further Education Curriculum*. Bilston College Publications.

Fullan, M. (1991) *The New Meaning of Educational Change*. London: Cassell, and New York: Teachers' College Press.

Furlong, A. (1992) *Growing Up in a Classless Society? School to Work Transitions*. Edinburgh: Edinburgh University Press.

Further Education Funding Council (1996) *Corporate Plan: 1996/7–1998/9*. Coventry: FEFC.

Further Education Funding Council (1996) *Student Numbers, Retention, Achievements and Destinations at Colleges in the Further Education Sector in England and Wales*. London: FEFC.

Gath, D. (1977) *Child guidance and delinquency in a London borough*. London: Oxford University Press.

Gewirtz, S., Ball, S. and Bowe, R. (1995) *Markets, Choice and Equity in Education*. Buckingham: Open University Press.

Gillborn, D. (1990) *'Race', Ethnicity and Education: Teaching and Learning in Multi-Ethnic Schools*. London: Unwin Hyman and Routledge.

Gillborn, D. (1995) *Racism and Antiracism in Real Schools: theory, policy, practice*. Buckingham: Open University Press.

Gillborn, D. (1997) 'Young, black and failed by school: the market, education reform and black students', *International Journal of Inclusive Education*, 1:1.

Gillborn, D. and Gipps, C. (1996) *Recent Research on the Achievements of Ethnic Minority Pupils.* Report for the Office for Standards in Education. London: HMSO.

Gilroy, P. (1987) *There Ain't No Black in the Union Jack.* London: Hutchinson.

Gipps, C. (1994) *Beyond Testing: Towards a Theory of Educational Assessment.* Lewes: The Falmer Press.

Gipps, C. and Murphy, P. (1994) *A Fair Test? Assessment, Achievement, Equity.* Buckingham: Open University Press.

Gipps, C. and Murphy, P. (1994) *A Fair Test? Assessment, Achievement and Equity.* Buckingham: Open University Press.

Glass, R. (1948) *The Social Background of a Plan: A Study of Middlesborough.* London: Routledge and Kegan Paul.

Glatter, R., Woods, P. and Bagley, C. (1995) *Parents and School Choice* (Impact Studies) Buckingham: Open University Press.

Glatter, R. Woods, P. and Bagley, C. (1997) 'Diversity, differentiation and hierarchy: school choice and parental preference', in Glatter, R., Woods, P. and Bagley, C. (eds) (v.i.).

Glatter, R., Woods, P. and Bagley, C. (eds) (1997) *Choice and Diversity in Schooling: Perspectives and Prospects.* London and New York: Routledge.

Gleeson, D. (1983) *Youth Training and The Search for Work.* London: Routledge

Gleeson, D. (1989) *The Paradox of Training.* Buckingham: Open University Press.

Gleeson, D. (1990) *Training and Its Alternatives.* Buckingham: Open University Press.

Gleeson, D. and Hodkinson, P. (1995), 'Ideology and Curriculum Policy: GNVQ and Mass Post-Compulsory Education in England and Wales', *British Journal of Education and Work,* 8:3.

Gleeson, D. and Mardle, G. (1980) *Further Education or Training? A Case Study of Day Release Education.* London: Routledge and Kegan Paul.

Gleeson, D. and McLean, M. (1994) 'Whatever happened to TVEI? – TVEI, Schooling and Curriculum', in *Journal of Education Policy,* 9:3.

Goldstein, H. (1995) *Multilevel Models in Educational and Social Research* (Revised Edition) London: Edward Arnold.

Goldstein, H. and Lewis, T. (1996) *Assessment: Problems, Developments and Statistical Issues.* Chichester: John Wiley.

Goldstein, H., Rasbash, J., Yang, M., Woodhouse, G., Pan, H., Nuttall, D. and Thomas, S. (1993) 'A multilevel analysis of school examination results', *Oxford Review of Education,* 19:4.

Gould, S. J. (1981) *The Mismeasure of Man.* New York: Norton.

Gray, J. (1981) 'A competitive edge: examination results and the probable limits of secondary school effectiveness.' *Educational Review,* 33:1.

Gray, J. (1982) 'Towards effective schools: Problems and progress in British research', *British Educational Research Journal,* 7:1.

Gray, J. and Jesson, D. (1987) 'Exam results and local authority league tables', in Harrison, A. and Gretton. J. (eds) (v.i.).

Gray, J., Jesson, D. and Jones, B. (1984) 'Predicting differences in examination results between local education authorities: Does school organisation matter?' *Oxford Review of Education,* 10:1.

Gray, J., Jesson, D. and Jones, B. (1986) 'The search for a fairer way of comparing schools' examination results', *Research Reports in Education*, 1:2.

Gray, J., Jesson, D. and Sime, N. (1990) 'Estimating differences in the examination performance of secondary schools in six LEAs: a multilevel approach to school effectiveness', *Oxford Review of Education*, 16:2.

Gray, J., Jesson, D., Goldstein, H., Hedger, K. and Rasbash, J. (1995) 'A multilevel analysis of school improvement: changes in schools' performance over time', *School Effectiveness and School Improvement*, 6:2.

Gray, J., McPherson, A. F. and Raffe, D. (1983) *Reconstructions of Secondary Education: theory, myth, and practice since the war*. London: Routledge and Kegan Paul.

Gray, J., Reynolds, D. and Fitz-Gibbon, C. and Jesson, D. (eds) (1996) *Merging Traditions : The Future of Research on School Effectiveness and School Improvement*. London: Cassell.

Green, A. (1986) 'Tertiary Modern FE', in Walkerdine, V. (ed) (v.i.).

Green, A. (1990) *Education and State Formation*. London: Macmillan.

Green, A. and Rikowski, G. (1995) 'Post-Compulsory Education and Training for the 21 Century', *Forum, 37*.

Hall, S. (1993) *Three Blind Mice: Rethinking New Ethnicities* (videocassette) University of East London: New Ethnicities Unit.

Hallam, S. and Toutounji, I. (1996) *What Do We Know about the Grouping of Pupils by Ability? A Research Review*. London: University of London Institute of Education.

Halpin, D., Power, S. and Fitz, J. (1997) 'Opting Into the Past? Grant Maintained Schools and the Reinvention of Tradition', in Glatter, R., Woods, P. and Bagley. C. (eds) (v.i.).

Halsey, A. H. (1981) 'Democracy for Education?' *New Society*, 28 May.

Halsey, A. H. (1986) *Change in British Society* (3rd edition). Oxford: Oxford University Press.

Halsey, A. H., Heath, A. and Ridge, J. (1990) *Origins and Destinations: Family, Class and Education in Modern Britain*. Oxford: Oxford University Press.

Hasley, A. H., Floud, J. and Anderson, C. A. (eds) (1961) *Education, Economy and Society*, New York: The Free Press.

Halstead, J. M. (ed) (1994) *Parental Choice and education: Principles, Policy and Practice*. London: Kogan Page.

Hamilton, D. (1996) 'Peddling feel-good factors', *Forum*, 38:2.

Hargreaves, A. and Reynolds, D. (eds) (1989) *Education Policies: Controversies and Critiques*. Lewes: The Falmer Press.

Hargreaves, D. (1996) 'Diversity and choice in school education: a modified libertarian view', *Oxford Review of Education*, 22:2.

Hargreaves, D. and Hopkins, D. (1991) *The Empowered School*. London: Cassell.

Harrison, A. and Gretton, J. (eds) (1987) *Education and Training UK*.

Hartley, D. (1994) 'Mixed Messages in Education Policy: Sign of the Times', *British Journal of Educational Studies*, 42:3.

Hartley, D. (1998) 'Repeat Prescription: The National Curriculum for Initial Teacher Training', *British Journal of Educational Studies*, 46:1.

Hatcher, R. (1997) 'New Labour, school improvement and racial inequality', *Multicultural Teaching*, 15:3.

Hayek, F. A. (1960) *The Constitution of Liberty*. London: Routledge and Kegan Paul.

Healey, Denis (1989) *The Time of My Life*. London: Michael Joseph.

Herrnstein, R. J. and Murray, C. (1994) *The Bell Curve: Intelligence and Class Structure in American Life*. New York: The Free Press.

Hewitt, R. (1996) *Routes of Racism: The Social Basis of Racist Action*. Stoke-on-Trent: Trentham Books.

Hill, D., Oakley Smith, B. and Spinks, J. (1990) *Local Management of Schools*. London: Paul Chapman Publishing.

Hindess, B. (1987) *Freedom, Equality, and the Market: Arguments on Social Policy*. London: Tavistock Publications.

Hindess, B. (ed) (1990) *Reactions to the Right*. London: Routledge.

Hirsch, D. (1994) *School: A Matter of Choice*. Paris: OECD.

Hirsch, D. (1997), 'Policies for school choice: what can Britain learn from abroad?' in Glatter, R., Woods, P. and Bagley, C. (eds) (v.s.).

Hodkinson, P. and Mattinson, K. (1994) 'A Bridge Too Far? The Problems Facing GNVQ', *Curriculum Journal*, 5:3.

Howe, D. (1997) 'A friend of John Major's has tried to convince me for years that the Prime Minister is passionately anti-racist. I've finally surrendered', *New Statesman*, 24 January.

Hughes, M. (1996) Parents, Teachers and Schools, in Bernstein, B. and Brannen, J. (eds) (v.s.).

Hughes, M., Wikley, F. and Nash, T. (1994) *Parents and Their Schools*. Oxford: Blackwell.

Hutton, W. (1995) *The State We're In*. London: Jonathan Cape.

Hutton, W. (1996) 'Fool's Gold in a Fool's Paradise', in *The Observer*, 2 June.

Hyland, T. (1994) *Competence, Education and NVQs: Dissenting Perspectives*. Cassell, London

Inglis, Bill (1991) 'The Labour Party's Education Policy on Primary and Secondary Education 1979–89', *British Journal of Educational Studies*, 39:1.

Jackson, B. and Marsden, D. (1962), *Education and the Working Class*. London: Routledge and Kegan Paul.

Jacoby, R. and Glauberman, N. (1995) *The Bell Curve Debate: History, Documents and Opinions*. New York: Times Books.

Jesson, D. and Gray, J. (1991) 'Slants on Slopes: Using Multi-Level Models to Investigate Differential School Effectiveness and its Impact on Pupils' Examination Results', *School Effectiveness and School Improvement*, 2:3.

John, M. (1997) 'Technology Head Resigns', in *The Times Educational Supplement*, 17 January.

Johnson, P. (1994) 'Gone is the time when Americans led the world in saying what they thought', in *The Spectator*, 26 November.

Jowett, S. (1995) *Allocating Secondary School Places: policy and practice*. Windsor: National Foundation for Educational Research.

Kamin, L. J. (1974) *The Science and Politics of IQ*. London: Penguin.

Kamin, L. J. (1995) 'Behind the curve', *Scientific American*, February.

Katz. M. (1965) 'From Boyce to Newsom: assumptions of British educational reports', *International Review of Education*, 11.

Kenny, J. (1996) 'Hardware alone is no substitute for a national strategy', in *The Times Educational Supplement Computer Update*, 18 October.

Kenway, J. (ed) (1994) *Economising Education: The Post-Fordist Directions*. Deakin: Deakin University Press.

Kerckhoff, A. C. (1993) *Diverging Pathways: Social Structure and Career Deflections*. Cambridge: Cambridge University Press.

Kerckhoff, A., Fogelman, K. and Manlove, J. (1997) 'Staying ahead: the middle class and school reform in England and Wales', *Sociology of Education*, 70.

Kerckhoff, A., Fogelman, K., Crook, D and Reeder, D. (1996*) Going Comprehensive in England and Wales*. London: Woburn Press.

Kinnock. N. (1986) *Making Our Way*. Oxford: Blackwell.

Kirkup, G., Laurillard, D., Stannett, C and Bates A. (1987*) Computer Based Learning: Introduction to Information Technology*. Buckingham: Open University Press.

Kliebard, H. (1996) 'Constructing the concept of curriculum on the Wisconsin frontier: how school restructuring sustained a pedagogical revolution', *History of Education*, 25:2.

Knight, C. (1990) *The Making of Tory Education Policy in Post-War Britain 1950–86*. London: The Falmer Press.

Labour Party (1988) *Parents in Partnership*. London: The Labour Party.

Labour Party (1989) *Meet the Challenge Make the Change*. London: The Labour Party.

Labour Party (1993) *Opening Doors to a Learning Society*. London: The Labour Party.

Labour Party (1995) *Diversity and Excellence*. London: The Labour Party.

Labour Party (1996) *Education Bulletin 6* (July/August) London: The Labour Party.

Labour Party (1997) *Education Bulletin* (April/May) London: The Labour Party.

Labour Party (1997) *New Labour: Because Britain deserves Better* (The Labour Party Manifesto) London: The Labour Party.

Lareau, A. (1989) *Home Advantage*. London: The Falmer Press.

Le Grand, J. (1998) 'The Third Way begins with Cora', *New Statesman*, 6 March.

Le Grand, J. and Bartlett, W. (eds) (1993) *Quasi-Markets and Social Policy*. London: Macmillan.

Levine, K. (1996) 'Literacy, Citizenship and Education', in Demaine, J. and Entwistle, H. (eds) (v.s.).

Lloyd, J. and Bilefsky, D. (1998), 'Transatlantic wonks at work', *New Statesman*, 27 March.

Mac an Ghaill, M. (1988) *Young, Gifted and Black: Student–Teacher Relations in the Schooling of Black Youth*. Milton Keynes: Open University Press.

Macbeth, A. M., McCreath, D. and Aitchisin, J. (1995) *Collaborate or Compete? Educational Partnerships in a Market Economy*. London: The Falmer Press.

MacPherson, A. and Willms, D. (1987) 'Equalisation and improvement: some effects of comprehensive re-organisation in Scotland', *Sociology*, 21:4.

Major, John (1997) *Britain: The Best Place in the World*. Text of a Speech to the Commonwealth Institute, 18 January. London: Conservative Central Office.

McCormick, R. (1992) 'Curriculum Development and New Information Technology', *Journal of Information Technology for Teacher Education*, 1:1.

McCrae, S., McGuire, M. and Ball, S. (1996) *Competition, 'Choice' and Hierarchy in a Post-16 Education and Training Market*. An unpublished paper, PPI-29, School of Education, Kings College, London.

McCulloch, G. (1989) *The Secondary Technical School*. London: The Falmer Press.

McCulloch, G. (1990) 'An Alternative Road? Problems and Possibilities of the Crowther Concept', in Gleeson, D. (ed) (1990) (v.s.).

McFarlane, A. (1997) 'Breakthrough in the lab', in *The Times Educational Supplement Computer Update*, 3 January.

McKenzie, J. (1993) *Education as a Political Issue*. Aldershot: Avebury Books.

McLean, N. (1997) 'Trying to get to grips with the IT order', in *The Times Educational Supplement Computer Update*, 14 March.

Merrtens, R. (1995) *Sharing Maths Cultures: IMPACT: Improving Mathematics for Parents, Children and Teachers in primary schools*. London The Falmer Press.

Miles, R. (1993) *Racism after 'Race Relations'*. London: Routledge.

Milne, K. (1998) 'The parable of the 31st child', *New Statesman*, 9 January.

Mirza, H. S. (1992) *Young, Female and Black*. London: Routledge.

Modood, T., Beishon, S. and Virdee, S. (1994) *Changing Ethnic Identities*. London: Policy Studies Institute.

Modood, T., Berthoud, R., Lakey, J., Nazroo, J., Smith, P., Virdee, S. and Beishon, S. (1997) *Ethnic Minorities in Britain: Diversity and Disadvantage*. London: Policy Studies Institute.

Moon, B. and Mortimore, P. (1989) *The National Curriculum: Straightjacket or Safety Net*. London: LEA publications.

Moon, B. and Shelton Mayes, A.(1994) *Teaching and Learning in the Secondary School*. London: Routledge.

Moore, R. (1988) 'Education, employment and recruitment', in Dale, R., Ferguson, R. and Robinson, A. (eds) (v.s.).

Mortimore, P., Sammons, P., Stoll, L., Lewis, D. and Ecob, R. (1988) *School Matters: The Junior Years*. Salisbury: Open Books.

Mullard, C. (1982) 'Multiracial education in Britain: from assimilation to cultural pluralism', in Tierney, J. (ed) (v.i.).

Murphy, R. J. L. (1987) 'Assessing a National Curriculum', in *Journal of Education Policy*, 2:4.

Murphy, R. J. L. (1989) 'National Assessment Proposals: Analysing the Debate', in Flude, M. and Hammer, M. (eds) (v.s.).

Murphy, R. J. L., Wilmut, J., Gillespie, J., Burke, P., Hadfield, M., Rainbow, R. and Wallis, J. (1995) *The Reliability of Assessment of NVQs*. University of Nottingham Report for NCVQ.

Murphy, R. J. L. and Broadfoot, P. (1995) *Effective Assessment and the Improvement of Education: A Tribute to Desmond Nuttall*. Lewes: The Falmer Press.

Murphy, R. J. L. and Joyes, G. (1997) 'Marks and grades aren't necessarily evil', in Watson, K. (ed) (v.i.).

Murphy, R. J. L., Burke, P., Gillespie, J., Rainbow, R. and Wilmut, J. (1997) *The Key Skills of Students Entering Higher Education*. University of Nottingham Report for the DfEE.

Nash, I. (1994) 'GNVQ falls victim to its own success', *The Times Educational Supplement*, 11 March.

National Commission on Education (1993) *Learning to Succeed*. London: Heinemann.

NCET (1993) *The future curriculum with IT: A seminar report*. Coventry: National Council for Educational Technology.

New, C. and David, M. E. (1985) *For the Children's Sake: Making Child Care more than Women's Business*. Harmondsworth: Penguin.

Nuttall, D. L. (1984) 'Doomsday or a new Dawn? The Prospects for a Common Examination at 16+', in Broadfoot, P. (ed) (v.s.).

Nuttall, D. L. (1987) The validity of assessments, in *European Journal of Psychology of Education*, 2:2.

Nuttall, D. L., Goldstein, H., Prosser, R. and Rasbash, J. (1989) 'Differential school effectiveness', in Creemers, B. P. M. and Scheerens, J. (eds) (v.s.).

O'Brien, M. (1984) 'The commatization of women: patriarchal fetishism in the sociology of education', *Interchange*, 15:2.

O'Brien, M. (1997) A unpublished paper reported on the *Panorama* programme *Missing Mum*. BBC Television, 3 February.

Oates, T. (1996) *The Development and Implementation of Key Skills in England*. London: National Council for Vocational Qualifications.

Orbach, S. (1997) 'Blaming Working Mothers', in *The Guardian* Magazine: Family Matters, 5 February.

Piore, M. and Sabel, C. (1984) *The Second Industrial Divide: Possibilities for Prosperity*. New York: Basic Books.

Piper, K. and McGaw, B. (1991) *Educational Assessment for Educational Policy and Strategy*. A paper at the UNESCO Round Table on the Impact of Evaluation and Assessment on Educational Policy in Africa, Nairobi.

Power, M. J. et al. (1967) 'Delinquent Schools?' *New Society*, 10.

Power, M. J., Benn, R. T. and Morris, J. N. (1972) 'Neighbourhood, school and juveniles before the courts', *British Journal of Criminology*, 12.

Pring, R. (1995) 'The community of education people: the 1994 Lawrence Stenhouse Memorial Lecture', printed in the *British Journal of Educational Studies*, 43:2.

Pring, R. and Walford, G. (eds) (1997) *Affirming the Comprehensive Ideal*. London: The Falmer Press.

Radice, G. (1986) *Equality and Quality: A Socialist Plan for Education*. London: The Fabian Society.

Radice, G.(1989) *Labour's Path to Power: The New Revisionism*. London: Macmillan.

Ranson, S. (1994) *Toward the Learning Society*. London: Cassell.

Rattansi, A. and Reeder, D. (eds) (1992) *Rethinking Radical Education*. London: Lawrence and Wishart.

Reay, D. (1996) 'Contextualising Choice: Social Power and Parental Involvement', *British Educatonal Research Journal*, 22:5.

Reay, D. (1997) 'Feminist theory, habits and social class: disrupting notions of classlessness', *Women's Studies International Forum*, 20:2.

Reay, D. and Ball, S. (1997) 'Spoilt for choice? The working classes and educational markets', *Oxford Review of Education*, 23:1.

Reeder, D. (1979) 'A recurring debate: education and industry', in Bernbaum, G. (ed) *Schooling in Decline*. London: Macmillan.

Reeves, F. (1983) *British Racial Discourse: A Study of British Political Discourse about Race and Race-Related Matters*. Cambridge: Cambridge University Press.

Reynolds, D. (1976) 'The delinquent school', in Woods, P. (ed) (v.i.).

Reynolds, D. (1982) 'The search for effective schools', *School Organisation*, 2:3.

Reynolds, D. (1987) 'The Effective School' (The 1986 Association of Educational Psychologists Lecture) printed in *Educational Psychology in Practice*, October.

Reynolds, D. (1991) 'Changing Ineffective Schools', in M. Ainscow (ed) (v.s.).

Reynolds, D. (1996a) The Effective School: An Inaugural Lecture, *Evaluation and Research in Education*, 9:2.

Reynolds, D. (1996b) 'Turning around ineffective schools: some evidence and some speculations', in Gray, J., Reynolds, D. and Fitz-Gibbon, C. and Jesson, D. (eds) (1996) (v.s.).

Reynolds, D. (1997) 'East–West Trade-Off', in *The Times Educational Supplement*, 27 June.

Reynolds, D. and Cuttance, P. (eds) (1992) *School Effectiveness : Research, Policy and Practice*. London: Cassell.

Reynolds, D. and Farrell, S. (1996) *Worlds Apart? – A Review of International Studies of Educational Achievement Involving England*. London: HMSO.

Reynolds, D., Creemers, B. P. M. and Peters, T. (eds) (1989) *School effectiveness and improvement: Selected proceedings of the first international congress for school effectiveness*. Groningen, Netherlands: RION.

Reynolds, D., Creemers, B. P. M., Bird, J. and Farrell, S. (1994) 'School effectiveness: the need for an international perspective', in Reynolds, D., Creemers, B. P. M., Nesselrodt, P., Schaffer, E., Stringfield, S. and Teddlie, C. (eds) *Advances in School Effectiveness Research and Practice*. Oxford: Pergamon Press.

Reynolds, D., Sammons, P., Stoll, L., Barber, M. and Hillman, J. (1996a) 'School Effectiveness and School Improvement in the United Kingdom', in Creemers, B. P. M. and Osinga, N. (eds) (v.s.).

Reynolds, D., Sammons, P., Stoll, L., Barber, M. and Hillman, J. (1996b) 'School effectiveness and school improvement in the United Kingdom', *School Effectiveness and School Improvement*, 7:2.

Ribbens, J. (1994) *A Feminist Sociology of Child Rearing*. London: Sage.

Roberts, K. (1987) *School Leavers and their Prospects*. Open University Press.

Robertson, D (1994) 'Flexibility and mobility in further and higher education: policy continuity and progress', *Journal of Further and Higher Education*, 17:1.

Robinson, J. and Burke, C. (1994) *Tradition, Culture and Ethos: The Impact of the Further and Higher Education Act (1992) on Sixth Form Colleges and their Futures*. A unpublished mimeo.

Rogers, L. and Wild, P. (1996) 'Data-logging: effects on practical science', *Journal of Computer Assisted Learning*, 12:3.

Rooker, J. (1993) 'Funding the Future', *Education Today and Tomorrow*, 46:2.

Rutter, M., Maughan, B., Mortimore, P. and Ouston, J. (1979) *Fifteen Thousand Hours : Secondary schools and their effects on children*. London: Open Books.

Sammons, P. and Reynolds, D. (1997) 'A Partisan Evaluation: John Elliott on School Effectiveness', *Cambridge Journal of Education*, 27:1.

Sammons, P., Nuttall, D. and Cuttance, P. (1993) 'Differential school effectiveness: Results from a re-analysis of the Inner London Education Authority's junior school project data', *British Educational Research Journal*, 19:4.

Sammons, P., Nuttall, D., Cuttance, P. and Thomas, S. (1995) 'Continuity of school effects: a longitudinal analysis of primary and secondary school effects on GCSE performance', *School Effectiveness and School Improvement*, 6:4.

Sanderson, M. (1994) *The Missing Stratum: Technical School Education in England, 1900–1990s*. London: The Athlone Press.

Sayer, J. (1989) *Towards the General Teaching Council*. London: The Education Management Unit.

SCAA (1997) *Expectations in Information Technology at Key Stages 1 and 2*. London: SCAA Publications.

Seldon, A. (1986) *The Riddle of the Voucher*. London: Institute of Economic Affairs.

Seldon, A. (1988) 'Thoughts for the New Left', *The Guardian*, 13 June.

Sewell, T. (1997) *Black Masculinities and Schooling: How Black Boys Survive Modern Schooling*. Stoke-on-Trent: Trentham.

Sexton, S. (1987) *Our Schools: A Radical Policy*. London: Institute of Economic Affairs.

Shulman, L. S. (1992) 'Those who understand: Knowledge growth in teaching', reprinted in Moon, B. and Shelton Mayes, A. (1994) (v.s.).

Simon, B. (1978) *Intelligence, Psychology, Education*. London: Lawrence Wishart.

Skilbeck, M. (1976) 'Three Educational Ideologies', in *Curriculum Design and Development*, (E203 Unit 3: Ideologies and Values) Milton Keynes: Open University Press.

Slavin, R. E. (1990) 'Achievement effects of ability grouping in secondary schools: a best evidence synthesis', *Review of Educational Research*, 60:3.

Slavin, R. E. (1996) *Education for All*. Lisse: Swets and Zeitlinger.

Smith, D. J. and Tomlinson, S. (1989) *The School Effect: A study of multi-racial comprehensives*. London: Policy Studies Institute.

Smith, T. and Noble, M. and Smith, G. (1995) *Education Divides: Poverty and schooling in the 1990s*. London: Child Poverty Action Group.

Smithers, A. and Robinson, P. (1993) *Changing Colleges: Further Education in the Market Place*. London: The Council for Industry and Higher Education.

Spours, K. and Young, M. F. D. (1997) 'Dearing and Beyond: Steps and Stages to a Unified 14 – 19 Qualifications System', in *British Journal of Education and Work*, 9:3.

Steedman (1983) *Examination Results in Selective and Non-Selective Schools*. London: National Children's Bureau.

Steedman, J. (1980) *Progress in Secondary Schools*. London: National Children's Bureau.

Sternberg, R. J. (1996) 'Myths, countermyths and truths about intelligence', *Educational Researcher*, 25:2.

Stevenson, D. (1997) *Information and Communications Technology in UK Schools: An Independent Inquiry*. London: Dennis Stevenson.

Stoll, L. and Fink, D. (1996) *Changing Our Schools*. Buckingham: Open University Press.

Stoll, L. and Myers, K. (1997) *No Quick Fixes: Perspectives on Schools in Difficulty*. Lewes: The Falmer Press.

Stringfield, S., Ross, S. and Smith, L. (eds) (1996) *Bold Plans for School Restruc-turing*. New Jersey: Lawrence Erlbaum.

Taylor Report (1977) *A New Partnership For Our Schools* (Department of Education and Science and Welsh Office) London: HMSO.

Taylor, T. (1995) 'Movers and shakers: high politics and the origins of the National Curriculum', *The Curriculum Journal*, 6:2.

Teacher Training Agency (1997) *Standards for the award of qualified teacher status*. London: Teacher Training Agency.

Teddlie, C. and Reynolds, D. (1998) *The International Handbook of School Effectiveness Research*. Lewes: The Falmer Press.

Teles, S. (1998) 'A blend of help and hassle', *New Statesman*, 6 March.

Thatcher, M. (1993) *The Downing Street Years*. London: HarperCollins.

Thomas, H. (1990) 'From Local Financial Management to Local Management of Schools', in Flude, M. and Hammer, M. (eds) (1990) (v.s.).

Thomas, S. and Mortimore, P. (1994) *Report on value added analysis of the 1993 GCSE examination results in Lancashire*. London: Institute of Education.

Thomas, S., Sammons, P. and Mortimore, P. (1995) 'Determining what adds value to student achievement', *Educational Leadership International*, 58:6.

Thompson, K. (1992) 'Religion, Values and Ideology', in Bocock, R. and Thompson, K. (eds) (v.s.).

Tierney, J. (ed) (1982) *Race, Migration and Schooling*. London: Holt, Rinehart and Winston.

Tizard, B., Blatchford, P., Burke, J., Farquhar, C. and Plewis, I. (1988) *Young Children at School in the Inner City*. London: Lawrence Erlbaum Associates.

Tomlinson, S. (1997) 'Diversity, choice and ethnicity: the effects of educational markets on ethnic minorities', *Oxford Review of Education*, 23:1)

Tooley, J. (1995) 'A measure of freedom', *The Times Higher Education Supplement*, 7 July.

Tooley, J. (1996) *Education without the State*. London: Institute of Economic Affairs Education and Training Unit.

Torrance, H. (1995) *Evaluating Authentic Assessment*. Buckingham: Open University Press.

Troyna, B. (1991) 'Underachievers or underrated? The experiences of pupils of South Asian origin in a secondary school', *British Educational Research Journal*, 17:4)

Troyna, B. (1993) *Racism and Education: Research Perspectives*. Buckingham: Open University Press.

Troyna, B. (1994) 'The "Everyday World" of Teachers? Deracialised discourses in the sociology of teachers and the teaching profession', *British Journal of Sociology of Education*, 15:3.

Troyna, B. and Siraj-Blatchford, I. (1993) 'Providing support or denying access? The experiences of students designated as "ESL" and "SN" in a multi-ethnic secondary school', *Educational Review*, 45:1.

Tymms, P. (1995) 'Influencing educational practice through performance indicators', *School Effectiveness and School Improvement*, 6:2.

Vincent, C. and Tomlinson, S. (1997) 'Home-School relationships: "the swarming of disciplinary mechanisms?"' *British Educational Research Journal*, 23:3.

Vincent. C. and Ball, S. (1996) 'We heard it on the grape vine', unpublished paper to the British Educational Research Association, September.

Walford, G. (1994) *Choice and Equity in Education*. London: Cassell.

Walford, G. (1997) 'Privatization and selection', in Pring, R. and Walford, G. (eds) (v.s.).

Walker, M. (1998) 'The Third Way International', *New Statesman*, 27 March.

Walkerdine, V. (1997) 'Don't rush back to the kitchen, mum', *The Times Educational Supplement*, 7 February.

Walkerdine, V. (ed) (1986) *Is there Anyone Here from Education?* Brighton: The Falmer Press.

Walkerdine, V. and Lucey, H. (1989) *Democracy in the Kitchen*. London: Virago.

Wall Street Journal (1994) 'Mainstream Science on Intelligence', 13 December, A18.

Walsh, V. and Morley, L. (eds) (1996) *Breaking Boundaires: Women in Higher Education*. London: Taylor and Francis.

Watkins, P. (1992) 'Class, The Labour Process and Work (ESA 845)', in *Economy and Schooling*. Geelong: Deakin University.

Watkins, P. (1993) 'Japanisation and the Management of Education', *International Journal of Education Management*, 7:2.

Watson, K. (ed) (1997) *Educational Dilemmas: Debate and Diversity*. London: Cassell.

West, A. (1994) 'Choosing schools: the consumers' perspective', in Halstead, J. M. (ed) (v.s.).

West, A., David, M. E., Noden, P., Edge, A. and Davies, J. (1997) *Parental choice, involvement and expectations of achievement in education* (Clare Market paper No. 13) London: London School of Economics Centre for Educational Research.

West, A., Pennell, H. and Noden, P. (1997) *Admissions to Secondary School: towards a national policy?* London: Research and Information on State Education.

Whatford, C. (1996) 'Interviews with comprehensive pupils are the sting in the tail', in *The Times Educational Supplement*, 2 February.

White Paper (1991) *Education and Training for the 21 Century*. Cmnd. 1536. London: HMSO.

White Paper (1994) *Competitiveness: Helping Business to Win*. Cmnd. 2563. London: HMSO.

White Paper (1995) *Competitiveness: Forging Ahead*. Cmnd. 2867. London: HMSO.

White Paper (1997) *Excellence in Schools*. Cmnd. 3681. London: HMSO.

Whitty, G. (1985) *Sociology and School Knowledge: curriculum theory, research and politics*. London: Methuen.

Whitty, G. (1992) 'Lessons from Radical Curriculum Initiatives', in Rattansi, A. and Reeder, D. (eds) (v.s.).

Whitty, G., Edwards, T. and Gewirtz, S. (1993) *Specialisation and Choice in Urban Education: the City Technology College Experiment*. London and New York: Routledge.

Whitty, G., Halpin, D. and Power, S. (1996) 'Self-managing schools in the market place: the experience of England, the USA and New Zealand', paper presented at Fourth Quasi-Markets seminar at the University of Bristol, March.

Whitty, G., Power, S. and Halpin, D. (1998) *Devolution and Choice in Education: The School, The State and The Market*. Buckingham: Open University Press.

Wiener, M. (1981) *English Culture and the Decline of the Industrial Spirit, 1850–1980*. Cambridge: Cambridge University Press.

Wilby, P. (1998) 'This may be the end of the LEA show', *New Statesman*, 20 March.

Wild, P. (1989) 'The effectiveness of INSET in CAL and IT: an evaluation of the work of an advisory teacher', *Computers and Education*, 16:4.

Williams, R. (1965) *The Long Revolution*. London: Pelican Books.

Willms, D. (1985) 'The balance thesis: contextual effects of ability on pupils "O" grade examination results', *Oxford Review of Education*, 11:1.

Willms, D. (1986) 'Social class segregation and its relationship to pupils' examination results in Scotland', *American Sociological Review*, 51:2.

Willms, D. (1987) 'Differences between Scottish Education Authorities in their examination attainments', *Oxford Review of Education*, 13:3.

Willms, D. and Cuttance, P. (1985) 'School effects in Scottish secondary schools', *British Journal of Sociology of Education*, 6:3.

Wilmut, J. (1994) *Agreement Trialling*. Ilminster: Wessex Publications.

Wilmut, J. (1995) *The Teacher's Role in Assessment*. A paper to the SCAA/NCVQ International Conference on General and Vocational Education 14–19 in London, November.

Witte, J. (1995) *Private and Public Education in Wisconsin: Implications for the Choice Debate* (unpublished paper) Madison: University of Wisconsin.

Wolf, A. (1995) *Competence-Based Assessment*. Buckingham: Open University Press.

Wolfendale, S. and Topping K. (1996) (eds) *Family Involvement in Literacy: Effective Partnerships in Education*. London and New York: Cassell.

Wood, R. (1991) *Assessment and Testing: A Survey of Research*. Cambridge: Cambridge University Press.

Wood, R. and Power, C. N. (1987) 'Aspects of the competence-performance distinction: educational, psychological and measurement issues', in *Journal of Curriculum Studies*, 19:4.

Woodhead, C. (1996) 'Boys who learn to be losers: On the white male culture of failure', in *The Times*, 6 March.

Woodhouse, G. and Goldstein, H. (1988) 'Educational Performance Indicators and LEA league tables', *Oxford Review of Education*, 14:3.

Woods, P. (1993) 'Responding to the Consumer: Parental Choice and School Effectiveness', *School Effectiveness and School Improvement*, 4:3.

Woods, P. (ed) (1976) *The process of schooling*. London: Routledge and Kegan Paul.

Wright, C. (1986) 'School Processes: An Ethnographic Study', in Eggleston, J., Dunn, D. and Anjali, M. (eds) (v.s.).

Young, M. (1992) 'A Curriculum for the 21st Century.' A paper presented at the international workshop on *Mutual Enrichment and Academic and Vocational Education in Upper Secondary Education*. Institute for Educational Research, University of Jyväskylä, Finland, 23–26 September.

Young, M. (1993) 'A Curriculum for the 21st Century? Towards a new basis for overcoming academic/vocational division', *British Journal of Educational Studies*, 41:3.

Index